M000287202

The best projects from a year of *Bead&Button* magazine

Creative Beading

Vol. 7

KALMBACH BOOKS

Kalmbach Books
21027 Crossroads Circle
Waukesha, Wisconsin 53186
www.Kalmbach.com/Books

© 2012 Kalmbach Books
All rights reserved. Except for brief excerpts for review, this book may not be reproduced in part or in whole by electronic means or otherwise without written permission of the publisher.

The jewelry designs in *Creative Beading Vol. 7* are the copyrighted property of the authors, and they may not be taught or sold without permission. Please use them for your education and personal enjoyment only. For technical and artistic reasons relating to photographic reproduction and the printing process, colors reproduced in these photographs are not exact representations of the original designs.

Published in 2012
17 16 15 14 13   2 3 4 5 6

Manufactured in the China

ISBN: 978-0-87116-482-7

The material in this book has appeared previously in *Bead&Button* magazine. *Bead&Button* is registered as a trademark.

Editor: *Elisa Neckar*
Technical Editor: *Julia Gerlach*
Proofreader: *Stacy Werkheiser*
Art Director: *Lisa Bergman*
Layout Designer: *Lisa Schroeder and Rebecca Markstein*
Illustrator: *Kellie Jaeger*
Photographers: *Bill Zuback and Jim Forbes*

Publisher's Cataloging-in-Publication Data

Creative beading : the best projects from a year of Bead&Button magazine.

    v. : ill.

Annual

Vol. [1] (2006)-

Description based on: vol. 7 (2012).

Latest issue consulted: vol. 7 (2012).

Material in each volume appeared in the previous year's issues of Bead&Button magazine.

Includes index.

1. Beadwork--Periodicals. 2. Beads--Periodicals. 3. Jewelry making--Periodicals. I. Kalmbach Publishing Company. II. Title: Bead&Button magazine.

TT860 .C743

745.594/2

Contents

22

32

38

56

58

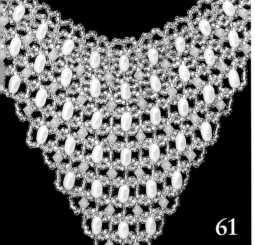

61

71

100

114

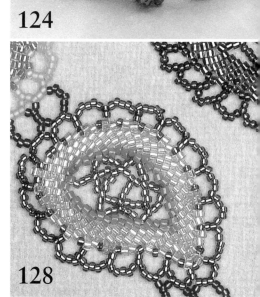

124

128

136

OTHER TECHNIQUES 206

192

222

230

232

244

Introduction

Welcome to the seventh volume of *Creative Beading*, the annual roundup of projects from *Bead&Button*, the original beading magazine. Besides being a collection of inspiring beading projects, the *Creative Beading* books are somewhat like little time capsules, providing a snapshot of the state of beading for a given time. If you pay attention, you'll be able to track the emergence of new tools, supplies, bead shapes, and design trends. In this volume, you'll find a few projects using Tila beads and elongated magatamas, two new bead shapes that were released this past year. You'll also find peanut beads, dagger beads, and rivolis, which continue to inspire designers around the world. And you'll find more base metal, as beaders have embraced the warm tones of copper and bronze during tight economic times and in the face of record prices for silver and gold.

In putting this book together, it was fun to pause and reflect on the year gone by. I tend to be very deadline-driven, always focused on the next task that needs to be completed. So, it was a real luxury to flip through this volume, admiring the beautiful designs and skilled handiwork, almost as if seeing them for the first time. I realized that I had intended to make several of these projects, but deadlines threatened and they were put aside for another day.

If you also let the demands of life get in the way of your beading pleasure, take this time to reclaim your seat at your beading table. With nearly 100 projects to choose from, it won't be hard too find a whole jewelry box full of designs that inspire you. From peyote stitch to herringbone, to stringing, wirework, kumihimo, and chain mail, the projects in this book cover an exciting range of techniques in a wide variety of styles. So, bring on the sticky notes (an extra-large pack!), flag those projects you want to do, and get ready to bead.

Happy beading,

Julia Gerlach

Julia Gerlach
Editor, *Bead&Button*

Tools & Materials

Excellent tools and materials for making jewelry are available in bead and craft stores, through catalogs, and on the Internet. Here are the essential supplies you'll need for the projects in this book.

TOOLS

Chainnose pliers have smooth, flat inner jaws, and the tips taper to a point. Use them for gripping, bending wire, and for opening and closing loops and jump rings.

Roundnose pliers have smooth, tapered, conical jaws used to make loops. The closer to the tip you work, the smaller the loop will be.

Use the front of a **wire cutters'** blades to make a pointed cut and the back of the blades to make a flat cut. Do not use your jewelry-grade wire cutters on memory wire, which is extremely hard; use heavy-duty wire cutters, or bend the memory wire back and forth until it breaks.

Crimping pliers have two grooves in their jaws that are used to fold or roll a crimp bead into a compact shape.

Make it easier to open split rings by inserting the curved jaw of **split-ring pliers** between the wires.

Beading needles are coded by size. The higher the number, the finer the beading needle. Unlike sewing needles, the eye of a beading needle is almost as narrow as its shaft. In addition to the size of the bead, the number of times you will pass through the bead also affects the needle size that you will use; if you will pass through a bead multiple times, you need to use a thinner needle.

A **hammer** is used to harden wire or texture metal. Any hammer with a flat head will work, as long as the head is free of nicks that could mar your metal. The light ball-peen hammer shown here is one of the most commonly used hammers for jewelry making.

A **bench block** provides a hard, smooth surface on which to hammer wire and metals pieces. An anvil is similarly hard but has different surfaces, such as a tapered horn, to help form wire into different shapes.

bench block

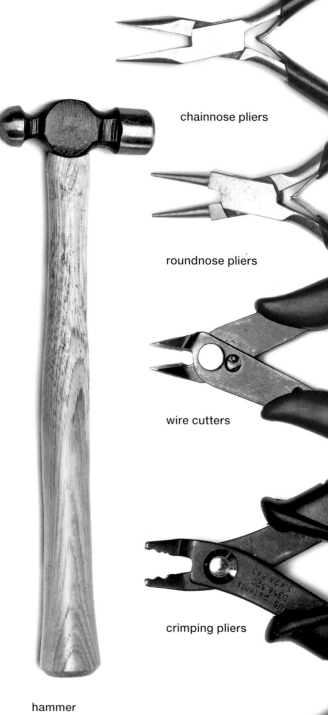

chainnose pliers

roundnose pliers

wire cutters

crimping pliers

hammer

beading needles

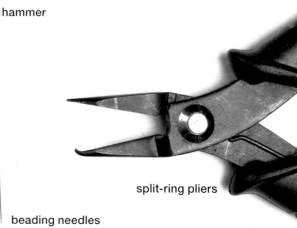

split-ring pliers

Tools & Materials

head pin

eye pin

jump rings

split ring

crimp beads

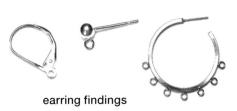

clasps

earring findings

FINDINGS

A **head pin** looks like a long, blunt, thick sewing pin. It has a flat or decorative head on one end to keep beads on. Head pins come in different diameters (gauges) and lengths.

Eye pins are just like head pins except they have a round loop on one end instead of a head. You can make your own eye pins from wire.

A **jump ring** is used to connect components. It is a small wire circle or oval that is either soldered closed or comes with a split so it can be opened and closed.

Split rings are used like jump rings but are much more secure. They look like tiny key rings and are made of springy wire.

Crimp beads and tubes are small, large-holed, thin-walled metal beads designed to be flattened or crimped into a tight roll. Use them when stringing jewelry on flexible beading wire.

Clasps come in many sizes and shapes. Some of the most common (clockwise from the top left) are the toggle, consisting of a ring and a bar; slide, consisting of one tube that slides inside another; lobster claw, which opens when you pull on a tiny lever; S-hook, which links two soldered jump rings or split rings; and box, with a tab and a slot.

Earring findings come in a huge variety of metals and styles, including (from left to right) lever back, post, hoop, and French hook. You will almost always want a loop (or loops) on earring findings so you can attach beads.

WIRE

Wire is available in a number of materials and finishes, including brass, gold, gold-filled, gold-plated, fine silver, sterling silver, anodized niobium (chemically colored wire), and copper. Brass, copper, and craft wire are packaged in 10- to 40-yd. (9.1–37 m) spools, while gold, silver, and niobium are sold by the foot or ounce. Wire thickness is measured by gauge — the higher the gauge number, the thinner the wire. It is available in varying hardnesses (dead-soft, half-hard, and hard) and shapes (round, half-round, square, and others).

STITCHING & STRINGING MATERIALS

Selecting beading thread and cord is one of the most important decisions you'll make when planning a project. Review the descriptions below to evaluate which material is best for your design.

Threads come in many sizes and strengths. Size (diameter or thickness) is designated by a letter or number. OO and A/O are the thinnest; B, D, E, F, and FF are subsequently thicker. **Cord** is measured on a number scale; 0 corresponds in thickness to D-size thread, 1 equals E, 2 equals F, and 3 equals FF.

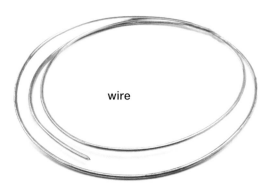

wire

Parallel filament nylon, such as Nymo or C-Lon, is made from many thin nylon fibers that are extruded and heat-set to form a single-ply thread. Parallel filament nylon is durable and easy to thread, but it can be prone to fraying and stretching. It is best used in bead weaving and bead embroidery.

Plied nylon thread, such as Silamide, is made from two or more nylon threads that are extruded, twisted together, and coated or bonded for further strength, making them strong and durable. It is more resistant to fraying than parallel filament nylon, and some brands do not stretch. It's a good material to use for twisted fringe, bead crochet, and beadwork that needs a lot of body.

Plied gel-spun polyethylene (GSP), such as Power Pro or DandyLine, is made from polyethylene fibers that have been spun into two or more threads that are braided together. It is almost unbreakable, it doesn't stretch, and it resists fraying. The thickness can make it difficult to make multiple passes through a bead. It is ideal for stitching with larger beads, such as pressed glass and crystals.

Parallel filament GSP, such as Fireline, is a single-ply thread made from spun and bonded polyethylene fibers. It's extremely strong, it doesn't stretch, and it resists fraying. However, crystals will cut through parallel filament GSP, and smoke-colored varieties can leave a black residue on hands and beads. It's most appropriate for bead stitching.

Polyester thread, such as Gutermann, is made from polyester fibers that are spun into single yarns and then twisted into plied thread. It doesn't stretch and comes in many colors, but it can become fuzzy with use. It is best for bead crochet or bead embroidery when the thread must match the fabric.

Flexible beading wire is composed of wires twisted together and covered with nylon. This wire is stronger than thread and does not stretch. The higher the number of inner strands (between 3 and 49), the more flexible and kink-resistant the wire. It is available in a variety of sizes. Use .014 and .015 for stringing most gemstones, crystals, and glass beads. Use thicker varieties, .018, .019, and .024, for heavy beads or nuggets. Use thinner wire, .010 and .012, for lightweight pieces and beads with very small holes, such as pearls. The thinnest wires can also be used for some bead-stitching projects.

flexible beading wire

nylon threads

parallel filament GSP

Tools & Materials

SEED BEADS

A huge variety of beads is available, but the beads most commonly used in the projects in this book are **seed beads**. Seed beads come in packages, tubes, and hanks. A standard hank (a looped bundle of beads strung on thread) contains 12 20-in. (51 cm) strands, but vintage hanks are often much smaller. Tubes and packages are usually measured in grams and vary in size.

cube beads

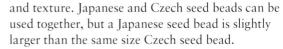

seed beads

Seed beads have been manufactured in many sizes ranging from the largest, 5º (also called "E beads"), which are about 5 mm wide, to tiny size 20º or 22º, which aren't much larger than grains of sand. (The symbol º stands for "aught" or "zero." The greater the number of aughts, e.g., 22º, the smaller the bead.) Beads smaller than Japanese 15ºs have not been produced for the past 100 years, but vintage beads can be found in limited sizes and colors. The most commonly available size in the widest range of colors is 11º.

Most round seed beads are made in Japan and the Czech Republic. **Czech seed beads** are slightly irregular and rounder than **Japanese seed beads**, which are uniform in size and a bit squared off. Czech beads give a bumpier surface when woven, but they reflect light at a wider range of angles. Japanese seed beads produce a uniform surface

triangle beads

drop beads

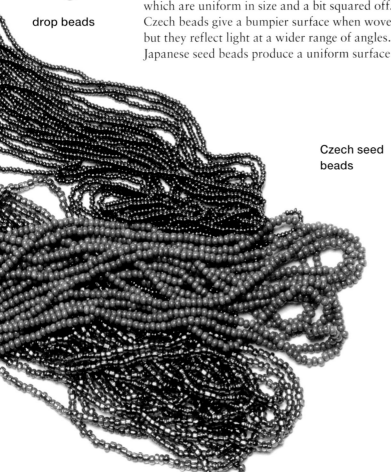

Czech seed beads

and texture. Japanese and Czech seed beads can be used together, but a Japanese seed bead is slightly larger than the same size Czech seed bead.

Seed beads also come in sparkly cut versions. Japanese **hex-cut** or hex beads are formed with six sides. **2-** or **3-cut** Czech beads are less regular. **Charlottes** have an irregular facet cut on one side of the bead.

Japanese **cylinder beads**, otherwise known as Delicas (the Miyuki brand name), Toho Treasures (the brand name of Toho), and Toho Aikos are extremely popular for peyote stitch projects. These beads are very regular and have large holes, which are useful for stitches requiring multiple thread passes. The beads fit together almost seamlessly, producing a smooth, fabric-like surface.

Bugle beads are thin glass tubes. They can be sized by number or length, depending on where they are made. Japanese size 1 bugles are about 2 mm long, but bugles can be made even longer than 30 mm. They can be hex-cut, straight, or twisted, but the selection of colors, sizes, shapes, and finishes is limited. Seed beads also come in a variety of other shapes, including **triangles, cubes,** and **drops.**

In stitches where the beads meet each other end to end or side by side — peyote stitch, brick stitch, and square stitch — try using Japanese cylinder beads to achieve a smooth, flat surface. For a more textured surface, use Czech or round Japanese seed beads. For right-angle weave, in which groups of four or more beads form circular stitches, the rounder the seed bead, the better; otherwise you risk having gaps. Round seed beads also are better for netting and strung jewelry.

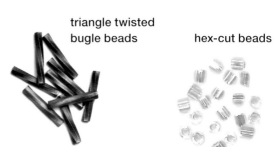

triangle twisted bugle beads

hex-cut beads

Basics

THREAD AND KNOTS

Adding thread

To add a thread, sew into the beadwork several rows or rounds prior to the point where the last bead was added, leaving a short tail. Follow the thread path of the stitch, tying a few half-hitch knots (see "Half-hitch knot") between beads as you go, and exit where the last stitch ended. Trim the short tail.

Conditioning thread

Use beeswax or microcrystalline wax (not candle wax or paraffin) or Thread Heaven to condition nylon beading thread and Fireline. Wax smooths nylon fibers and adds tackiness that will stiffen your beadwork slightly. Thread Heaven adds a static charge that causes the thread to repel itself, so don't use it with doubled thread. Both conditioners help thread resist wear. To condition, stretch nylon thread to remove the curl (Fireline doesn't stretch). Lay the thread or Fireline on top of the conditioner, hold it in place with your thumb or finger, and pull the thread through the conditioner.

Ending thread

To end a thread, sew back through the last few rows or rounds of beadwork, following the thread path of the stitch and tying two or three half-hitch knots (see "Half-hitch knot") between beads as you go. Sew through a few beads after the last knot, and trim the thread.

Half-hitch knot

Pass the needle under the thread bridge between two beads, and pull gently until a loop forms. Cross back over the thread between the beads, sew through the loop, and pull gently to draw the knot into the beadwork.

Overhand knot

Make a loop with the thread. Pull the tail through the loop, and tighten.

Square knot

[1] Cross one end of the thread over and under the other end. Pull both ends to tighten the first half of the knot.
[2] Cross the first end of the thread over and under the other end. Pull both ends to tighten the knot.

Stop bead

Use a stop bead to secure beads temporarily when you begin stitching.

Choose a bead that is different from the beads in your project. Pick up the stop bead, leaving the desired length tail. Sew through the stop bead again in the same direction, making sure you don't split the thread. If desired, sew through it one more time for added security.

Surgeon's knot

[1] Cross one end of the thread over and under the other twice. Pull both ends to tighten the first half of the knot.
[2] Cross the first end of the thread over and under the other end. Pull both ends to tighten the knot.

Basics

STITCHES

Brick stitch

[1] To work the typical method, which results in progressively decreasing rows, work the first row in ladder stitch (see "Ladder stitch") to the desired length, exiting the top of the last bead added.

[2] Pick up two beads, sew under the thread bridge between the second and third beads in the previous row, and sew back up through the second bead added. To secure this first stitch, sew down through the first bead and back up through the second bead.

[3] For the remaining stitches in the row, pick up one bead per stitch, sew under the thread bridge between the next two beads in the previous row, and sew back up through the new bead. The last stitch in the new row will be centered above the last two beads in the previous row, and the new row will be one bead shorter than the previous row.

Increasing

To increase at the start of the row, repeat step 1 above, then repeat step 2, but sew 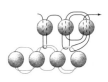 under the thread bridge between the first and second beads in the previous row. To increase at the end of the row, work two stitches off of the thread bridge between the last two beads in the previous row.

Crossweave technique

Crossweave is a beading technique in which you string one or more beads on both ends of a length of thread or cord and then cross the ends through one or more beads.

Herringbone stitch
Flat

[1] Work the first row in ladder stitch (see "Ladder stitch") to the desired length, exiting the top of an end bead in the ladder.

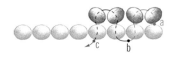

[2] Pick up two beads, and sew down through the next bead in the previous row (a–b). Sew up through the following bead in the previous row, pick up two beads, and sew down through the next bead (b–c). Repeat across the first row.

[3] To turn to start the next row, sew down through the end bead in the previous row and back through the last bead of the pair just added (a–b). Pick up two beads, sew down through the next bead in the previous row, and sew up through the following bead (b–c). Continue adding pairs of beads across the row.

Tubular

[1] Work a row of ladder stitch (see "Ladder stitch") to the desired length using an even number of beads. Form it into a ring to create the first round (see "Ladder stitch: Forming a ring"). Your thread should exit the top of a bead.

[2] Pick up two beads, sew down through the next bead in the previous round (a–b), and sew up through the following bead. Repeat to complete the round (b–c).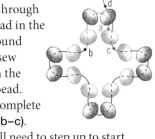

[3] You will need to step up to start the next round. Sew up through two beads — the next bead in the previous round and the first bead added in the new round (c–d).

[4] Continue adding two beads per stitch. As you work, snug up the beads to form a tube, and step up at the end of each round until your rope is the desired length.

Twisted tubular

[1] Work a ladder and two rounds of tubular herringbone as explained above.

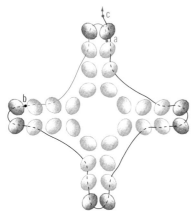

[2] To create a twist in the tube, pick up two beads, sew down through one bead in the next stack, then sew up through two beads in the following stack (a–b). Repeat around, adding two beads per stitch. Step up to the next round through three beads (b–c). Snug up the beads. The twist will begin to appear after the sixth round. Continue until your rope is the desired length.

Ladder stitch
Making a ladder

[1] Pick up two beads, and sew through them both again, positioning the beads side by side so that their holes are parallel (a–b).
[2] Add subsequent beads by picking up one bead, sewing through the previous bead, then sewing through the new bead (b–c). Continue for the desired length.

This technique produces uneven tension, which you can correct by zigzagging back through the beads in the opposite direction or by choosing the "Crossweave method" or "Alternative method."

Crossweave method

[1] Thread a needle on each end of a length of thread, and center a bead.
[2] Working in crossweave technique, pick up a bead with one needle, and cross the other needle through it (a–b and c–d). Add all subsequent beads in the same manner.

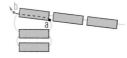

Alternative method

[1] Pick up all the beads you need to reach the length your project requires. Fold the last two beads so they are parallel, and sew through the second-to-last bead again in the same direction (a–b).

[2] Fold the next loose bead so it sits parallel to the previous bead in the ladder, and sew through the loose bead in the same direction (a–b). Continue sewing back through each bead until you exit the last bead of the ladder.

Forming a ring

With your thread exiting the last bead in the ladder, sew through the first bead and then through the last bead again. If using the "Crossweave method" or "Alternative method" of ladder stitch, cross the threads from the last bead in the ladder through the first bead in the ladder.

Netting

Netting produces airy, flexible beadwork that resembles a net and can be worked vertically, horizontally, or in the round. Netting starts with a base row or round of beads upon which subsequent rows or rounds are stitched. Subsequent rows or rounds are added by picking up a given odd number of beads, and sewing through the center bead of the next stitch in the previous row or round. The instructions for netting vary for each project, but some common variations include three-, five-, and seven-bead netting. The number of beads per stitch determines the drape of the overall piece. More beads per stitch produce larger spaces and a more fluid drape.

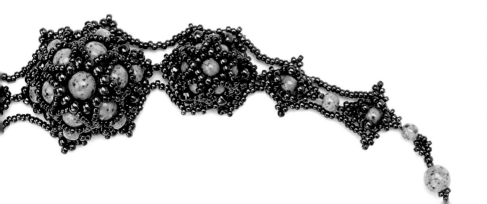

Basics

Peyote stitch

Flat even-count

[1] Pick up an even number of beads, leaving the desired length tail (a–b). These beads will shift to form the first two rows as the third row is added.

[2] To begin row 3, pick up a bead, skip the last bead added in the previous  step, and sew back through the next bead, working toward the tail (b–c). For each stitch, pick up a bead, skip a bead in the previous row, and sew through the next bead until you reach the first bead picked up in step 1 (c–d). The beads added in this row are higher than the previous rows and are referred to as "up-beads."

[3] For each stitch in subsequent rows, pick up a bead, and sew through the next up-bead in the previous row (d–e). To count peyote stitch rows, count the total number of beads along both straight edges.

Flat odd-count

Odd-count peyote is the same as even-count peyote, except for the turn on odd-numbered rows, where the last bead of the row can't be attached in the usual way because there is no up-bead to sew through.

Work the traditional odd-row turn as follows:

[1] Begin as for flat even-count peyote, but pick up an odd number of beads. Work row 3 as in even-count, stopping before adding the last bead.

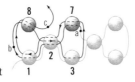

[2] Work a figure-8 turn at the end of row 3: Pick up the next-to-last bead (#7), and sew through #2, then #1 (a–b). Pick up the last bead of the row (#8), and sew through #2, #3, #7, #2, #1, and #8 (b–c).

[3] In subsequent odd-numbered rows, pick up the last bead of the row, sew under the thread bridge between the last two edge beads, and sew back through the last bead added to begin the next row.

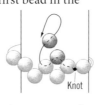

Tubular

Tubular peyote stitch follows the same stitching pattern as flat peyote, but instead of sewing back and forth, you work in rounds.

[1] Start with an even number of beads tied into a ring (see "Square knot").

[2] Sew through the first bead in the ring. Pick up a bead, skip a bead in the ring, and sew through the next bead. Repeat to complete the round.

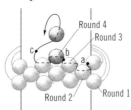

[3] To step up to start the next round, sew through the first bead added in round 3 (a–b). Pick up a bead, and sew through the next bead in round 3 (b–c). Repeat to complete the round.

[4] Repeat step 3 to achieve the desired length, stepping up after each round.

Circular

Circular peyote is worked in continuous rounds like tubular peyote, but the rounds stay flat and radiate outward from the center as a result of increasing the number of beads per stitch or using larger beads. If the number or size of the beads is not sufficient to fill the spaces between stitches, the circle will not lie flat.

Bezels

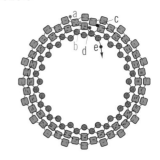

[1] Pick up enough seed beads to fit around the circumference of a rivoli or stone, and sew through the first bead again to form a ring (a–b).

[2] Pick up a bead, skip the next bead in the ring, and sew through the following bead (b–c). Continue working in tubular peyote stitch to complete the round, and step up through the first bead added (c–d).

[3] Work the next two rounds in tubular peyote using beads one size smaller than those used in the previous rounds (d–e). Keep the tension tight to decrease the size of the ring.

[4] Position the rivoli or stone in the bezel cup. Using the tail thread, repeat steps 2 and 3 to work three more rounds on the other side of the stone.

Increasing

[1] At the point of increase, pick up two beads instead of one, and sew through the next bead.

[2] When you reach the pair of beads in the next row, sew through the first bead, pick up a bead, and sew through the second bead.

Decreasing

[1] At the point of decrease, sew through two up-beads in the previous row.

[2] In the next row, when you reach the two-bead space, pick up one bead.

Zipping up or joining

To join two sections of a flat peyote piece invisibly, match up the two pieces so the end rows fit together. "Zip up" the pieces by zigzagging through the up-beads on both ends.

Right-angle weave
Flat strip

[1] To start the first row of right-angle weave, pick up four beads, and tie them into a ring (see "Square knot"). Sew through the first three beads again.

[2] Pick up three beads. Sew through the last bead in the previous stitch (**a–b**), and continue through the first two beads picked up in this stitch (**b–c**).

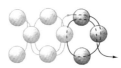

[3] Continue adding three beads per stitch until the first row is the desired length. You are stitching in a figure-8 pattern, alternating the direction of the thread path for each stitch.

Adding rows

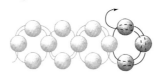

[1] To add a row, sew through the last stitch of row 1, exiting an edge bead along one side.

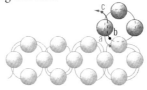

[2] Pick up three beads, and sew through the edge bead your thread exited in the previous step (**a–b**). Continue through the first new bead (**b–c**).

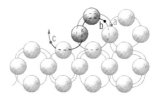

[3] Pick up two beads, and sew back through the next edge bead in the previous row and the bead your thread exited at the start of this step (**a–b**). Continue through the two new beads and the following edge bead in the previous row (**b–c**).

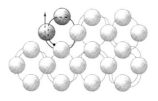

[4] Pick up two beads, and sew through the last two beads your thread exited in the previous stitch and the first new bead. Continue working a figure-8 thread path, picking up two beads per stitch for the rest of the row.

Square stitch

[1] String all the beads needed for the first row, then pick up the first bead of the second row. Sew through the last bead of the first row and the first bead of the second row again. Position the two beads side by side so that their holes are parallel.

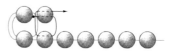

[2] Pick up the next bead of row 2, and sew through the corresponding bead in row 1 and the new bead in row 2. Repeat across the row.

Basics

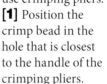

Crimping

Use crimp beads to secure flexible beading wire. Slide the crimp bead into place, and squeeze it firmly with chainnose pliers to flatten it. For a more finished look, use crimping pliers:

[1] Position the crimp bead in the hole that is closest to the handle of the crimping pliers.

[2] Holding the wires apart, squeeze the pliers to compress the crimp bead, making sure one wire is on each side of the dent.

[3] Place the crimp bead in the front hole of the pliers, and position it so the dent is facing the tips of the pliers. Squeeze the pliers to fold the crimp in half.

Opening and closing loops and jump rings

[1] Hold a loop or a jump ring with two pairs of pliers, such as chainnose, flatnose, or bentnose pliers.

[2] To open the loop or jump ring, bring the tips of one pair of pliers toward you, and push the tips of the other pair away from you.

[3] The open jump ring. Reverse the steps to close.

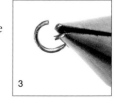

Plain loop

[1] Using chainnose pliers, make a right-angle bend in the wire directly above a bead or other component or at least ¼ in. (6 mm) from the end of a naked piece of wire. For a larger loop, bend the wire further in.

[2] Grip the end of the wire with roundnose pliers so that the wire is flush with the jaws of the pliers where they meet. The closer to the tip of the pliers that you work, the smaller the loop will be. Press downward slightly, and rotate the wire toward the bend made in step 1.

[3] Reposition the pliers in the loop to continue rotating the wire until the end of the wire touches the bend.

[4] The plain loop.

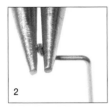

Wrapped loop

[1] Using chain-nose pliers, make a right-angle bend in the wire about 2 mm above a bead or other component or at least 1¼ in. (3.2 cm) from the end of a naked piece of wire.

[2] Position the jaws of the roundnose pliers in the bend. The closer to the tip of the pliers that you work, the smaller the loop will be.

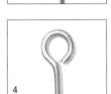

[3] Curve the short end of the wire over the top jaw of the roundnose pliers.

[4] Reposition the pliers so the lower jaw fits snugly in the loop. Curve the wire downward around the bottom jaw of the pliers. This is the first half of a wrapped loop.

[5] To complete the wraps, grasp the top of the loop with one pair of pliers.

[6] With another pair of pliers, wrap the wire around the stem two or three times. Trim the excess wire, and gently press the cut end close to the wraps with chainnose pliers.

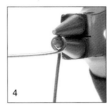

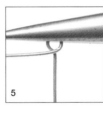

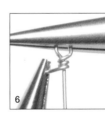

Loops, wrapped above a top-drilled bead

[1] Center a top-drilled bead on a 3-in. (7.6 cm) piece of wire. Bend each wire end upward, crossing them into an X above the bead.

[2] Using chainnose pliers, make a small bend in each wire end so they form a right angle.

[3] Wrap the horizontal wire around the vertical wire as in a wrapped loop. Trim the excess wrapping wire.

Single-Stitch
Projects

Crystal building blocks

Stitch peyote bezels around crystal cubes for an easy and elegant necklace

designed by **Liisa Turunen**

A simple pattern of pearls and bezeled crystals makes an accessory that's perfect for everyday wear or a night out.

stepbystep

Bezels

[1] Attach a stop bead to the center of 1 yd. (.9 m) of Fireline or thread (Basics, p. 13), leaving an 8-in. (20 cm) tail. Pick up an 8 mm cube crystal and 11 11º cylinder beads. Sew through the cube again, positioning the cylinders along one edge of the cube **(figure 1)**.
[2] Pick up 11 cylinders, and sew through the cube again, positioning the beads along the edge opposite the cylinders added in step 1 **(figure 2)**.

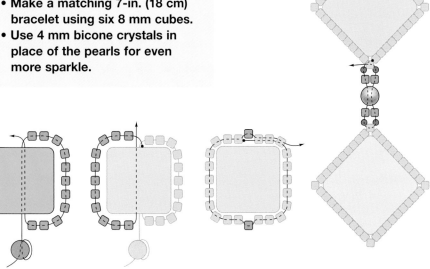

materials

necklace 22½ in. (57.2 cm)

- **12** 8 mm cube crystals in each of **2** colors: A, B
- **27** 4 mm pearls
- 8 g 11º cylinder beads
- 5 g 15º seed beads
- clasp
- Fireline 6 lb. test, or nylon beading thread, size D
- beading needles, #12

[6] Remove the stop bead, and, using the tail, repeat steps 4 and 5 to complete the bezel. Sew through the beadwork to exit a corner cylinder in the center round, tying a few half-hitch knots (Basics) as you go. Repeat with the working thread, exiting an opposite corner. Do not trim the threads.

[7] Repeat steps 1–6 for a total of 24 cubes, 12 of each color.

Necklace

[1] Pick up a 15º, a cylinder, a 4 mm pearl, a cylinder, and a 15º. Sew through the corresponding corner bead in a cube of contrasting color. Pick up a 15º and a cylinder, and sew back through the 4 mm. Pick up a cylinder and a 15º, and sew through the corner cylinder your thread exited at the start of this step (figure 4). Retrace the thread path, and end the thread (Basics).

[2] Repeat step 1 to connect the remaining cubes, alternating colors. Do not end the thread on the end cubes.

Clasp

[1] With the thread exiting a corner cylinder in the center round of an end cube, pick up a 15º, a cylinder, a 4 mm, a 15º, a cylinder, a 15º, a 4 mm, a 15º, a cylinder, three 15ºs, half of the clasp, and three 15ºs. Skip the last three 15ºs, clasp, and three 15ºs, and sew through the next seven beads.

[2] Pick up a cylinder and a 15º, and sew through the cylinder your thread exited at the start of step 1. Retrace the thread path through the clasp connection a few times, and end the thread.

[3] Repeat steps 1 and 2 on the other end of the necklace. ○

[3] Sew through the 11 cylinders added in step 1, pick up a cylinder, and sew through the next 11 cylinders. Pick up a cylinder, and sew through the next three cylinders (figure 3).

[4] Work two rounds of tubular peyote stitch (Basics) using cylinders, and step up through the first cylinder added in each round.

[5] Work a round of peyote using 15º seed beads, keeping firm tension so that this round is snug against the top edge of the cube.

EDITOR'S NOTES:
- Make a matching 7-in. (18 cm) bracelet using six 8 mm cubes.
- Use 4 mm bicone crystals in place of the pearls for even more sparkle.

FIGURE 1   FIGURE 2   FIGURE 3   FIGURE 4

Daring daggers

Earn points for style and flair with this clever design that incorporates dagger beads in a flat peyote stitch foundation

designed by **Marcia Rose**

Whether you choose dagger beads in bold and bright or earthy matte colors, this bracelet will demand attention.

stepbystep

[1] On a comfortable length of Fireline, attach a stop bead (Basics, p. 13), leaving a 10-in. (25 cm) tail. Pick up 12 8º seed beads, then work a row of flat even-count peyote stitch (Basics) using 8ºs.

[2] Work a row of peyote using color A 5 x 16 mm dagger beads (photo a). Push the daggers up and hold them out of the way as you work. Make sure they end up pointing in the same direction.

[3] Work two rows using 8ºs (photo b).

[4] Repeat steps 2 and 3 until you have six rows of As, ending with two rows of 8ºs.

[5] Repeat steps 2 and 3, using color B 5 x 16 mm daggers instead of As, for a total of six rows of Bs, ending with two rows of 8ºs.

[6] Continue as in steps 4 and 5 until you reach the desired length minus the length of the clasp, ending and adding thread (Basics) as needed.

[7] Sew through the beadwork to exit an 8º in the last row, with your needle pointing toward the other edge of the bracelet. Sew through the first loop of half of the clasp and the next 8º in the row (photo c). Repeat to attach the remaining loops of the clasp. Retrace the thread path, then exit an 8º in the last row next to a loop of the clasp.

[8] Pick up an 8º, and sew through the next 8º in the row to conceal the thread connecting the peyote strip to the clasp (photo d). Repeat to complete the row, and end the working thread.

[9] Remove the stop bead, and attach the clasp on the other end of the bracelet. ◗

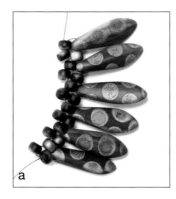

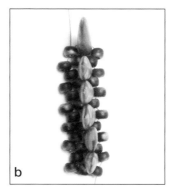

a

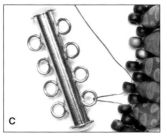

b

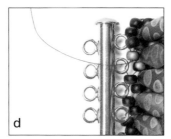

c

d

DESIGNER'S NOTES:

- **Alternate as few or as many colors of daggers as you wish.**
- **Pick up six 8ºs in step 1 to make a bracelet half the width. Use a two-strand clasp instead of a four-strand clasp.**
- **Use 5 x 12 mm drop beads (right) instead of daggers for a softer look. These glass drops have an organic feel to them.**
- **5 x 16 mm daggers a little too dramatic? Take a stab at using 3 x 10 mm daggers (bottom) to create a more subtle version of this bracelet while still boasting an edgy style.**

materials

beige bracelet 8 in. (20 cm)

- 5 x 16 mm dagger beads
  114 color A (cream with gold/bronze dots)
  114 color B (matte opaque white with gold dots)
- 3–4 g 8º seed beads (gold)
- 4-strand slide clasp
- Fireline 6 lb. test
- beading needles, #12

brown/teal bracelet colors:

- 5 x 6 mm dagger beads color A (tortoise shell with rainbow dots); color B (matte teal with rainbow dots)
- 8º seed beads (8RY852, frosted jet Apollo)

green bracelet colors:

- 5 x 6 mm dagger beads color A (lime green); color B (lime green with bronze dots)
- 8º seed beads (nickel plated)

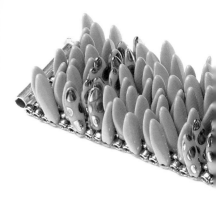

Don't miss a beat

Large seed beads allow this playful pattern to work up in double time

designed by **Collette Hunt**

Holidays have a way of sneaking up on us, so any time is a good time to work on a handmade ornament. Combine flat and circular peyote to create this beaded drum. It lends a personal touch to any tree, or you can tuck a tiny trinket inside and use it as a designer gift box.

step by step

Drum body

[1] On a comfortable length of thread, pick up four color B 8º seed beads, 10 color A 8º seed beads, and two Bs, leaving a 12-in. (30 cm) tail. These beads, shown lighter in **figure 1**, make up the first two rows of peyote stitch and will shift as the third row is added.

[2] Working in flat even-count peyote stitch (Basics, p. 13), refer to **figure 1**, picking up one 8º per stitch:
Row 3: One B, five As, and two Bs.
Row 4: One B, one A, one B, four As, and one B.
Row 5: One B, four As, one B, one A, and one B.
Row 6: One B, two As, one B, three As, and one B.

Rows 7–8: In each row: One B, three As, one B, two As, and one B.
Row 9: One B, two As, one B, three As, and one B.
Row 10: One B, four As, one B, one A, and one B.
Row 11: One B, one A, one B, four As, and one B.
Row 12: One B, five As, and two Bs.
Row 13: Two Bs, five As, and one B.
Row 14: One B, five As, and two Bs.
Row 15: One B, one A, one B, four As, and one B.
Row 16: One B, four As, one B, one A, and one B.
Row 17: One B, two As, one B, three As, and one B.
Rows 18–19: In each row: One B, three

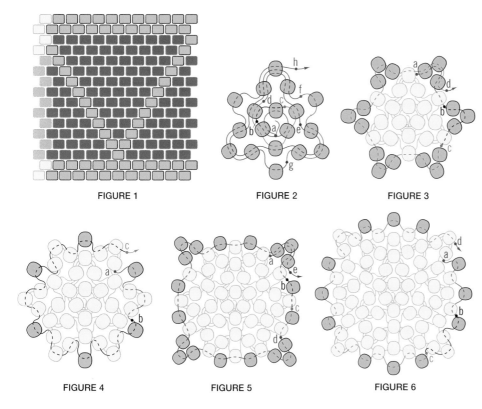

FIGURE 1

FIGURE 2

FIGURE 3

FIGURE 4

FIGURE 5

FIGURE 6

materials

drum 2 x 1½ in. (5 x 3.8 cm)

- 8 4 mm pearls
- 6–7 g 8º seed beads,
  in each of 2 colors: A, B
- 8 15º seed beads
- nylon beading thread, size D
- beading needles, #10

DESIGNER'S NOTES:

- If the body of your drum is not as sturdy as you would like, cut a strip of thin cardboard 5⅞ x 1⅜ in. (14.9 x 3.5 cm), and roll it into a cylinder. Tape the ends together, and insert it into the drum body before stitching the drumheads in place.
- If you want to use the drum as a gift box, secure the top drumhead to the drum body with only a few stitches to form a hinge.
- A drum stitched with 15º seed beads instead of 8º seed beads makes a darling charm or pendant (below).

As, one B, two As, and one B.

Row 20: One B, two As, one B, three As, and one B.

Row 21: One B, four As, one B, one A, and one B.

Row 22: One B, one A, one B, four As, and one B.

Row 23: One B, five As, and two Bs.

Row 24: Two Bs, five As, and one B.

[3] Repeat rows 3–24 twice, then repeat rows 3–22 to complete the strip, ending and adding thread (Basics) as needed.

[4] Zip up (Basics) the first and last rows, and retrace the join. Don't end the working thread or tail.

Drumheads

[1] On 1½ yd. (1.4 m) of thread, pick up three Bs, leaving a 6-in. (15 cm) tail. Tie the beads into a ring with a square knot (Basics), and sew through the first B again (figure 2, a–b).

[2] Work in circular peyote stitch (Basics) as follows:

Round 2: Pick up a B, and sew through the next B in the ring (b–c). Repeat twice, and step up through the first B added in this round (c–d).

Round 3: Pick up three Bs, and sew through the next B in the previous round (d–e). Repeat twice, then sew through the three Bs added in the first stitch of this round (e–f).

Round 4: Pick up a B, and sew through the three Bs in the next stitch of the previous round (f–g). Repeat once. Repeat again, but sew through only two Bs in the next stitch of the previous round (g–h).

Round 5: Pick up three Bs, and sew through the next B in the previous round (figure 3, a–b). Pick up three Bs, and sew through the center B of the next stitch added in round 3 (b–c). Repeat these two stitches twice, then sew through the three Bs added in the first stitch of this round (c–d).

Round 6: Pick up a B, and sew through the three Bs in the next stitch of the previous round (figure 4, a–b). Repeat four times. Repeat again, but sew through only two Bs in the next stitch of the previous round (b–c).

Round 7: Pick up three Bs, and sew through the next B in the previous round (figure 5, a–b). Pick up a B, and sew through the center B of the next stitch added in round 5 (b–c). Pick up a B, and sew through the next B in the previous round (c–d). Repeat these three stitches three times, then sew through the three Bs added in the first stitch of this round (d–e).

Round 8: Work two peyote stitches with Bs (figure 6, a–b). Work one stitch with a B, and sew through the three Bs of the

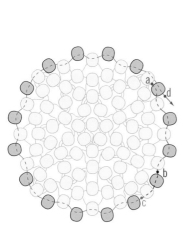

FIGURE 7

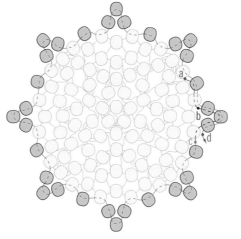

FIGURE 8

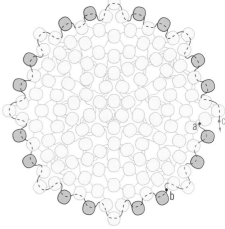

FIGURE 9

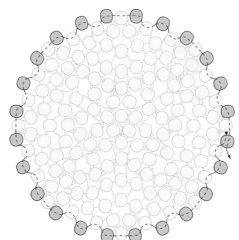

FIGURE 10

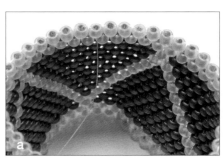

next stitch added in round 7 (b–c). Repeat these three stitches twice. Repeat again, but sew through only two Bs in the next stitch of the previous round (c–d).

Round 9: Work three peyote stitches with Bs (figure 7, a–b). Pick up a B, and sew through the center B of the next stitch added in round 7 (b–c). Repeat these four stitches three times, then step up through the first B added in this round (c–d).

Round 10: Work one peyote stitch with a B (figure 8, a–b). Work one stitch with three Bs (b–c). Repeat these two stitches around, then sew through the beadwork to exit the three Bs added in the second stitch of this round (c–d).

Round 11: Work a peyote stitch with a B, then pick up a B, and sew through the three Bs in the next stitch of the previous round (figure 9, a–b). Repeat these two stitches around, but in the last stitch, sew through only the first two Bs in the next stitch of the previous round (b–c).

Round 12: Work a round of peyote stitch with Bs, sewing through the Bs in the previous round and the center Bs of the stitches added in round 10 (figure 10). End the working thread and tail.

[3] Make a second drumhead.

Assembly

[1] Using the working thread from the drum body, sew through the beadwork to exit an edge B, positioning the needle to point toward the inside of the drum body (photo a).

[2] Sew through an edge B on a drumhead, and sew through the next edge bead on the drum body with the needle pointing toward the outside of the drum body (photo b). Sew through the next edge bead on the drum body toward the inside.

[3] Repeat step 2 around, centering the drumhead inside the inner rim of the drum body. End the working thread.

[4] Repeat steps 1–3 on the other end of the drum body using the tail.

[5] Add 1 yd. (.9 m) of thread, and exit a point B on the drum body. Pick up a 4 mm pearl and a 15° seed bead. Skip the 15°, and sew back through the pearl and the point B (photo c). Continue to sew through the diagonal row of Bs to exit the point B on the opposite edge of the drum body. Repeat this step around to add a pearl and a 15° to each point.

[6] Exit a top edge B of the drum body. Pick up 37 Bs, and sew through the opposite top edge B (photo d). Sew through the beadwork to retrace the thread path, and end the thread. ●

Frame it

Create a frame for a favorite focal bead

designed by **Sue Sloan**

Suspend a focal bead in the center of a peyote stitch frame to display it as a mini masterpiece. You can adjust the size and shape of the frame to highlight any bead in your stash.

step by step

Frame

Determine the dimensions of the frame: On a scrap of Fireline, pick up an odd number of color B 11º seed beads to equal the length of the focal bead and an odd number of Bs to equal the width of the focal bead. Use these numbers to start the frame in step 1.

[1] On 3 yd. (2.7 m) of Fireline, center the following beads: two color A 11º seed beads, the odd number of Bs that equals the length of the focal bead plus two more Bs, two As, the odd number of Bs that equals the width of the focal bead plus two more Bs, and a repeat of all the beads just picked up. Tie the beads into a ring with a square knot (Basics, p. 13). Wind half of the thread around

materials

**pendant 1–2 x 1½–2½ in.
(2.5–5 x 3.8–6.4 cm)**

- focal or art-glass bead
- 4 8º seed beads
- 11º seed beads
  1 g color A
  2–3 g color B
- Fireline 6 lb. test
- beading needles, #12
- bobbin (optional)

necklace 12–20 in. (30–51 cm)

- assorted beads of your choice
- clasp
- 2 crimp beads
- 2 crimp covers (optional)
- flexible beading wire, .015
- chainnose or crimping pliers
- wire cutters

EDITOR'S NOTE:
To make it easier to fit your needle through the beadwork, work the bail off of the center beads along one of the top edges, and add the focal bead prior to zipping up in step 8.

a bobbin if desired, and sew through the first A with the working thread.

[2] To work a corner stitch, pick up two As, and sew through the next A (figure 1, a–b). Pick up a B, skip a bead, and sew through the following B (b–c). Using Bs, work in peyote stitch (Basics) until you sew through the next A (c–d). Repeat this pattern of As and Bs to complete the round, and step up through the first A picked up at the start of this step (d–e).

[3] Work an increase round: Work a corner stitch with two As, then work in peyote with Bs until you sew through the next A (e–f). Repeat this pattern of As and Bs to complete the round, and step up through the first A picked up at the start of this step (f–g).

[4] Work another increase round as in step 3.

[5] Work another increase round, but pick up an 8º seed bead instead of two As at each corner, and step up through the first 8º picked up at the start of this step. Do not end the thread.

[6] To work the other side of the frame, unwind the other half of the thread from the bobbin, and thread a needle on it. Pick up two As, and sew through the next B (figure 2, a–b). Using Bs, work in peyote stitch until you reach the next A (b–c). Repeat this pattern of As and Bs to complete the round, and step up through the first A picked up at the start of this step (c–d).

[7] To complete this side of the frame, work as in steps 2–4.

[8] Zip up the edges of the frame (Basics), sewing through the 8º in each corner. Do not end the thread.

[9] With the shorter thread, sew through the beadwork to exit the center of one side of the frame. Pick up an 8º, the focal bead, and an 8º, and sew through the center of the opposite side of the frame. Sew back through the 8º, focal bead, and 8º (figure 3), and retrace the thread path a few times to reinforce the connection. End this thread (Basics) but not the other.

Bail
[1] With the remaining thread, sew through the beadwork to the place

where you want to add a bail. Determine how wide you want the bail to be, and work in peyote stitch to add the desired number of As or Bs at the center of the outer edge (figure 4).

[2] Using the beads just added as the first row, work in even- or odd-count peyote stitch to make the bail strip as wide as desired. End and add thread (Basics) if needed.

[3] Roll the strip into a tube, and zip up the last row to the first row. End the thread.

Tubes (optional)
[1] On 1 yd. (.9 m) of Fireline, work a strip of even- or odd-count peyote as wide and long as desired using As or Bs.

[2] Zip up the last row to the first row to create a tube. End the thread.

[3] Make as many tubes as desired.

Assembly
[1] Determine the desired finished length of your necklace, add 6 in. (15 cm), and cut a piece of beading wire to that length. Center the frame, and string the necklace with assorted beads and optional tubes.

[2] On each end, string a crimp bead and half of the clasp, and go back through the crimp bead and the next few beads. Test the fit, and add or remove beads as necessary. Crimp the crimp beads (Basics), and trim the excess wire. Close a crimp cover over each crimp if desired. ●

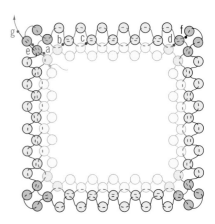

FIGURE 1

FIGURE 2

FIGURE 3

FIGURE 4

Create this
fun cuff
with peyote
triangles

PEYOTE STITCH

Triangles
in transition

designed by **Linda K. Landy**

Directions are given for
the bracelet on the left.
To make the bracelet on
the right, use As instead
of Bs in round 8 of the
first side and round 1 of
the second side of the
triangle.

If you love peyote stitch, you'll flip over this bracelet. Stitch the triangles, position them to form a band, and sew a connecting row between them. Add a clasp and voilà!

Measure your wrist, and add 1 in. (2.5 cm) to determine the length needed for the bracelet. Instructions are written for a 7¼-in. (18.4 cm) bracelet. For a 6½-in. (16.5 cm) bracelet, pick up 17 color A 11º seed beads for each leg of the triangle in step 1 of "Triangles." Add or subtract As in increments of two for smaller or larger triangles. The number of corner beads remains the same regardless of the size of the triangles.

stepbystep

Triangles

[1] On 3 yd. (2.7 m) of thread, center two color B 11º seed beads, 19 color A 11º seed beads, two Bs, 19 As, two Bs, and 19 As. Wrap half of the thread around a bobbin or piece of cardboard. Tie the beads into a ring with a square knot (Basics, p. 13), and sew through the first two Bs. The beads in the ring form the first two rounds of the peyote stitch triangle.

[2] Work the first side of the triangle in peyote stitch (Basics):

Round 3: Pick up an A, skip the next A in the ring, and sew through the following A. Repeat until you sew through the next B (figure 1, a–b). To create a corner, pick up two Bs, and sew through the next B (b–c). Snug up the thread to keep the Bs from twisting. Repeat for the remaining two legs of the triangle, adding two Bs

at each corner. Step up through the first A added in this round (c–d).

Rounds 4–6: Repeat round 3, increasing one A per leg per round, and stepping up after each round, until there is a stack of five Bs at each corner (figure 2).

Round 7: Work 10 peyote stitches using As. With the thread exiting the first B in the next stack, pick up a 3 mm magatama, and sew through the next B in the stack (figure 3, a–b). Repeat for the remaining two legs of the triangle, but work 14 stitches with As instead of 10. Then work four stitches with As, and step up through the first A added in this round (b–c).

Round 8: Work in peyote using Bs until you reach the corner. Without picking up a bead, sew through the first B, the 3 mm, and the next B. Repeat for the remaining two legs of the triangle, work the last four stitches using Bs, and step up through the first B added in this step. Tie a couple of half-hitch knots (Basics), but do not trim the thread.

[3] Remove the bobbin from the tail, and sew through the A adjacent to the bead the thread is exiting (figure 4, point a).

[4] Work the second side of the triangle in peyote stitch:

Round 1: Work to the next corner using Bs. Without

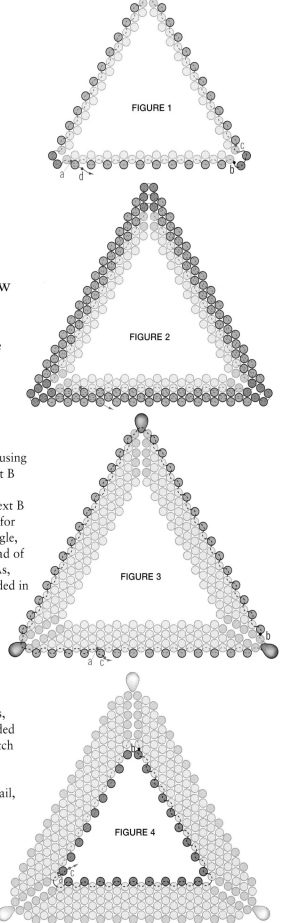

FIGURE 1

FIGURE 2

FIGURE 3

FIGURE 4

FIGURE 5

FIGURE 6

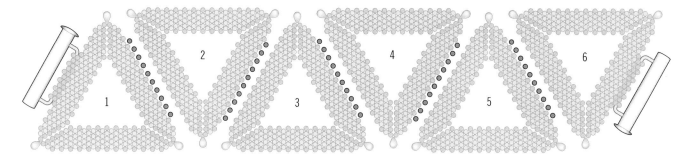

FIGURE 7

FIGURE 8

EDITOR'S NOTE:
Due to the geometric nature and width of this cuff, allow room for a comfortable fit.

picking up a bead, sew through the first A on the next leg of the triangle (a–b). Repeat for the remaining two legs of the triangle, and step up through the first B added in this round (b–c).

Round 2: Work to the corner using As, pick up two Bs to make the corner, and snug up the thread to keep the corner beads from twisting. Repeat for the remaining two legs of the triangle, and step up.

Rounds 3–6: Repeat rounds 3–6 of the first side of the triangle, ending with five Bs in each corner and stepping up to each new round.

Round 7: Work to the corner using As. Without picking up a bead, sew through the B, the 3 mm, and the B of round 7 of the first side of the triangle. Repeat for the remaining two legs of the triangle, work the remaining stitches of the first leg using As, and step up.

[5] Zip up (Basics) the sides of the triangle. At each corner, sew through the B, the 3 mm, and the B. Tie a few half-hitch knots, but do not trim the thread.

[6] Repeat steps 1–5 to make a total of six triangles.

Clasp

[1] To attach the clasp to a triangle, exit the fourth A from the corner of round 7, pick up a B, and sew through the next A in round 7. Repeat for a total of six stitches using Bs (figure 5).

[2] Sew through the A adjacent to the bead your thread is exiting (figure 6), and work six stitches using Bs.

[3] Sew through the beadwork to exit the first B added in step 1, and work five stitches using Bs.

[4] Sew through the beadwork to exit the first B added in step 2, and work five stitches using Bs. Work five more rows of odd-count peyote on this side. Wrap the strip of peyote around the bar of half of the clasp, keeping the clasp halves connected, and zip up the ends. Retrace the thread path to secure the connection, and end the thread (Basics).

[5] Repeat steps 1–4 to attach the other half of the clasp to another triangle.

Assembly

[1] Arrange the triangles on your work surface as shown in figure 7, and measure the beadwork to determine the number of connecting rows needed to make your bracelet the desired length.

materials
bracelet 7¼ x 2 in. (18.4 x 5 cm)
- **18** 3 mm magatama beads
- 11º seed beads
  40 g color A
  8 g color B
- 10 x 30 mm slide clasp with bars
- nylon beading thread, size D
- beading needles, #12
- bobbin or cardboard

[2] On triangle 1, on the leg indicated in figure 7, exit the second B from the corner in the center round (figure 8), pick up a B, and sew through the next B in the row. Repeat for a total of 10 Bs. If your bracelet needs more length, work two additional rows. Retrace the thread path, but do not end the thread.

[3] Repeat step 2 with triangles 2–5.

[4] Attach two triangles by lining up the connecting row of one triangle with the corresponding row of Bs on the next triangle. Zip up the Bs. Retrace the thread path, and end the thread. Repeat with the remaining triangles. ●

Ruffles around

Increase rounds of peyote to produce a beaded bead with a fun and frilly edge

designed by **Pascal Pinther**

This beaded bead can be used in many ways. Strung on wire or a head pin with a loop, you can wear it as a pendant. Or follow the Design Options instructions on p. 36 to make lively links for a bracelet or a funky pair of earrings.

The materials list calls for 11º seed beads for all the colors, but using the natural size differences between brands helps this beaded bead take shape. The color A 11º seed beads should be largest, so use Japanese seed beads that have a more cylindrical shape or 10º cylinder beads. The color B 11ºs should be a bit smaller, so use regular Japanese 11º rocaille seed beads. The color C 11ºs should be smallest, so use Czech seed beads, which have a slightly thinner profile than Japanese seed beads and have a range of sizes within each hank.

stepbystep

[1] On 2½ yd. (2.3 m) of Fireline, pick up 12 color A 11º seed beads. Tie the beads into a ring with a square knot (Basics, p. 13), leaving a 6-in. (15 cm) tail, and sew through the first A in the ring **(figure, a–b)**. The As in the ring will shift to make up the first two rounds of circular peyote stitch (Basics) as the third round is added.

[2] Work subsequent rounds of circular peyote using tight tension as follows:

Round 3: Work a round of peyote stitch using one A per stitch for a

Pascal's pendant (above) uses 10º seed beads for color A, 11º Japanese seed beads for color B, and 11º Czech seed beads for color C. The green version (p. 36) features 10º cylinder beads for color A and 11º Japanese seed beads for colors B and C.

materials

beaded bead 1⅜ x ⅞ in. (3.5 x 2.2 cm)
- **48** 4 mm bicone crystals
- 1 g 11º seed beads in each of **3** colors: A, B, C
- Fireline 6 lb. test
- beading needles, #12

Design options

To make a pendant: On a head pin, string a 10 mm bicone crystal, the large opening of a bead cap or decorative cone, the beaded bead, and a 6 mm bicone crystal, and make a plain or wrapped loop (Basics).

To make a pair of earrings: On a head pin, string one to three accent beads as desired, a beaded bead, and one to three accent beads. Make a plain or wrapped loop. Open the loop (Basics) of an earring finding, and attach the dangle. Repeat for a second earring.

To make a beaded bead link: Cut 5 in. (13 cm) of 20-gauge wire. Make a plain or wrapped loop on one end. String an 8 mm bicone crystal, a beaded bead, and an 8 mm bicone. Make a plain or wrapped loop on the other end. Connect multiple links with jump rings (Basics) to make a necklace or bracelet.

total of six stitches. Step up through the first A added in this round **(b–c)**. End the tail (Basics).

Round 4: Work a round of two-drop peyote stitch using two As per stitch. Step up through the first A added in this round **(c–d)**.

Round 5: Work an increase round of peyote: Pick up an A, and sew through the next A in the same stitch of the previous round. Pick up an A, and sew through the first A in the next stitch of the previous round. Repeat to complete the round, increasing the round to 12 stitches. Step up through the first A added in this round **(d–e)**.

Round 6: Work a round of peyote using one A per stitch. Step up through the first A added in this round **(e–f)**.

Round 7: Work a round of two-drop peyote using two As per stitch, and step up through the first A added in this round **(f–g)**.

Round 8: Work an increase round of peyote: Pick up a color B 11º seed bead, and sew through the second A in the same stitch of the previous round. Pick up a B, and sew through the first A in the next stitch of the previous round. Repeat to complete the round,

increasing the round to 24 stitches. Step up through the first B added in this round **(g–h)**. The circle of peyote will begin to curl more after each subsequent round.

Round 9: Work a round of two-drop peyote using two Bs per stitch, and step up through the first B added in this round **(h–i)**.

Round 10: Work an increase round of peyote: Pick up a B, and sew through the second B in the same stitch of the previous round. Pick up a B, and sew through the first B in the next stitch of the previous round. Repeat to complete the round, increasing the round to 48 stitches. Step up through the first B added in this round **(i–j)**.

Round 11: Work a round of two-drop peyote using two color C 11º seed beads per stitch, and step up through the first two Cs added in this round **(j–k)**.

Round 12: Work a round of peyote using one C per stitch, sewing through both Cs in each stitch of the previous round. Step up through the first C added in this round **(k–l)**.

[3] Pick up a C, a 4 mm bicone crystal, and a C, and sew through the next C in the previous round. Repeat to complete the round **(l–m)**. End the working thread. ●

This purple version uses all 11° Japanese seed beads, creating wavy center rounds and tighter ruffles.

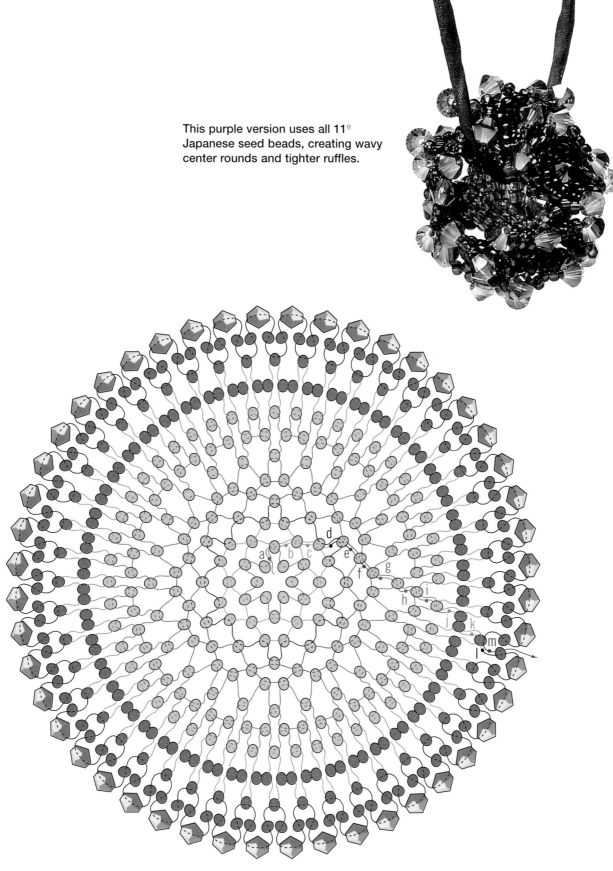

FIGURE

Loop de loop

Loopy beaded beads light up lampworked glass in this necklace

designed by **Jessica Fehrmann**

Experiment with larger or graduated sizes of lampworked glass beads to make your own look.

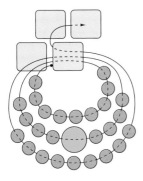

FIGURE

Embellish peyote tubes with loops to complement lampworked beads. Attach drop beads to chain to complete the textured look.

stepbystep

Beaded beads

[1] On a comfortable length of Fireline, attach a stop bead (Basics, p. 13), leaving a 6-in. (15 cm) tail. Working in flat even-count peyote stitch (Basics), use 11º cylinder beads to make a strip that is two beads wide and eight rows long with four beads on each straight edge. Zip up (Basics) the ends of the strip to form a tube, but do not end the threads. String the tube on a short piece of beading wire as you work the next step. This will help you locate the opening of the tube later.

[2] Exiting a cylinder in the tube, pick up nine 15º seed beads. Sew through the same cylinder in the tube to create a loop. Pick up four 15ºs, a 6º seed bead, and four 15ºs, and sew through the same cylinder in the tube. Make a third loop using nine 15ºs **(figure)**.

[3] Sew through an adjacent cylinder in the tube, and repeat step 2. Repeat around the tube, occasionally substituting a 3 mm drop bead for the 6º, to add three loops around each cylinder. For a more random look, change the location of the 6º in each loop. Remove the stop bead, and end the threads (Basics).

[4] Repeat steps 1–3 for a total of eight beaded beads.

EDITOR'S NOTE:
You can purchase 4.5 mm jump rings for the drop beads and 5.5 mm jump rings for the 6º beads if you do not want to make your own. Add or omit jump ring dangles on the chain to get the look you desire.

Strung centerpiece

[1] Cut a 10-in. (25 cm) piece of beading wire, and string a 6º, a beaded bead, a 6º, a bead aligner (flat side first), a lampworked bead, and a bead aligner (pointed side first). Repeat the pattern to string all the beaded beads and lampworked beads. End with the last beaded bead followed by a 6º.

[2] Cut two 5-in. (13 cm) pieces of chain.

[3] On each end of the beading wire, string a crimp bead, a wire guard, and an end link of a chain. String the wire back through the crimp bead, making sure each crimp bead is up against the adjacent 6º. Crimp the crimp beads (Basics), and trim the tails. Using chainnose pliers, close a crimp cover over each crimp if desired.

materials
necklace 18 in. (46 cm)
- **7** 12–14 mm lampworked beads
- 6 g 3 mm drop beads
- 6 g 6º seed beads
- 3 g 11º cylinder beads
- 10 g 15º seed beads
- **14** 3.5 x 5 mm bead aligners
- clasp
- 24 in. (61 cm) 22-gauge sterling silver wire, half-hard
- 10 in. (25 cm) chain, 6–7 mm links
- **2** crimp beads
- **2** crimp covers (optional)
- **2** wire guards
- Fireline 6 lb. test
- flexible beading wire, .019
- beading needles, #12
- **2** pairs of chainnose pliers
- crimping pliers
- stepped roundnose pliers
- flush wire cutters

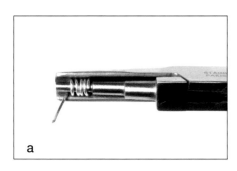

a

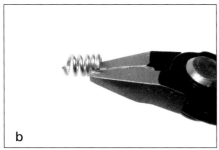

b

Jump ring dangles

[1] Wrap the 22-gauge wire around the smallest step of the stepped roundnose pliers four or five times to make a coil (photo a).

[2] Remove the coil from the pliers, and find the end of the wire at one end of the coil. This is the start of the first jump ring. Using flush cutters, cut the coil parallel to the end of the wire to separate the first jump ring (photo b). Continue cutting one coil at a time until you have four or five small jump rings.

[3] Repeat steps 1 and 2 until you have 20–30 small jump rings.

[4] To create medium jump rings, coil the wire around the medium step of the pliers, and repeat steps 1 and 2 until you have 25–30 medium jump rings.

[5] Open a small jump ring (Basics), attach a drop bead and a link of a chain, and close the jump ring. Repeat to add a drop to every other link. Use the medium jump rings to attach 6°s to each link so that the rings hang opposite the small jump ring dangles.

[6] Open a medium jump ring, attach half of the clasp to an end link of a chain, and close the jump ring. Repeat on the other chain. ○

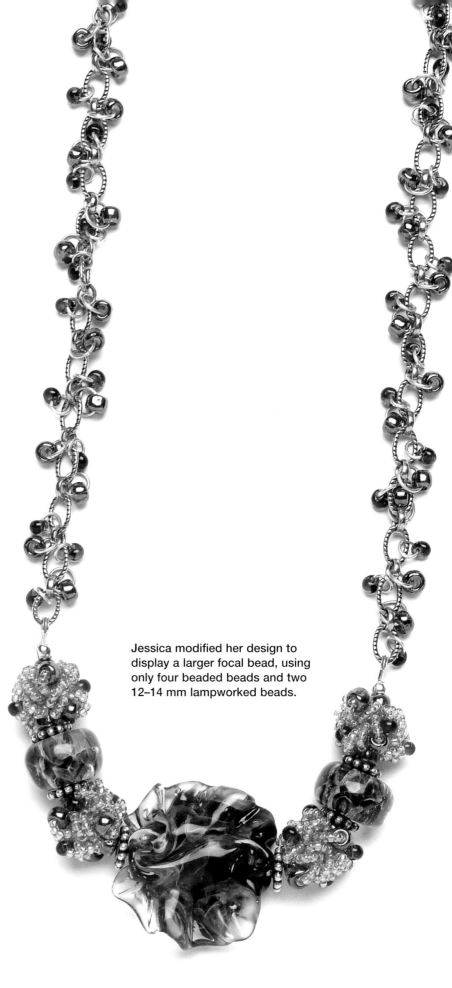

Jessica modified her design to display a larger focal bead, using only four beaded beads and two 12–14 mm lampworked beads.

HERRINGBONE STITCH

That's a wrap

Twisted tubular herringbone winds around itself to hang a pretty pendant

designed by **Melissa Grakowsky**

materials

necklace 16 in. (41 cm)
centerpiece 3 in. (7.6 cm)

- 28 x 16 mm pendant
- **6** 6 mm rondelles
- **36** 4 mm fire-polished glass beads
- 2–3 g 3 mm magatama fringe beads
- 8º seed beads
  8–10 g color D
  3–4 g color E
- 11º seed beads
  5–6 g color A
  1 g color B
  3–4 g color C
- 4–5 g 15º seed beads
- Fireline 6 lb. test
- beading needles, #12

This clever technique could be used to suspend a stone donut or other pendant with a large hole.

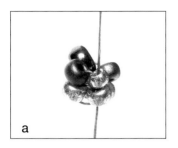

a

b

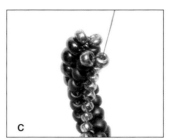

c

d

e

f

g

h

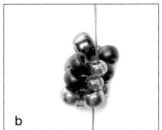

i

Utilizing several sizes of beads allows ordinary stitches to be used in extraordinary ways.

stepbystep

Neck strap

[1] On 3 yd. (2.7 m) of Fireline, make a four-bead ladder (Basics, p. 13) with color B 11º seed beads, leaving an 18-in. (46 cm) tail. Form the ladder into a ring (Basics).

[2] Work in tubular herringbone stitch (Basics) for the first round: Pick up a 15º seed bead and a color A 11º seed bead for the first stitch, pick up a color D 8º seed bead and an A for the second stitch, and step up through two beads (photo a).

[3] Continue the bead sequence established in step 2, but switch to modified twisted tubular herringbone stitch: Step up through only the first bead in the new round instead of two beads (photo b). Work a total of 50 rounds.

[4] Work a round of tubular herringbone using Bs (photo c), a round using 4 mm fire-polished beads (photo d), and a round using Bs (photo e).

[5] Working in tubular herringbone, continue in the bead sequence from step 2 for 20 rounds, stepping up through two beads.

[6] Repeat step 4.

[7] Work as in step 3 for a total of 50 rounds.

[8] Repeat step 4.

[9] Stitch the central portion of the neck strap: Working in tubular herringbone, pick up a color C 11º seed bead and an A for the first stitch, pick up a D and an A for the second stitch, and step up through two beads. Work a total of 85 rounds to make a neck strap that when complete will have an overall length of 16 in. (41 cm). Note: 11 rounds equal about 1 in. (2.5 cm); to change the final length of the neck strap, add or omit rounds in this section. End and add thread (Basics) as needed.

[10] Repeat step 4.

[11] Repeat steps 3–7.

[12] To finish the end, repeat step 4. Exiting an end B, pick up a B, sew through a B in the opposite stitch, the adjacent B, back through the new B, into the remaining B

in the first stitch, and through the next 4 mm in the previous round (photo f).

[13] Sew through the beads in the last round to exit an A. Pick up three 3 mm fringe beads, skip one A in the same column, and sew through the next three As (photo g). Repeat until you reach the last cluster of 4 mms before the long curve of the central portion of the neck strap. Exit a 4 mm.

[14] Sew through the adjacent 4 mm so the thread is facing the nearest end of the neck strap. Pick up enough As to make a loop that will accommodate the end cluster of 4 mms, and sew through the adjacent 4 mm (photo h). Retrace the thread path of the loop, and end the thread.

[15] Repeat steps 12–14 on the other end of the neck strap using the tail.

Centerpiece

[1] On 3 yd. (2.7 m) of Fireline, make a four-bead ladder with two Cs and two Ds, leaving an 18-in. (46 cm) tail. Form the ladder into a

ring. Work in tubular herringbone stitch using two As in the first stitch and two Ds in the second. As you work, the tube will begin to curve (photo i). Work a total of 62 rounds.

[2] Exiting a D in the last round, pick up a color E 8º seed bead, and sew through the D your thread just exited (photo j). Sew through the adjacent D, pick up an E, and sew through the D your thread just exited. Work a modified ladder stitch by sewing through the two Es just added (photo k).

[3] Pick up two Es, and sew down through the adjacent E in the previous round and up through the next two stacked Es. Work a modified ladder stitch to join the two Ds and two Es in this round, and exit an E (photo l). Work a total of 23 stitches.

[4] Work the next stitch by picking up only one E, working a ladder stitch thread

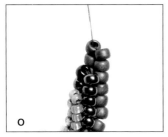

path to join it to both Ds in the same round (photo m). Repeat for a total of 16 stitches, then switch back to picking up two Es (photo n) for the remaining stitches.

[5] To stagger the length of the columns of each color, work two rounds of tubular herringbone, adding Ds and Es but omitting the Cs. Work two modified ladder stitches, adding Es only (photo o). Repeat using the tail.

[6] Exit a C at one end, and join the two end stitches of Cs using a ladder stitch thread path (photo p).

[7] Sew through the bead-work to exit an end D. Pick up a D, and sew through the D on the other end (photo q). Sew through the adjacent D, and repeat on the other side.

[8] Exit an end E, join the end four Es as in step 6, and end the thread.

[9] Center 1 yd. (.9 m) of Fireline in the two center Es at the top of the pendant.

[10] Pick up a fringe bead, an A, a 4 mm, an A, and a fringe bead. Skip two Es, and sew through the next two Es (photo r). Repeat once, but sew through the last centered E and an E in the next stitch. The column this E is in will be referred to as the first column.

[11] Pick up three fringe beads, skip an E in the first column, and sew through the next E in the adjacent column (photo s). Sew through the next E in the first column. Repeat three times.

[12] Pick up a 6 mm rondelle and a B. Skip the B, and sew back through the 6 mm. Sew through the next E in the adjacent column, then sew through the next E in the first column (photo t). Pick up three fringe beads, skip an E in the first column, and sew through the next E in the adjacent column. Sew through the next E in the first column. Repeat twice.

[13] Repeat steps 10–12 using the tail.

[14] For a top-drilled pendant with a hole drilled front to back, pick up four Bs, the pendant, and four As, and sew through the E on the opposite surface. Repeat with the adjacent pair of end Es, and end the thread. For a top-drilled pendant with a hole drilled side to side, add both sets of Bs to the front Es first (photo u), then add the As to the back Es.

Assembly

Position the centerpiece in each end of the neck strap, wrap the twisted sections around each other, and attach each end cluster of 4 mms to the appropriate loop of As. ◐

Larger beads at the ends of the rope slip into hidden loops for security.

HERRINGBONE STITCH

Elegance
squared

Create a clever collar with two-hole Tila beads

designed by **Diane Fitzgerald**

Is there anything that gets your creative juices flowing more than a different bead shape? Try two-hole Tila beads!

step by step

Herringbone unit

[1] On 2 yd. (1.8 m) of Fireline, leaving a 12-in. (30 cm) tail, sew through both holes of a Tila bead. Tie the working thread and tail together with a square knot (Basics, p. 13), and sew back through the second hole.

[2] Working in ladder stitch (Basics), pick up two 8º hex-cut beads, and sew through the second hole of the Tila bead and the 8ºs (figure 1, a–b). Pick up two 8ºs, and work another stitch (b–c).

[3] Working in modified ladder stitch (see "Tila beads," p. 46), pick up a Tila bead, and sew through the previous pair

FIGURE 1

of 8ºs, the first hole of the Tila bead, and the second hole of the Tila bead (c–d).

[4] Continue working in ladder stitch and modified ladder stitch to add an alternating pattern of a Tila bead and two pairs of 8ºs for a total of three sets.

[5] With your thread exiting up out of the end pair of 8ºs, pick up a Tila bead, and sew down through its second hole and the second pair of 8ºs (figure 2, a–b).

[6] Sew up through the first hole of the next Tila bead, pick up four 8ºs, and sew down through the second hole of the Tila bead (b–c).

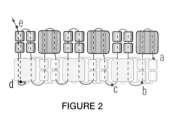

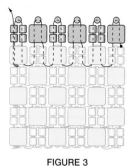

FIGURE 2

FIGURE 3

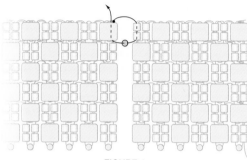

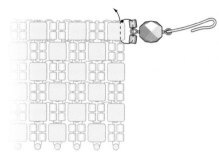

FIGURE 4

FIGURE 5

FIGURE 6

[7] Sew up through the next pair of 8ºs, and repeat steps 5 and 6 across the row **(c–d)**.

[8] At the end of the row, sew under the adjacent thread bridge, and sew back up through the end hole of the Tila bead and the corresponding pair of 8ºs **(d–e)**.

[9] Work three more rows as in steps 5–8, alternating Tila beads and groups of 8ºs to create a checkerboard pattern.

[10] Work the sixth row as in steps 5–8, but pick up an 11º seed bead between the two holes of each Tila bead and between each pair of 8ºs **(figure 3)**. End the working thread (Basics) but not the tail.

[11] Make 11 to 13 units.

8 mm units

[1] On a head pin, string an 8 mm round faceted fire-polished bead, and make a plain loop (Basics).

[2] Using eye pins instead of a head pin, repeat step 1 five times.

[3] Open the loop (Basics) of the head pin unit, attach a loop of an eye pin unit, and close the loop. Open the remaining loop of the eye pin unit, attach a loop of another eye pin unit, and close the loop. Repeat to connect four eye pin units **(photo a)**.

[4] Open a loop of the remaining eye pin unit, attach the hook clasp, and close the loop **(photo b)**.

Assembly

Turn the herringbone units so the edge 11ºs are at the bottom of each unit.

[1] To connect the herringbone units, thread a needle on the tail of one unit, and exit the end edge hole of a Tila bead. Sew through the end pair of 8ºs of the next unit, pick up an 11º, and sew through the hole of the Tila bead your thread just exited **(figure 4)**. Retrace the thread path, and end the thread. Repeat to connect all the units.

[2] Thread a needle on the remaining tail, and sew through the Tila bead to exit the end edge hole. Pick up an 8º, the loop of the 8 mm clasp unit, and an 8º, and sew through the hole of the Tila bead your thread just exited **(figure 5)**. Retrace the thread path.

[3] Pick up two 11ºs, and sew under the thread bridge between the two holes of the end Tila bead **(figure 6, a–b)**. Pick up an 11º, and sew under the thread bridge between the first pair of 8ºs. Pick up an 11º, and sew under the thread bridge between the next 8º and Tila bead **(b–c)**.

materials

necklace 16 in. (41 cm)

- 6 8 mm round faceted fire-polished beads (bronze)
- 18 g Tila beads (bronze matte)
- 17 g 8º hex-cut beads (bronze)
- 3 g 11º seed beads (bronze)
- hook clasp
- 1-in. (2.5 cm) head pin
- 5 1-in. (2.5 cm) eye pins
- Fireline 6 lb. test
- beading needles, #10 or #12
- chainnose pliers
- roundnose pliers
- wire cutters

Repeat across all the units, ending and adding thread (Basics) as needed.

[4] Sew through the end edge pair of 8ºs, pick up an 8º, the end loop of the connected 8 mm units, and an 8º, and sew through the pair of 8ºs your thread just exited. Retrace the thread path, and end all remaining threads. ●

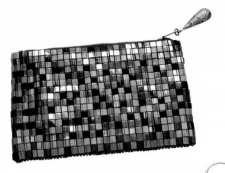

Diane used Tila beads to make this purse in square stitch and these earrings in ladder stitch.

Tila beads

Miyuki's Tila beads measure about 5 x 5 mm by 2 mm thick, and they have two parallel holes. The name, Tila, is familiar to both English and Japanese beaders. In Japanese, "tila" sounds like the word for "flat" while in English the word suggests "tiles," which these beads resemble.

Currently, there are few two-hole beads on the market. Besides Tila beads, a similar style is produced in the Czech Republic. The Czech variety is made of press-molded glass. In contrast, Miyuki's Tila beads are manufactured similar to other Japanese extruded beads, such as seed beads, cylinder beads, and hex-cut beads.

Two-hole beads not only provide interesting opportunities in bead weaving, stringing, bead embroidery, and mosaic tile work, they also offer a smooth contrast of texture when combined with other beads.

You can use many different stitches with Tila beads, such as peyote, square, and herringbone. When working with Tila beads, it is best to use medium tension, as it helps to keep your work flat as you stitch. Use doubled thread for durability. The beads have a flat side and a more rounded side, so when seeking continuity in a piece, it helps to be mindful of which side you pick up.

The following are just a few sample stitches you can work with Tila beads.

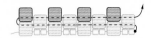

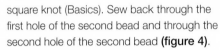

FIGURE 1   FIGURE 2   FIGURE 3

Peyote stitch
Row 1
Attach a stop bead (Basics, p. 13). Pick up a Tila bead and a 6 mm bugle or two or three 11º seed beads, 10º cylinder beads, or 8º hex-cut beads. The beads should equal the length of the Tila bead. Repeat for the desired length of the row (figure 1).

Row 2
Pick up a Tila bead, and sew through the second hole of the previous Tila bead. Repeat across the row (figure 2).

Remaining rows
Continue as in row 2 (figure 3) for the desired length. Finish as in row 1, adding seed beads, cylinders, bugles, or hex-cuts between the remaining holes of the end row of Tila beads.

Ladder stitch
First two beads
Pick up two beads, place them side by side, and tie the thread ends with a square knot (Basics). Sew back through the first hole of the second bead and through the second hole of the second bead (figure 4).

FIGURE 4

FIGURE 5

Remaining beads
Pick up a new bead, and sew through the second hole of the previous bead and the hole your thread just exited. Sew through the second hole of the new bead (figure 5). Repeat for the desired length.

Herringbone stitch
Base row
Using an even number of beads, work a row in ladder stitch to the desired length. Turn the beadwork so your thread is exiting upward from an end hole.

First bead of a new row
Pick up a Tila bead, and sew down through the second hole and the corresponding hole in the previous row. Sew up through the first hole of the next bead (figure 6).

Remaining beads
Repeat the steps for "First bead of a new row" for the length of the row. To turn, sew under the thread bridge of the previous stitch and back up through the hole your thread just exited (figure 7).

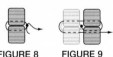

FIGURE 6   FIGURE 7

Square stitch
First two beads
Pick up two beads, place them side by side, and tie the thread ends with a square knot (Basics) (figure 8).

First two rows
Pick up two beads, and stack them side by side. Sew back through the corresponding holes of the previous pair of beads and the first bead just added (figure 9). Repeat for the desired length (figure 10).

Preparing for the next row
Sew back through the first hole of all the beads in the second row and through the second hole of the first bead (figure 11).

Third row
Pick up a bead, and sew through the second hole of the previous bead and the corresponding hole of the next bead (figure 12). Repeat for the desired length (figure 13).

Remaining rows
Repeat the steps for "Preparing for the next row" and "Third row" for as many rows as desired.

FIGURE 8   FIGURE 9   FIGURE 10

FIGURE 11   FIGURE 12

FIGURE 13

Keep it in line

Peanut beads provide a unique advantage to right-angle weave. They mimic the structure of cubic right-angle weave without sacrificing drape or having to stitch time-consuming layers.

Peanut beads lend texture and substance to right-angle weave

designed by **Maggie Roschyk**

materials

necklace 19 in. (48 cm)
- **3** 10 mm sew-on crystals (indicolite)
- 50–60 g 2 x 4 mm peanut beads (nickel plated)
- 5-strand clasp
- Fireline 6 lb. test
- beading needles, #12

EDITOR'S NOTE:

To make a matching bracelet, work a section as in step 1 of "Centerpiece" with five stitches per row for five rows. Center a crystal, and stitch it in place. On one side of the section, work a strip off of the first two rows that is two stitches wide and five stitches long. Repeat off of the last two rows, then connect the strips as in step 3 of "Neck straps." Repeat to the desired length, and add a clasp as for the necklace.

The clean lines and geometric shapes that define Art Deco inspired me to design this necklace. Incorporating peanut beads, with their rounded ends, allows the beadwork a soft drape while maintaining a stylish edge.

As with many styles of seed beads, you'll want to cull your peanut beads and discard any that are misshapen. Work with comfortable lengths of Fireline, ending and adding thread (Basics, p. 13) as needed.

stepbystep

Centerpiece

[1] Pick up four 2 x 4 mm peanut beads, leaving a 6-in. (15 cm) tail. Working in right-angle weave (Basics), make a strip of beadwork six stitches wide. Add rows (Basics) of six stitches each until you have a total of 15 rows.
[2] Work a decrease row: Sew through the second-to-last stitch in the last row, and exit the end bead (figure 1, a–b).

Work four right-angle weave stitches off of the previous row (b–c).
[3] Repeat step 2, but work two stitches instead of four, exiting the end bead of the last stitch (c–d).
[4] To create the point, pick up a bead, and sew through the end bead in the adjacent stitch of the last row (d–e).
[5] Sew through the beadwork to exit a center bead in the second row. Sew through one hole of a sew-on crystal and back through an adjacent bead. Retrace the thread path, then sew through the beadwork to exit next to the remaining hole of the sew-on crystal. Sew through the crystal, then sew through an adjacent bead. Retrace the thread path. Stitch the other two crystals into place, spacing as desired.

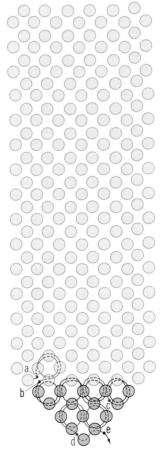

FIGURE 1

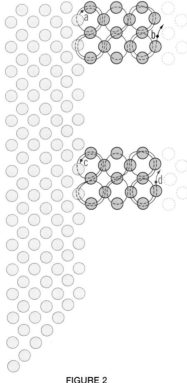

○ 2 x 4 mm peanut beads

FIGURE 2

Keep an eye out for new colors and sizes, like these 4 x 6 mm peanut beads.

Neck straps

[1] On one side of the centerpiece, exit the side bead of the top row (figure 2, point a). Working in right-angle weave off of the side beads of the first two rows, make a neck strap two stitches wide (a–b) and 56 rows long.

[2] Make a second neck strap two stitches wide and 65 rows long off of the side beads of the seventh and eighth rows (c–d).

[3] Connect the end rows of the neck straps with a row of five stitches: Work two stitches off of the end beads of the shorter strap, work a third stitch facing the longer strap but not connected to it (figure 3, a–b), then work two stitches off of the end beads of the longer strap (b–c).

[4] Sew through the beadwork in the last row, positioning the thread to work three more rows of five stitches each. Exit an end bead in the last row.

[5] Add the clasp: Sew through a loop of half of the clasp, and sew back through the end bead (figure 4, a–b). Repeat (b–c). Retrace the thread path a few times, then sew through the beadwork to exit the end bead in the next stitch of the last row. Attach the remaining loops of this half of the clasp in the same manner.

[6] Repeat steps 1–5 on the other side of the centerpiece. ●

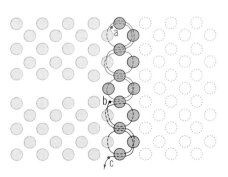

FIGURE 3

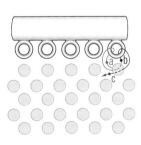

FIGURE 4

Dazzling diamonds

designed by **Samantha Mitchell**

Embellish crystal links of right-angle weave with more crystals to produce maximum sparkle

Crystals with special finishes add extra pizzazz, while jet black crystals lend a classic look to this easy-to-wear bracelet.

These bracelets work up so quickly, you'll want to make them in all your favorite colorways — plus more to give as gifts.

stepbystep

[1] On 3 yd. (2.7 m) of Fireline, leaving an 8-in. (20 cm) tail, pick up a repeating pattern of an 11º seed bead and two 4 mm bicone crystals four times. Sew through the first 11º and 4 mm again to form a ring (figure 1).

[2] Pick up an 11º, a 3 mm bicone crystal, and an 11º. Skip the next 4 mm, 11º, and 4 mm, and sew through the next 4 mm, 11º, and 4 mm (figure 2, a–b). Repeat, and sew through the next 11º, 3 mm, 11º, 4 mm, and 11º (b–c). Retrace the thread path of the outer 12 beads, exiting the bottom 11º.

[3] Pick up a repeating pattern of two 4 mms and an 11º three times, then pick up two 4 mms. Sew through the 11º your thread exited at the start of this step and the first 4 mm picked up (figure 3).

[4] Repeat steps 2 and 3 until you reach the desired bracelet length, minus the length of the clasp, and repeat step 2 again. End the working thread and tail (Basics, p. 13).

[5] Open a jump ring (Basics), slide it through an end 11º, and attach half of the clasp. Close the jump ring. Repeat on the other end. ●

EDITOR'S NOTE:
If you have a hard time finding metal beads, you can substitute 11º Japanese seed beads, but chances are the end seed bead won't accommodate a jump ring. Instead, make a loop of 11º seed beads at each end to attach the clasp using jump rings.

materials
bracelet 7½ in. (19.1 cm)
- **96** 4 mm bicone crystals
- **24** 3 mm bicone crystals
- **85** 11º metal seed beads
- clasp
- **2** 4 mm jump rings
- Fireline 6 lb. test
- beading needles, #12
- **2** pairs of pliers

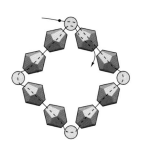

FIGURE 1

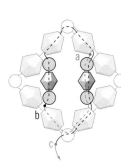

FIGURE 2

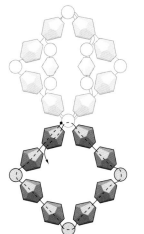

FIGURE 3

Pearls in a half shell

Lustrous pearls rest in
a basket of crystals

designed by **Samantha Mitchell**

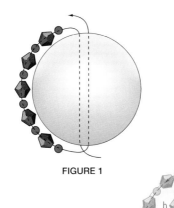

FIGURE 1

FIGURE 2

Nestle pearls in cute cups of crystals. Any round bead will work for this design, but make sure the hole is large enough for several thread paths plus the beading wire.

step by step

Embellished pearls

[1] On 1 yd. (.9 m) of Fireline, pick up a 12 mm pearl, leaving a 6-in. (15 cm) tail.

[2] Pick up a repeating pattern of an 11º seed bead and a color A 3 mm bicone crystal five times, then pick up an 11º. Sew through the pearl again (**figure 1**). Repeat three times.

[3] Sew through six beads in the first loop, exiting the third A. Pick up a 15º seed bead, a color B 3 mm bicone crystal, and a 15º. Sew through the third A in the next loop (**figure 2, a–b**). Pick up a 15º, a B, and a 15º. Sew through the third A in the first loop. Sew through the remaining beads in the first loop, the pearl, and the first six beads in the next loop (**b–c**).

[4] Connect the remaining loops as in step 3, and end the working thread and tail (Basics, p. 13).

[5] Repeat steps 1–4 to make a total of six embellished pearls.

Bracelet assembly

[1] Cut 12 in. (30 cm) of beading wire, and string a crimp bead and half of the clasp on one end. Go back through the crimp bead, and crimp it (Basics). Trim the tail.

[2] String a 6 mm bicone crystal, an A, a 6 mm, and an embellished pearl. Repeat five times, then string a 6 mm, an A, and a 6 mm.

[3] String a crimp bead and the other half of the clasp, and crimp as before. ●

materials

bracelet 7¾ (19.7 cm)

- **6** 12 mm pearls or beads
- **14** 6 mm bicone crystals
- 3 mm bicone crystals
  127 color A
  36 color B
- 2 g 11º seed beads
- 2 g 15º seed beads
- clasp
- **2** crimp beads
- flexible beading wire, .010–.012
- Fireline 4 or 6 lb. test
- beading needles, #12
- crimping pliers
- wire cutters

Mosaic medallions

Dangle tilework look-alikes from your ears

designed by **Liz Stahl**

Use pearls, gemstones, or an assortment of beads from your stash to create these earrings today.

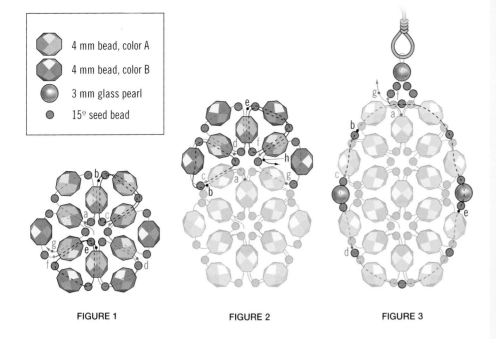

materials

green pair of earrings 1 in. (2.5 cm)
- 4 mm round fire-polished beads
  22 color A (opaque pale green stardust, czechbeads.com)
  16 color B (stone green luster, czechbeads.com)
- **6** 3 mm glass pearls (light gold)
- 1–2 g 15º seed beads (Miyuki 457L, metallic light bronze)
- pair of earring findings
- Fireline 6 lb. test
- beading needles, #12

apricot-and-green earring colors:
- 4 mm round fire-polished beads
  color A (opaque rose and topaz luster, shipwreckbeads.com)
  color B (stone green luster, czechbeads.com)
- 3 mm glass pearls (light gold)
- 15º seed beads (Miyuki 457L, metallic light bronze)

Color key:
- 4 mm bead, color A
- 4 mm bead, color B
- 3 mm glass pearl
- 15º seed bead

FIGURE 1

FIGURE 2

FIGURE 3

Use right-angle weave to work up a quick pair of earrings with a center of sweet fire-polished bead flowers and an edging in a complementary or contrasting color.

stepbystep

Medallion

Lower medallion

[1] On 26 in. (66 cm) of Fireline, pick up a repeating pattern of a 15º seed bead and a color A 4 mm fire-polished bead three times, leaving an 8-in. (20 cm) tail. Sew through all six beads again to form a ring. Tie a square knot (Basics, p. 13), and sew through the next two beads to exit an A (figure 1, a–b).

[2] Pick up a 15º, an A, a 15º, an A, and a 15º, and sew through the A your thread exited at the start of this step and the first four beads just added (b–c).

[3] Pick up a 15º, an A, a 15º, a color B 4 mm fire-polished bead, and a 15º, and sew through the A your thread exited at the start of this step and the first two beads just added (c–d).

[4] Pick up a 15º, a B, a 15º, an A, and a 15º, and sew through the A your thread exited at the start of this step and the first four beads just added (d–e).

[5] Repeat step 3 (e–f).

[6] Join the ends to form a ring: Pick up a 15º, a B, and a 15º, and sew through the adjacent A from step 1. Pick up a 15º, and sew through the A in the last stitch (f–g).

[7] Sew through the beadwork to exit the inside A between the two As on the outer edge (figure 2, point a). With the tail, sew through the center ring of 15ºs. End the tail (Basics).

Upper medallion

[1] Sew through the next 15º and A along the outer edge (a–b).

[2] Pick up a 15º, a B, a 15º, an A, and a 15º, and sew through the A your thread exited at the start of this step (b–c) and the first four beads just added (c–d).

[3] Pick up a 15º, an A, a 15º, a B, and a 15º. Sew through the A your thread exited at the start of this step and the first two beads just added (d–e).

[4] Repeat step 2 (e–f).

[5] Pick up a 15º, and sew through the adjacent A in the lower medallion (f–g). Pick up a 15º, a B, and a 15º, and sew through the A your thread exited at the start of this step (g–h). Sew through all six 15ºs in the center ring, and snug up the beads.

Edging

[1] Sew through the beadwork to exit the top inside A in the upper medallion (figure 3, point a). Sew through the next 15º, B, and 15º along the outer edge (a–b). Pick up a 15º, and sew through the next 15º and B (b–c).

[2] Pick up a 15º, a 3 mm pearl, and a 15º, and sew through the following B and 15º along the outer edge (c–d).

[3] Pick up a 15º, and sew through the next 15º, B, and 15º. Repeat this stitch twice, but in the last repeat, sew through only a 15º and a B (d–e).

[4] Repeat step 2, then pick up a 15º, and sew through the next 15º, B, and 15º. Pick up a 15º, and sew through the next 15º (e–f).

[5] Pick up two 15ºs, a 3 mm pearl, and an earring finding, and sew back through the 3 mm. Pick up two 15ºs, and sew through the three 15ºs your thread exited at the start of this step (f–g). Retrace the thread path of the earring connection, and end the thread.

[6] Make a second earring. ○

DESIGNER'S NOTE:

Substitute 4 mm bicone crystals for the color B fire-polished beads to add even more glamour.

RAW beauty

A hidden layer of right-angle weave provides the structure for this clever bangle

designed by **Donna Pagano Denny**

materials

bracelet 6½ in. (16.5 cm)

- **39–43** 4 mm bicone crystals
- 18–20 g 11º seed beads
- 4 g 15º seed beads
- clasp
- **2** 6 mm jump rings
- Fireline 6 lb. test
- beading needles, #12
- **2** pairs of pliers

Sparkling crystals adorn the spine of a simple yet stunning bracelet.

EDITOR'S NOTES:

- **In steps 3 and 4 of "Embellishment," use 11º's in a complementary color for an entirely different look.**
- **Make a flat bracelet (below) using just the three-row strip of right-angle weave and following the same technique to embellish.**

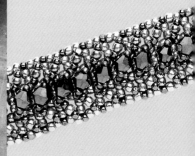

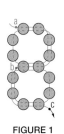

FIGURE 1

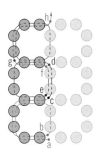

FIGURE 2

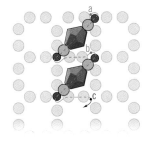

FIGURE 3

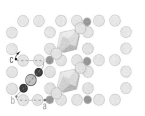

FIGURE 4

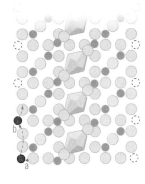

FIGURE 5

step by step

Measure your wrist, and subtract the length of the clasp to determine how long to stitch the band. A 6½-in. (16.5 cm) bracelet requires a right-angle weave strip that is about 39 stitches long.

Right-angle weave strips

[1] On 3 yd. (2.7 m) of Fireline, pick up eight 11º seed beads, and sew through the first six beads to form a ring (figure 1, a–b), leaving a 9-in. (23 cm) tail.
[2] Work a flat strip of right-angle weave (Basics, p. 13): Pick up six 11ºs, and sew through the last two 11ºs your thread exited at the start of this step and the first four 11ºs just added (b–c).
[3] Repeat step 2 until the strip is the desired length minus the length of the clasp. For the last stitch, sew through the first two beads picked up instead of four.
[4] To work the first stitch of the new row, pick up six 11ºs, and sew through the last two 11ºs your thread exited in the previous row (figure 2, a–b), the six 11ºs just added (b–c), and the next two 11ºs in the previous row (c–d).
[5] Pick up four 11ºs, and sew through the last two 11ºs added in the previous stitch (d–e), the two 11ºs your thread exited at the start of this step (e–f), and the first two 11ºs just added (f–g).

[6] Pick up four 11ºs, and sew through the next two 11ºs in the previous row, the two 11ºs your thread exited at the start of this stitch, and the four 11ºs just added (g–h).
[7] Continue in right-angle weave to the end of the first row. End the working thread (Basics) but not the tail.
[8] Repeat steps 1–7 to make a second strip of right-angle weave the same length as the first strip, then add a third row by repeating steps 4–7.

Embellishment

[1] Add 2 yd. (1.8 m) of Fireline (Basics) to the three-row strip of right-angle weave, and exit the two end 11ºs in the middle row (figure 3, point a).
[2] Pick up a 15º seed bead, an 11º, a 4 mm bicone crystal, an 11º, and a 15º, and sew through the next two parallel 11ºs in the middle row so the beads lie diagonally across the stitch (a–b). Repeat (b–c) to the end of the row.
[3] Sew through the bead-work to exit the two end 11ºs on an edge row (figure 4, a–b). Pick up a 15º, an 11º, and a 15º, and sew through the next two parallel 11ºs in the row so the beads lie diagonally across the stitch (b–c). Repeat to the end of the row.
[4] Sew through the bead-work to exit the two end 11ºs on the remaining edge row, and embellish as in step 3.

[5] Pick up a 15º, and sew through the next two 11ºs along the edge of the bracelet (figure 5, a–b). Repeat to the end of the strip, and snug up the beads. Sew through the beadwork to the other edge, and repeat. Do not end the working thread or tail.

Assembly

[1] Lay both strips of right-angle weave side by side on your work surface with the embellished strip face down and the two 9-in. (23 cm) tails on opposite ends. With the working thread of the embellished strip exiting a corner 15º, sew through the first two edge 11ºs on the two-row strip (figure 6, a–b) and the next 15º on the embellished strip (b–c). Continue to the end of the strips.
[2] Sew through the bead-work to exit a corner 15º on the other edge of the embellished strip, fold the strips so the edges are even, and join the edges as in step 1. End the working thread.

Clasp

[1] Using the 9-in. (23 cm) tail from the two-row strip of right-angle weave, sew through the beadwork to exit two end 11ºs on one end of the bracelet (figure 7, point a). Pick up seven 15ºs, and sew through the two adjacent end 11ºs toward the center of the bracelet to form a loop (a–b). Sew through the next two end 11ºs (b–c), and retrace the thread path.
[2] Sew through the bead-work to exit the two end 11ºs in the middle row of the embellished strip. Pick up four 11ºs, and sew through the two 11ºs your thread just exited to form a loop. Retrace the thread path, and end the thread.
[3] Open a jump ring (Basics), and attach the two loops created in steps 1 and 2 and half of the clasp. Close the jump ring.
[4] Using the 9-in. (23 cm) tail from the embellished strip, repeat steps 1–3 on the other end of the bracelet. ❍

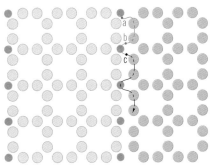

FIGURE 6

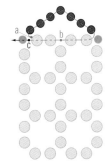

FIGURE 7

Beaded bead bounty

Create a bevy
of dimensional
beads and
embellished
cubes

designed by **Chris Prussing**

Miniature sculptures with endless
color combinations, these beaded
beads can be used as focal beads,
spacers, buttons, or toggles.

Use crossweave technique and pressed-glass bicones to make two different sizes and shapes of beaded beads.

stepbystep

Large beaded bead
Side one
[1] Thread a needle on each end of 2 yd. (1.8 m) of Fireline. With the right-hand needle, center a repeating pattern of an 11° seed bead and a 6 mm bicone four times. Cross the left-hand needle through the last 6 mm picked up (**figure 1**).
[2] Work in crossweave technique as follows: With the left-hand needle, pick up three 6 mms (**figure 2, a–b**). With the right-hand needle, cross through the last 6 mm picked up (**aa–bb**).
[3] With the left-hand needle, pick up two 6 mms (**bb–cc**). With the right-hand needle, sew through the adjacent 11° from step 1 (**b–c**), and cross through the last 6 mm picked up (**c–d**).
[4] With the left-hand needle, pick up two 6 mms (**d–e**). With the right-hand needle, sew through the adjacent bicone from step 1 (**cc–dd**), and cross through the last 6 mm picked up (**dd–ee**).
[5] Repeat steps 3 and 4 twice (**e–f** and **ee–ff**).

[6] With the right-hand needle, sew through the adjacent 11° from step 1 and the next 6 mm from step 2, and pick up a 6 mm (**f–g**). With the left-hand needle, cross through the last 6 mm picked up (**ff–gg**). Snug up the beads so the beadwork cups around the edge.

Side two
[1] Flip your work so the threads exit a 6 mm on the lower right, and continue working in crossweave technique following **figure 3**: With the left-hand needle, pick up a 6 mm, an 11°, and a 6 mm (**a–b**). With the right-hand needle, cross through the last 6 mm picked up (**aa–bb**).
[2] With the left-hand needle, pick up two 6 mms (**bb–cc**). With the right-hand needle, sew through the adjacent 6 mm from "Side one," and cross through the last 6 mm picked up (**b–c**).
[3] With the left-hand needle, pick up an 11° and a 6 mm (**c–d**). With the right-hand needle, sew through the next 6 mm from "Side one," and cross through the last 6 mm picked up (**cc–dd**).
[4] Repeat steps 2 and 3 twice (**d–e** and **dd–ee**).
[5] With the right-hand needle, sew through the adjacent 6 mm from "Side one" and the first 6 mm picked up in step 1 of "Side two," and pick up a 6 mm (**e–f**). With the left-hand needle, cross through the last 6 mm picked up (**ee–ff**). Snug up the beads.
[6] With each needle, sew through the next 11°, 6 mm, and 11°, and cross through the remaining 6 mm (**f–g** and **ff–gg**).

materials
large beaded bead 1 x 1 in. (2.5 x 2.5 cm)
- **32** 6 mm Czech pressed-glass bicone beads
- **18** 3 mm round fire-polished beads, bicone crystals, pearls, or drop beads
- **8** 11° seed beads
- **1–2 g** 15° seed beads
- Fireline 6 lb. test
- beading needles, #12

cube bead ⅝ x ⅝ in. (1.6 x 1.6 cm)
- **12** 6 mm Czech pressed-glass bicone beads
- **4** 3 mm round fire-polished beads, bicone crystals, pearls, or drop beads
- **8** 11° seed beads
- **1–2 g** 15° seed beads
- Fireline 6 lb. test
- beading needles, #12

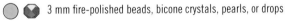
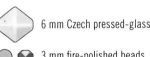

6 mm Czech pressed-glass bicone beads

3 mm fire-polished beads, bicone crystals, pearls, or drops

11° seed beads

15° seed beads

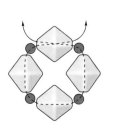

FIGURE 1

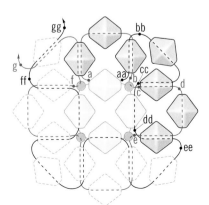

FIGURE 2

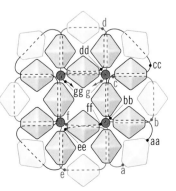

FIGURE 3

Embellishment

[1] The center of the beaded bead has four 6 mms. Sew through the beadwork with both needles to exit each end of a center 6 mm.

[2] With each needle, pick up four 15º seed beads. With one needle, pick up a 3 mm bead, then cross the other needle through it **(figure 4, a–b and aa–bb)**. With each needle, pick up four 15ºs, and cross through the next parallel 6 mm **(b–c and bb–cc)**. Snug up the beads.

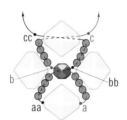

FIGURE 4

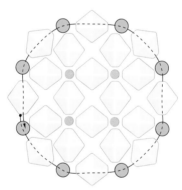

FIGURE 5

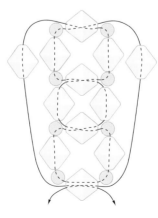

FIGURE 6

[3] Repeat step 2 five times, keeping a firm tension to create a ring of embellishment around the center of the bead.

[4] Working perpendicular to the first ring of embellishment, repeat step 2 around the center of the bead to embellish the rest of the bead. End one thread (Basics, p. 13).

[5] With the remaining needle, sew through the beadwork to exit a 6 mm along the perimeter of the beaded bead. Pick up a 3 mm bead, and sew through the next 6 mm along the perimeter. Repeat around the bead **(figure 5)**, and end the thread.

Cube bead

[1] Thread a needle on each end of 1 yd. (.9 m) of Fireline, and work step 1 of "Large beaded bead: Side one."

[2] Work in crossweave technique with firm tension as follows: With each needle, pick up a 6 mm. With one needle, pick up a 6 mm, and cross the other needle through it.

[3] With each needle, pick up an 11º, a 6 mm, and an 11º. With one needle, pick up a 6 mm, and cross the other needle through it.

[4] With each needle, pick up a 6 mm, and cross through the parallel 6 mm at the other end of the strip **(figure 6)**. Snug up the beads.

[5] With each needle, pick up four 15ºs. With one needle, pick up a 3 mm bead, then cross the other needle through it. With each needle, pick up four 15ºs, and cross through the next parallel 6 mm. Snug up the beads.

[6] To create a hole for stringing the cube in a project: With each needle,

pick up four 15ºs. With one needle, pick up a 15º, and cross the other needle through it. With each needle, pick up a 15º. With one needle, pick up a 15º, and cross the other needle through it. With each needle, pick up four 15ºs, and cross through the next parallel 6 mm **(photo)**.

[7] Repeat steps 5 and 6, then sew through the beadwork to exit a perpendicular 6 mm.

[8] Repeat step 5, sew through the beadwork to exit the next parallel 6 mm, and repeat step 5 again. End the threads. ○

More project ideas

Button covers, bracelet links, or pins

[1] Follow steps 1–6 of "Large beaded bead: Side one" to make a half bead.

[2] With one needle, sew through the beadwork to exit a 6 mm along the perimeter. Pick up an 11º, and sew through the following 6 mm. Repeat to complete the round, pulling the thread tight to further cup the bead.

[3] Embellish the bead as in "Embellishment," keeping in mind you are only embellishing half a bead.

[4] With both needles, sew through the beadwork, tying a couple of half-hitch knots (Basics), but do not trim the threads.

[5] Make several half beads, and use the remaining threads to sew them to 12 mm fabric buttons (above), 12 mm perforated disks for bracelet links, or a mesh dome with pin-back finding.

EDITOR'S NOTES:

- To attach a "Large beaded bead" in a project, exit a 6 mm on the perimeter of the bead.
- To use these beads in a strung necklace (above right), make the cubes into links by stringing them on wire and making wrapped or plain loops (Basics) on both ends. Attach lengths of chain, or sew through the loops to attach a large beaded bead.

Filigree gorget

Interwoven layers of beads result in a fabric-like drape

designed by **Gretchen Grammer**

This lacy necklace is reminiscent of jewelry from the Edwardian era with its ethereal lightness and delicate style.

stepbystep

Row 1

[1] Thread a needle on each end of 2 yd. (1.8 m) of Fireline, and center 16 15°s seed beads. With the right-hand needle, cross through the last four 15°s to form a chain unit (figure 1).

[2] Work in crossweave technique as follows: With the left-hand needle, pick up eight 15°s. With the right-hand needle, pick up four 15°s, and cross through the last four 15°s picked up with the left-hand needle (figure 2).

[3] Repeat step 2 to make a total of 79 chain units.

[4] For the 80th unit, pick up eight 15°s with the left-hand needle, and pick up four 15°s with the right-hand needle. Tie the two threads together with a square knot (Basics, p. 13) to form the last chain unit, and end the threads (Basics).

Row 2

Position the chain vertically so you are working down the chain toward yourself (Editor's Note, p. 63). Thread a needle on each end of 2 yd. (1.8 m) of Fireline, and center 16 15°s. Work in crossweave technique as follows:

Unit 1: With the left-hand needle, sew through the first chain unit created in the previous row from front to back, and cross through the last four 15°s added to form a chain unit (figure 3, a–aa).

Unit 2: With the left-hand needle, sew through the next chain unit in the previous row from back to front, and pick up eight 15°s (a–b). With the right-hand needle, pick up four 15°s, and cross through the last four 15°s picked up with the left-hand needle (aa–bb).

Unit 3: With the left-hand needle, pick up eight 15°s, and sew through the next chain unit in the previous row from front to back. With the right-hand needle, pick up four 15°s, and cross through the last four 15°s picked up with the left-hand needle.

Units 4–27: Alternate between working units 2 and 3.

Unit 28: With the left-hand needle, sew through the next chain unit in the previous row from back to front, and pick up four 15°s and a 5 mm pearl. With the right-hand needle, pick up four 15°s, and cross through the pearl.

Unit 29: With the left-hand needle, pick up eight 15°s, and sew through the next chain unit in the previous row from front to back. With the right-hand needle, pick up four 15°s, and cross through the last four 15°s picked up with the left-hand needle.

Units 30–53: Alternate between working units 28 and 29.

Units 54–79: Alternate between working units 2 and 3.

Unit 80: With the left-hand needle, sew through the last chain unit in the previous row from back to front, and pick up eight 15°s. With the right-hand needle, pick up four 15°s. Tie the two threads together with a square knot to form the last chain unit, and end the threads.

Row 3

[1] Thread a needle on each end of 2 yd. (1.8 m) of Fireline, and center 12 15°s. Work in crossweave technique as follows:

Unit 1: With the left-hand needle, sew through the 29th chain unit in the previous row from back to front, and pick up a 15°, a 3 mm bicone crystal, and a 15°. With the right-hand needle, cross through the 15°, 3 mm, and 15° just added.

Unit 2: With the left-hand needle, pick up eight 15°s, and sew through the next chain unit in the previous row from front to back. With the right-hand needle, pick up four 15°s, and cross through the last four 15°s picked up with the left-hand needle.

Unit 3: With the left-hand needle, sew through the next chain unit from back to front, and pick up five 15°s, a 3 mm bicone crystal, and a 15°. With the right-hand needle, pick up four 15°s, and cross through the last 15°, 3 mm, and 15° picked up with the left-hand needle.

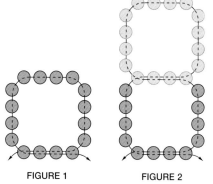

FIGURE 1   FIGURE 2

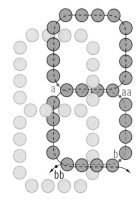

FIGURE 3

[2] Alternate between working units 2 and 3 for a total of 23 chain units.

[3] With the left-hand needle, pick up eight 15°s, and sew through the next chain unit in the previous row from front to back. With the right-hand needle, pick up four 15°s. Tie the two threads together with a square knot to form the last chain unit, and end the threads.

Row 4

[1] Thread a needle on each end of 2 yd. (1.8 m) of Fireline, and center 12 15°s. Work in crossweave technique as follows:

Unit 1: With the left-hand needle, sew through the second chain unit in the previous row from back to front, and pick up a pearl. With the right-hand needle, cross through the pearl.

Unit 2: With the left-hand needle, pick up eight 15°s, and sew through the next chain unit in the previous row from front to back. With the right-hand needle, pick up four 15°s, and cross through the last four 15°s picked up with the left-hand needle.

Unit 3: With the left-hand needle, sew through the next chain unit from back

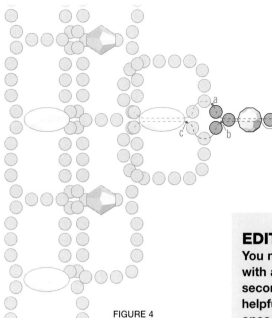

FIGURE 4

Elegant and airy, this design is equally beautiful in a high-contrast or more subdued color scheme.

EDITOR'S NOTE:

You may find it easier to secure the first row to a piece of Styrofoam with a T-pin and work down the chain toward yourself. In this way, the second row will be to the right of the first row. You might also find it helpful to use quilter's tape to secure the chain to your work surface once you begin the decrease (rows 3–13). For the last row, it is easiest to pick up the necklace. Be sure you are always working on the front of the necklace when you add a pearl or a crystal.

to front, and pick up four 15ºs and a pearl. With the right-hand needle, pick up four 15ºs, and cross through the pearl.

[2] Alternate between working units 2 and 3 across the row until you reach the second-to-last chain unit in the previous row. Repeat step 3 of "Row 3."

Rows 5–13

Alternate working as in "Row 3" and "Row 4," decreasing a unit on each end of each subsequent row and ending on "Row 3." You will not need as much thread as the rows get shorter.

Row 14

[1] Thread a needle on each end of 2 ft. (61 cm) of Fireline. Work in crossweave technique as follows:

Unit 1: With the left-hand needle, sew through the second chain unit in the previous row from back to front, and pick up eight 15ºs and a 5 mm pearl. With the right-hand needle, pick up four 15ºs, and cross through the pearl.

Unit 2: With the left-hand needle, pick up eight 15ºs, and sew through the next chain unit in the previous row from front to back. With the right-hand

needle, pick up four 15ºs, and cross through the eight 15ºs picked up with the left-hand needle, the pearl, and the last two 15ºs picked up by the right-hand needle in the first stitch of this row.

[2] Pick up two 15ºs, a 4 mm round crystal, and a 15º. Skip the last 15º, and sew back through the 4 mm and the next 15º (figure 4, a–b). Pick up a 15º, and sew through the two adjacent 15ºs in the second stitch of the previous row (b–c). Retrace the thread path to the other end of the thread. Tie the threads together with a square knot, and end the threads.

Clasp

[1] Open a 6 mm jump ring (Basics), and attach the end chain unit of "Row 1" and the S-hook or lobster claw clasp. Close the jump ring.

[2] Open a 6 mm jump ring, and attach the remaining end chain unit of "Row 1" and the 2-in. (5 cm) piece of chain. Close the jump ring.

[3] On a head pin, string a 5 mm pearl, and make the first half of a wrapped loop (Basics). Slide the end of the chain into the loop, and complete the wraps. ●

materials

necklace 17½ in. (44.5 cm)

- **50** 5 mm rice-shaped pearls
- **4 mm** round crystal
- **42** 3 mm bicone crystals
- **20 g** 15º seed beads
- S-hook or lobster claw clasp
- 2 in. (5 cm) chain, 3–5 mm links
- 1½-in. (3.8 cm) head pin
- **2** 6 mm jump rings
- Fireline 6 lb. test
- beading needles, #12
- chainnose pliers
- roundnose pliers
- wire cutters

Crisscrossed Crystals

Sew a simple, elegant bracelet in crystals and pearls

designed by **Nancy Sebestyen**

Creative use of crossweave technique produces a classic look that's quick to stitch.

materials

bracelet 7¼ in. (18.4 cm)
- 26 6 mm crystal pearls
- 14 4 mm bicone crystals
- 39 3 mm crystal pearls
- 52 3 mm bicone crystals in each of 2 colors: A, B
- 2 8º seed beads
- 2–3 g 11º seed beads
- 2–3 g 15º seed beads
- clasp
- Fireline 6 lb. test
- beading needles, #12

Combine sparkly bicone crystals with shimmering pearls to create a pretty little adornment for your wrist.

step by step

Base

[1] Thread a needle on each end of 3 yd. (2.7 m) of Fireline. Center one half of the clasp. Over both needles, string an 8º seed bead (figure 1, a–b and aa–bb).

[2] With each needle, pick up two 11º seed beads. With one needle, pick up a 4 mm bicone crystal, and cross the other needle through it (b–c and bb–cc).

[3] With each needle, pick up two 11ºs, a 6 mm pearl, a 15º seed bead, a color A 3 mm bicone crystal, a 15º, a 3 mm pearl, a 15º, an A, and a 15º. Sew through the 6 mm again (c–d and cc–dd).

[4] Repeat steps 2 and 3 until you have a total of 13 units, and repeat step 2 again.

[5] With each needle, pick up two 11ºs. Over both needles, string an 8º and the other half of the clasp (figure 2). Retrace the thread path to reinforce the connection, and cross through the last 4 mm.

Embellishment

[1] With each needle, pick up a 15º, a color B 3 mm bicone crystal, and a 15º. Over both needles, string a 3 mm pearl (figure 3, a–b and aa–bb).

[2] With each needle, pick up a 15º, a B, and a 15º, and cross the needles through the next 4 mm in the base (b–c and bb–cc).

[3] Repeat steps 1 and 2 for the length of the bracelet.

[4] Sew through the beadwork, and retrace the thread path to reinforce the connection to the clasp half added in step 1 of "Base." End both threads (Basics, p. 13). ◗

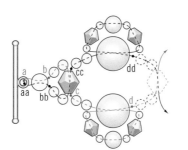

FIGURE 1

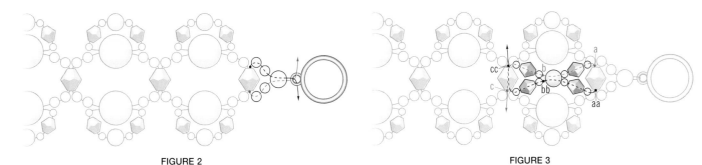

FIGURE 2

FIGURE 3

EDITOR'S NOTE:

To make a multicolored variation, use a single color each of 6 mm pearls, 4 mm bicone crystals, and 3 mm pearls, and a random assortment of 3 mm bicone crystals.

Dimensional crossweave technique mimics the look of cubic right-angle weave

Diamond

Embellish diamond-shaped components of cubic crossweave with tiny sparkling crystals, pearls, and metal accents for feminine finishing touches.

stepbystep

Base

[1] Thread a needle on each end of a comfortable length of 8 lb. Fireline, and center three 11º seed beads. With one needle, pick up an 11º, and cross the other needle through it.

[2] With each needle, pick up an 11º. With one needle, pick up an 11º, and cross the other needle through it. Repeat (figure 1).

[3] With each needle, pick up an 11º. Cross both needles through the end 11º in the first stitch (figure 2).

[4] With one needle, sew through a top 11º on the adjacent side (figure 3, a–b). Sew through the ring of four 11ºs on this side (b–c). Repeat with the other needle on the opposite side.

[5] Cross the needles through a bottom 11º on the adjacent side (figure 4). This completes the unit and positions the thread to build subsequent units. There are six sides per unit, which all look the same. The 11º your threads exit after completing each unit determines the direction of the new unit.

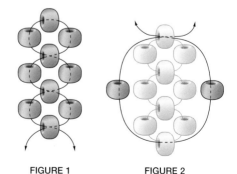

FIGURE 1   FIGURE 2

deluxe

designed by **Grace Nehls**

[6] Continue working in cubic crossweave technique to build a subsequent unit off of a previous unit: With each needle, pick up an 11º. With one needle, pick up an 11º, and cross the other needle through it. Repeat **(figure 5)**. With each needle, pick up an 11º. Cross the needles through the top 11º opposite the bottom 11º your thread exited at the start of this step **(figure 6)**. Repeat steps 4 and 5.

[7] Repeat step 6 to stitch a total of 13 units. With each needle, sew through the beadwork, and cross both needles through the bottom 11º on the side adjacent to the one you've been working off of. This changes the direction of the new row, making it perpendicular to the previous row **(figure 7)**.

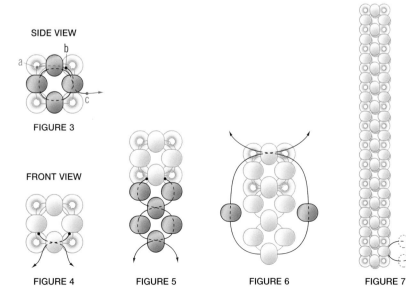

SIDE VIEW

FIGURE 3

FRONT VIEW

FIGURE 4

FIGURE 5

FIGURE 6

FIGURE 7

EDITOR'S NOTES:
- Use glass 11º seed beads in place of metal 11ºs for the base if desired, using only 6 lb. Fireline throughout the project.
- Work steps 1–8 of "Base" with fewer units to create a single zigzag chain. Embellish as desired.

materials
bracelet 8 in. (20 cm)
- **10** 6 mm bicone crystals
- **7** 6 mm disk beads or margarita crystals
- **10** 4 mm button pearls
- **316** 2 mm round crystals
- **12 g** 11º metal seed beads
- 15º seed beads
  3 g color A, 1 g color B
- **7** 10 mm bead caps
- Fireline 6 lb. and 8 lb. test
- beading needles, #12

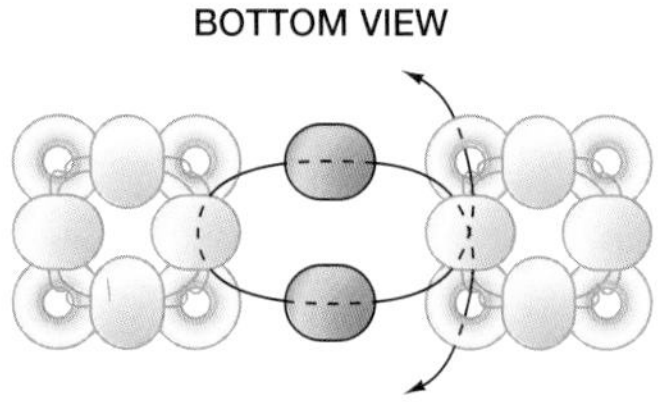

BOTTOM VIEW

FIGURE 9

FIGURE 10

FIGURE 8

[8] Repeat step 6 to stitch a total of 12 units, not counting the end unit of the previous row. With each needle, sew through the beadwork, and cross both needles through the bottom 11º on the side adjacent to the one you've been working off of, as in step 7. Make a total of five zigzag rows, ending and adding thread (Basics, p. 13) as needed.

[9] To create the first diamond, repeat step 6 to stitch a total of six units, not counting the end unit of the previous row. With each needle, sew through the beadwork, and cross both needles through the bottom 11º on the adjacent side working back toward the bracelet instead of away from it. Work a row of six units, not counting the end unit from the previous row. With each needle, sew through the beadwork, and cross both needles through the bottom 11º facing the last long row. Work a row of four units, not counting the end unit from the previous row **(figure 8)**.

[10] Join two units: With each needle, pick up an 11º, and cross the needles

through the corresponding bottom 11º in the center unit of the last long row, and sew through the adjacent side 11ºs **(figure 9)**. Cross the needles through the adjacent top 11º. With each needle, pick up an 11º, and cross the needles through the top 11º in the previous unit. With each needle, sew through the side 11ºs to complete the unit. With each needle, follow the crossweave thread path through the center unit of the long row, and cross the needles through the bottom 11º opposite the 11º your threads exited at the start of this step.

[11] To complete the next diamond, stitch six units as in step 6. With each needle, sew through the beadwork, cross both needles through the bottom 11º facing the next long row, and stitch four units **(figure 10)**. Join the end unit to the center unit of the next long row as in step 10.

[12] Repeat step 11 three times, then work as in step 9 to complete the end diamond. Join the last unit as in step 10, and end the threads.

Embellishments

[1] Thread a needle on each end of a comfortable length of 6 lb. Fireline, and center a 2 mm round crystal. With each needle, sew through a top 11º in the end unit on one end of the base **(photo a)**. (Note: We substituted 11º seed beads for the 2 mms in **photos a–f**.) With each needle, pick up a 2 mm, and sew through the next top 11º **(photo b)**. Repeat, adding a 2 mm between all the top 11ºs along the outer edge of the base, ending and adding thread as needed.

[2] Repeat step 1 to add a 2 mm between the top 11ºs along the inner edge of the base.

[3] Repeat steps 1 and 2 on the bottom of the base using color A 15º seed beads. End the threads.

[4] Working with a single needle, add a comfortable length of 6 lb. Fireline to one end of the base, exiting a top 11º in the end unit. Pick up a 10 mm bead cap, a 6 mm disk bead or margarita crystal, and a color B 15º seed bead.

Skip the B, and sew back through the disk, the bead cap, and the top 11º opposite the 11º your thread exited at the start of this embellishment (photo c). Retrace the thread path.

[5] Sew through the beadwork along the side of the diamond to exit a top 11º in the corner unit. Pick up a 4 mm button pearl and a B. Skip the B, and sew back through the pearl and the opposite top 11º in the corner unit (photo d). Retrace the thread path. Sew through the beadwork to add a pearl embellishment to the opposite corner unit of the same diamond.

[6] Sew through the beadwork to exit a side 11º in the center unit joining the first two diamonds. Pick up a 6 mm bicone crystal and three Bs. Skip the Bs, and sew back through the bicone and the side 11º (photo e). Retrace the thread path, then sew through the beadwork to exit the opposite side 11º. Repeat the bicone embellishment on this side, then sew through the beadwork to exit a top 11º in the same center unit. Repeat the embellishment added in step 4.

[7] Repeat the embellishments in steps 4–6 for the remaining diamonds, ending and adding thread as needed.

Toggle bar

[1] Thread a needle on each end of a comfortable length of 6 lb. Fireline, and stitch a row of nine units as in steps 1–6 of "Base."

[2] With one needle, exit an end 11º, pick up a 2 mm, and sew through the next end 11º. Repeat around the end 11ºs. Exit an edge 11º, pick up a 2 mm, and sew through the next edge 11º. Repeat to add a 2 mm between the 11ºs along all four edges and the 11ºs on the other end.

[3] Exiting an end 11º, pick up a pearl and a B. Skip the B, and sew back through the pearl and the opposite end 11º. Retrace the thread path, and end

the thread. With the remaining thread, repeat the pearl embellishment on the other end. Retrace the thread path, and sew through the beadwork, exiting a center edge 11º.

[4] Connect the toggle to a diamond on one end of the base: Pick up a repeating pattern of a 2 mm and an 11º three times, then pick up a 2 mm. Sew through the bottom end A. Pick up a repeating pattern of a 2 mm and an 11º three times, then pick up a 2 mm, and sew through the edge 11º your thread exited at the start of this step (photo f). Retrace the thread path several times, and end the thread. ⊙

Substituting 11º seed beads for the 2 mm round crystals creates a casual and less-expensive accessory.

Disks & dots

Interwoven loops create a triple-strand effect with glass roundels and silver-plated beads

Pair a rich hue with metallic beads for a classic look.

materials

bracelet 8 in. (20 cm)
- **121** 6 mm roundels
- **184** 2.4 mm round silver-plated beads
- clasp
- **2** crimp beads
- flexible beading wire, .010
- chainnose pliers
- wire cutters

designed by **Lynne Soto**

Create an everyday bracelet in your favorite hues with an easy technique.

stepbystep

[1] Center half of the clasp on 4 ft. (1.2 m) of beading wire. With each end, pick up five 2.4 mm round beads. With one end, pick up a 6 mm roundel, and cross the other end through it **(photo a)**. Slide the loop along the wire so one end is 6 in. (15 cm) longer than the other.

[2] With one end, pick up a pattern of a 2.4 mm and a roundel four times. With the other end, pick up a pattern of a 2.4 mm and a roundel three times, then pick up a 2.4 mm, and cross the end through the last roundel picked up with the first end **(photo b)**.

[3] Repeat step 2 11 times.

[4] With each end, pick up five 2.4 mms. With one end, pick up the other half of the clasp. Cross the other end through it.

[5] With the longer end, pick up five 2.4 mms, and go through the end roundel. Snug up the beads.

[6] Pick up a pattern of a 2.4 mm and a roundel three times, then pick up a 2.4 mm. Go through the next centered roundel in the same direction as the wire path in step 5 **(photo c)**.

[7] Repeat step 6 11 times.

[8] Pick up five 2.4 mms, go through the clasp loop, and flip the bracelet so the flat side faces upward. Pick up five 2.4 mms, and go through the end roundel to position two strands of 2.4 mms on each side of the clasp.

[9] Pick up three 2.4 mms, a crimp bead, and three 2.4 mms, and go through the next centered roundel. Pick up two 2.4 mms, go back through the 2.4 mm next to the crimp bead, the crimp bead, and the next 2.4 mm, pick up two 2.4 mms, and go through the end roundel in the same direction it exited at the start of this step. Go through the first three 2.4 mms, the crimp bead, and the next 2.4 mm. Snug up the beads. Flatten the crimp bead with chainnose pliers, and trim the wire **(photo d)**.

[10] On the other end, pick up five 2.4 mms, and go through the end roundel to position two strands of 2.4 mms on each side of the clasp. Repeat step 9. ●

a

b

c

d

BEAD WEAVING

Romantic
rendezvous

Medallions take shape
in a feminine necklace

designed by **Sandra Lamoureux**

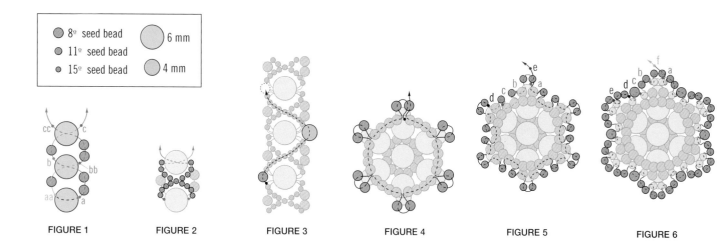

○ 8º seed bead	● 6 mm	
○ 11º seed bead		
○ 15º seed bead	● 4 mm	

FIGURE 1 FIGURE 2 FIGURE 3 FIGURE 4 FIGURE 5 FIGURE 6

Join domed components with dainty lines of seed beads for a dramatic look.

stepbystep

Large medallion

[1] Thread a needle on each end of 2 yd. (1.8 m) of Fireline, and center a 6 mm round bead.

[2] With the right-hand needle, pick up two 8º seed beads. With the left-hand needle, pick up an 8º and a 6 mm. Cross the right-hand needle through the 6 mm **(figure 1, a–b and aa–bb)**.

[3] Repeat step 2 **(b–c and bb–cc)** until you have a total of six 6 mms, keeping the pairs of 8ºs on one side and the single 8ºs on the other side.

[4] With the left-hand needle, pick up an 8º. With the right-hand needle, pick up two 8ºs. Cross both needles through the first 6 mm to form a ring.

[5] With each needle, pick up four 15º seed beads. With one needle, pick up a 15º, and cross the other needle through it. With each needle, pick up four 15ºs, and cross both needles through the next 6 mm in the ring **(figure 2)**.

[6] Repeat step 5 around the ring. With each needle, sew diagonally through the first nine 15ºs added in this round.

[7] With the needle exiting the inner (smaller) rim, pick up an 8º, and sew diagonally through the next nine 15ºs.

Pick up a 4 mm round bead, and sew diagonally through the next nine 15ºs **(figure 3)**. Repeat this step to complete the round.

[8] With the needle exiting a 15º along the outer (larger) rim, pick up a 4 mm, and sew diagonally through the next nine 15ºs. Pick up an 8º, and sew diagonally through the next nine 15ºs. Repeat this step to complete the round.

[9] With the needle exiting an 8º along the inner rim, sew through all the inner rim 8ºs, and step up through the first 8º.

[10] Pick up a 6 mm, and sew through the 8º opposite the one your thread just exited. Sew back through the 6 mm and the 8º your thread exited at the start of this step. Push the 6 mm down so it sits below the ring of 8ºs, and retrace the thread path. Tie a few half-hitch knots (Basics, p. 13), but don't trim the thread.

[11] With the needle exiting a 15º along the outer rim, pick up two 8ºs, and sew through the next two 8ºs. Repeat around the ring to add a pair of 8ºs between all the 8ºs in the previous round. Step up through the first 8º picked up in the first stitch of this round.

[12] Pick up two 8ºs, and sew through the next four 8ºs. Repeat to complete

the round, and step up through the first 8º added in this step **(figure 4)**.

[13] Pick up two 11º seed beads, and sew through the next 8º in the previous round **(figure 5, a–b)**. Pick up an 11º, and sew through the adjacent pair of 8ºs between the 6 mms in the outer rim **(b–c)**. Pick up an 11º, and sew through the next 8º in the previous round **(c–d)**.

[14] Repeat step 13 around the outer rim, and step up through the first 11º added **(d–e)**.

[15] Pick up two 11ºs, and sew through the next 11º **(figure 6, a–b)**. Repeat **(b–c)**. Pick up an 8º, and sew through the next 11º **(c–d)**. Pick up two 11ºs, and sew through the next 11º **(d–e)**.

[16] Repeat step 15 around the outer rim, and step up through the first 11º added **(e–f)**.

[17] Pick up an 11º, and sew through the next two 11ºs in the previous round **(figure 7, a–b)**. Pick up a 15º, and sew through the next 11º, 8º, and 11º **(b–c)**. Pick up a 15º, and sew through the next two 11ºs **(c–d)**.

[18] Repeat step 17 around the outer rim, and step up through the first 11º added **(d–e)**. End the thread (Basics).

[19] With the remaining thread, sew through the beadwork to exit a 15º next to a 4 mm. Pick up four 15ºs, sew through the 15º on the other side of the 4 mm, and sew through the 4 mm **(figure 8, a–b)**. Pick up three 15ºs,

Each successive round of beadwork builds dimension in the components.

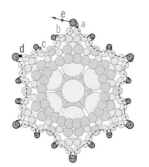

FIGURE 7

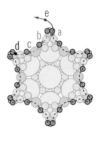

FIGURE 8   **FIGURE 9**   **FIGURE 10**

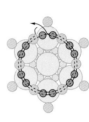

FIGURE 11   **FIGURE 12**   **FIGURE 13**   **FIGURE 14**

materials

bronze necklace 17 in. (43 cm)

- **8** 6 mm round Czech glass beads, gemstones, or pearls (marbleized blue)
- **69** 4 mm round Czech glass beads, gemstones, or pearls (marbleized blue)
- **5–7 g** 8º seed beads (antique bronze)
- **7–12 g** 11º seed beads (antique bronze)
- **7–12 g** 15º seed beads (antique bronze)
- Fireline 4 lb. test
- beading needles, #12

black bracelet colors:

- 6 mm and 4 mm round Czech glass beads (granite)
- 8º, 11º, and 15º seed beads (metallic brown iris)

DESIGN OPTIONS:

- Make more connectors for a longer necklace.
- Make a bracelet with fewer components.
- Make earrings with one or two components.

sew back through the 4 mm, pick up three 15ºs, and sew back through the 4 mm (b–c).

[20] Repeat step 19 around the outer rim, and end the thread.

Small medallions

[1] Thread a needle on each end of 1½ yd. (1.4 m) of Fireline, and center a 4 mm.

[2] With the right-hand needle, pick up an 11º. With the left-hand needle, pick up an 8º and a 4 mm. Cross the right-hand needle through the 4 mm **(figure 9)**.

[3] Repeat step 2 until you have a total of six 4 mms, keeping the 11ºs on one side and the 8ºs on the other side.

[4] With the right-hand needle, pick up an 11º. With the left-hand needle, pick up an 8º, and cross both needles through the first 4 mm to form a ring.

[5] With each needle, pick up three 15ºs. With one needle, pick up a 15º, and cross the other needle through it. With each needle, pick up three 15ºs, and cross the needles through the next 4 mm **(figure 10)**.

[6] Repeat step 5 around the ring. With each needle, sew diagonally through the first seven 15ºs added in this round.

[7] With the needle exiting the inner rim, pick up an 11º, and sew diagonally through the next seven 15ºs. Pick up an 8º, and sew through the next seven 15ºs

(figure 11). Repeat this step to complete the round.

[8] With the needle exiting the outer rim, pick up an 8º, and sew through the next seven 15ºs. Pick up an 11º, and sew through the next seven 15ºs. Repeat this step to complete the round.

[9] With the needle exiting an 11º along the inner rim, sew through all the 11ºs.

[10] Pick up a 4 mm, and sew through the 11º opposite the one your thread just exited. Sew back through the 4 mm and the 11º your thread exited at the start of this step. Push the 4 mm down so it sits below the ring of 11ºs, and retrace the thread path. Tie a few half-hitch knots, but do not trim the thread.

[11] With the needle exiting the outer rim, sew through the beadwork to exit an 8º nestled between two 4 mms. Pick up two 11ºs, skip an 8º, and sew through the next 8º. Repeat to complete the round, adding a pair of 11ºs between the 8ºs added in steps 2–4 **(figure 12)**. Step up through the first 11º added in this step.

[12] Pick up two 11ºs, and sew through the next 11º, 8º, and 11º. Repeat around the outer rim, and step up through the first 11º added in this step **(figure 13)**.

[13] Pick up two 15ºs, and sew through the next 11º **(figure 14, a–b)**. Pick up a 15º, and sew through the next

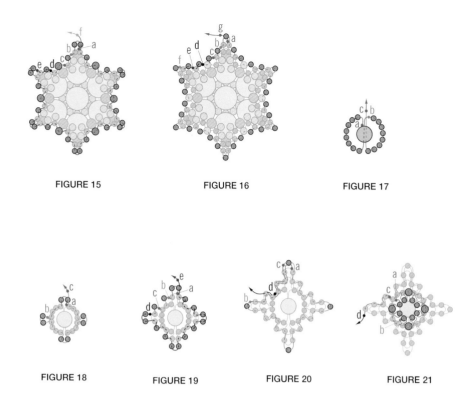

FIGURE 15

FIGURE 16

FIGURE 17

FIGURE 18

FIGURE 19

FIGURE 20

FIGURE 21

8º (b–c). Pick up a 15º, and sew through the next 11º (c–d).

[14] Repeat step 13 around the outer rim, and step up through the first 15º added (d–e).

[15] Pick up two 15ºs, and sew through the next 15º (figure 15, a–b). Pick up a 15º, and sew through the next 15º (b–c). Pick up an 11º, and sew through the next 15º (c–d). Pick up a 15º, and sew through the next 15º (d–e).

[16] Repeat step 15 around the rim, and sew through the first 15º added (e–f).

[17] Pick up a 15º, and sew through the next 15º (figure 16, a–b). Repeat (b–c). Pick up a 15º, and sew through the next 11º (c–d). Pick up a 15º, and sew through the next 15º (d–e). Repeat (e–f).

[18] Repeat step 17 around the outer rim, and step up through the first 15º added (f–g). End the thread.

[19] Make a total of four small medallions.

Connectors

[1] On 1 yd. (.9 m) of Fireline, pick up a 4 mm and eight 15ºs, and sew through the 4 mm again, leaving an 8-in. (20 cm) tail (figure 17, a–b). Pick up eight 15ºs, and sew through the 4 mm again (b–c). Sew through all the 15ºs again to form a 16-bead ring around the 4 mm.

[2] With your thread exiting the first 15º in either half of the ring, pick up two 15ºs, and sew through the next four 15ºs (figure 18, a–b). Repeat around the ring, and step up through the first 15º added (b–c).

[3] Pick up two 15ºs, and sew through the next 15º (figure 19, a–b). Pick up a 15º, skip the next 15º, and sew through the following two 15ºs (b–c). Pick up a 15º, skip the next 15º, and sew through the following 15º (c–d).

[4] Repeat step 3 to complete the round, and step up through the first 15º added (d–e).

[5] Pick up a 15º, and sew through the next eight 15ºs (figure 20, a–b). Repeat to complete the round (b–c). Sew through the beadwork to exit at **point d**.

[6] Pick up a 15º, an 11º, and a 15º. Skip two 15ºs in the 16-bead ring around the 4 mm, and sew through the next two 15ºs (figure 21, a–b). Repeat to complete the round (b–c), and sew through all the beads added in this round. Sew through the beadwork to exit at **point d**.

[7] With the tail, sew through the beadwork to exit the 15º on the opposite side of the connector. Do not end the threads.

[8] Make a total of 19 connectors with the following variations: Make 12 full connectors as in steps 1–7. Make five ¾ connectors as in steps 1–7, but in step 5 do not add a 15º in the last repeat. Make two ½ connectors as in steps 1–7, but in step 5, do not add a 15º in the second repeat and the last repeat.

Clasp

Toggle ring

[1] On 1 yd. (.9 m) of Fireline, pick up 20 15ºs, and sew through all of the beads again, leaving an 8-in. (20 cm) tail (figure 22, a–b). Pick up two 15ºs, and sew through the next five 15ºs (b–c). Repeat around the ring, and step up through the first 15º added (c–d).

[2] Pick up two 15ºs, and sew through the next 15º (figure 23, a–b). Pick up a 15º, skip the next 15º, and sew through the following three 15ºs (b–c). Pick up a 15º, skip the next 15º, and sew through the following 15º (c–d).

[3] Repeat step 2 around the ring, and step up through the first 15º added (d–e).

[4] Pick up two 15ºs, and sew through the next 15º (figure 24, a–b). Pick up a 15º, skip the next 15º, and sew through the following 15º (b–c). Repeat the last stitch three times (c–d).

[5] Repeat step 4 to complete the round, and step up through the first 15º added (d–e).

[6] Pick up a 15º, and sew through the next 15º added in step 4 (figure 25, a–b). Pick up a 15º, and sew through the next 15º (b–c). Pick up a 15º, and sew through the next two 15ºs (c–d). Pick up a 15º, and sew through the next 15º (d–e). Pick up a 15º, and sew through the next 15º (e–f).

[7] Repeat step 6 to complete the round, and step up through the first 15º added (f–g).

[8] With the tail, sew through the beadwork to exit at **figure 26, point a**. Pick up a 15º, an 11º, and a 15º, skip two 15ºs in the ring, and sew through the next three 15ºs (a–b). Repeat around the ring, and step up through the 15º directly above the 15º your thread exited at the start of this step (b–c).

[9] Pick up an 11º, an 8º, and an 11º, and sew through the beadwork as shown (figure 27, a–b). Repeat to complete the round (b–c). End the tail.

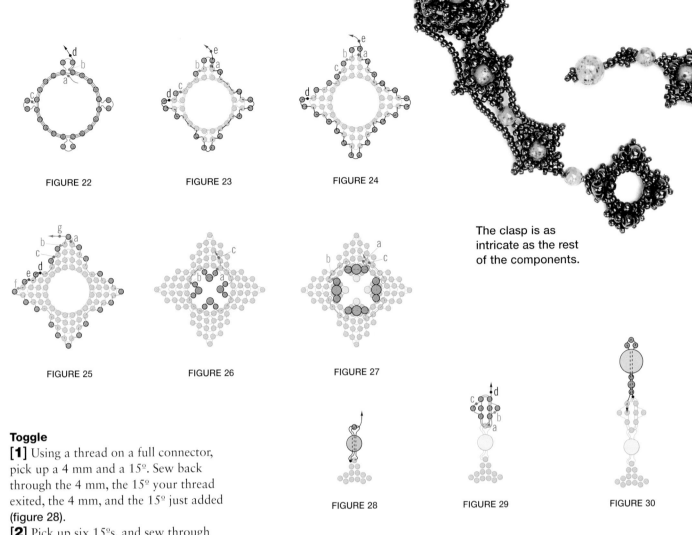

FIGURE 22

FIGURE 23

FIGURE 24

FIGURE 25

FIGURE 26

FIGURE 27

The clasp is as intricate as the rest of the components.

Toggle

[1] Using a thread on a full connector, pick up a 4 mm and a 15º. Sew back through the 4 mm, the 15º your thread exited, the 4 mm, and the 15º just added **(figure 28)**.

[2] Pick up six 15ºs, and sew through the 15º your thread just exited and the first 15º added **(figure 29, a–b)**. Pick up a 15º, skip the next 15º, and sew through the following two 15ºs **(b–c)**. Pick up a 15º, skip the next 15º, and sew through the following five 15ºs **(c–d)**.

[3] Pick up a 15º, an 11º, a 15º, a 6 mm, and three 15ºs. Skip the last three 15ºs, and sew back through all the beads just added **(figure 30)**. Retrace the thread path, sew through the beadwork to exit the toggle, and end the thread.

Assembly

[1] Arrange the components on your work surface with the large medallion in the center and a ¾ connector above it. On each side of the connector, place a 4 mm, a ¾ connector, a small medallion, a ½ connector, a small medallion, a ¾ connector, an alternating pattern of a 4 mm and a full connector six times, and half of the clasp.

[2] Use the tails of the connectors to attach each component to the next. To attach a medallion to a connector: With your thread exiting the point of one component, sew through the point of the next component, and retrace the thread path. To attach a connector, a 6 mm, and a connector: With your thread exiting the point of a connector, pick up a 6 mm, sew through the point of the next connector, and retrace the thread path.

[3] If needed, end and add thread (Basics). To embellish the connections, sew through the beadwork of a component, pick up enough 15ºs to reach the next component, allowing for drape, and sew through the next component **(figure 31)**. Repeat as desired, and end the threads. ●

FIGURE 28

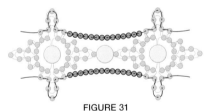

FIGURE 29

FIGURE 30

FIGURE 31

The back/inside of the medallions look like birds' nests.

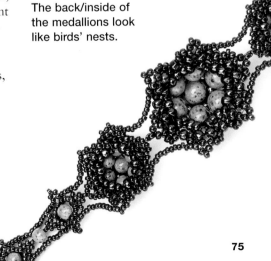

Heirloom treasures

Decorate your tree with bead-studded glass ornaments — or give them away as special gifts

designed by **Cathy Lampole**

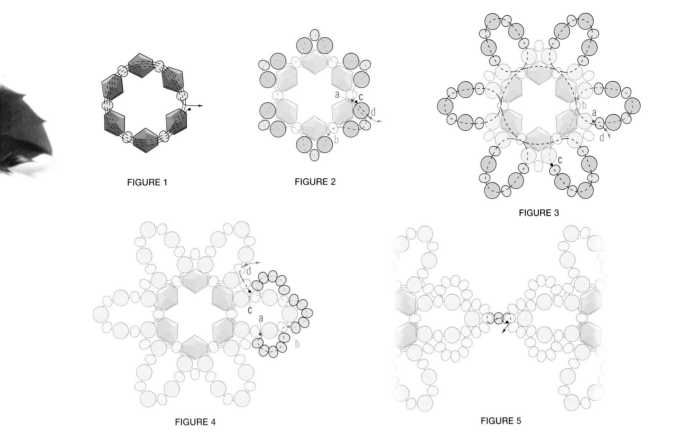

FIGURE 1

FIGURE 2

FIGURE 3

FIGURE 4

FIGURE 5

Resolve to make this the year you hang handmade ornaments on your tree. Create family memories of gathering in the glow of beautiful beaded glass globes reflecting twinkling lights.

stepbystep

Medallions

[1] On 1 yd. (.9 m) of thread, pick up an alternating pattern of a 6 mm bicone crystal and an 11º seed bead six times, leaving a 6-in. (15 cm) tail. Sew through the beads twice more to form a ring, and exit an 11º (figure 1).

[2] Pick up a 4 mm pearl, an 11º, and a pearl, and sew through the next 11º in the ring (figure 2, a–b). Repeat around the ring (b–c), and step up through the first pearl added in this step (c–d).

[3] Pick up an alternating pattern of an 11º and a pearl until you have four 11ºs and three pearls, and sew through the previous pearl (figure 3, a–b). Sew through the next 11º, bicone, and 11º in the ring and the next pearl (b–c).

[4] Repeat step 3 five times to form a total of six loops. Step up through the first 11º added in step 3 (c–d).

[5] Pick up five 11ºs, and sew through the next 11º in the loop (figure 4, a–b). Repeat twice (b–c). Sew through the 11º between the loops and the first 11º in the next loop (c–d). This completes the scalloped edging for the first loop.

[6] Repeat step 5 five times. Sew through the scalloped edging to exit the center 11º of a middle cluster. Set the medallion aside.

[7] Make a total of five medallions.

Connecting the medallions

[1] Place two medallions next to each other, and align the center 11º from which a working thread exits with a center 11º in a scallop opposite a working thread (photo a).

[2] Pick up an 11º, and sew through the center 11º in the opposite medallion. Sew back through the 11º just added and the 11º your thread exited at the start of this step (figure 5). Retrace the thread path twice. End the thread (Basics, p. 13).

materials

ornament cover

- 2⅝-in. (6.7 cm) diameter glass ball ornament
- 40 6 mm bicone crystals
- 45 4 mm bicone crystals
- 190 4 mm crystal pearls
- 11 g 11º Japanese seed beads
- nylon beading thread, size D
- beading needles, #12
- painter's tape

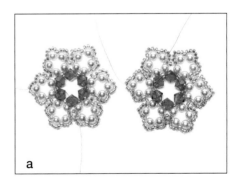

a

[3] Repeat steps 1 and 2 with the remaining medallions, connecting them to each other to form a band. End the remaining threads. Place the band of medallions on your ornament.

Top and bottom rings

[1] On 1 yd. (.9 m) of thread, pick up an alternating pattern of a 4 mm bicone crystal and a pearl 10 times. Sew through the beads twice more to form a ring, leaving a 6-in. (15 cm) tail, and exit a bicone.
[2] Pick up five 11°s, and sew through the next bicone to form a loop around a pearl. Repeat around the ring, exiting a pearl (photo b). Do not end the working thread or tail. Set the ring aside.
[3] Repeat steps 1 and 2 to make another ring.

Top ring attachment

[1] Place a ring on top of the ornament.
[2] Push the loop around the pearl from which the working thread exits upward toward the ornament bail. Pick up an 11°, a pearl, an 11°, a pearl, and an 11°, and sew through the center 11° of one of the upper medallion scallops.
[3] Pick up an 11°, a 4 mm bicone, and an 11°, and sew through the center 11° in the adjacent scallop of the next medallion.
[4] Pick up an 11°, a pearl, an 11°, a pearl, and an 11°, and sew through the pearl your thread exited in step 2 in the same direction. Snug up the beads (photo c). Sew through the next 4 mm bicone, pearl, 4 mm bicone, and pearl in the top ring.
[5] Repeat steps 2–4 around the ring to connect the remaining medallions to the top ring. End the threads.

Bottom ring attachment

[1] Estimate the position of the ring at the bottom of the ornament, and tape it in place.
[2] Using the working thread from the bottom ring, pick up 15 11°s, a 4 mm bicone, a 6 mm bicone, a 4 mm bicone, and an 11°, and sew through the center 11° of one of the lower scallops. If needed, adjust the number of 11°s

picked up to make the beaded ornament cover fit snugly.
[3] Sew back through all but the first two beads picked up in this step. Pick up two 11°s, sew through the pearl your thread exited in step 2 in the same direction, and snug up the beads.
[4] Sew through the next 4 mm bicone and pearl.
[5] Repeat steps 2–4 around the ring to connect the remaining medallions to the bottom ring (photo d). End the threads. ◗

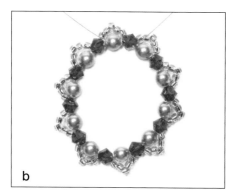

b

c

d

EDITOR'S NOTE:
Placing the ornament on a mug or glass will steady it so you can attach the medallions to the top and bottom rings.

Lemon squeezy

Brighten your wardrobe with light and luscious earrings

designed by **Jane Danley Cruz**

FIGURE 1

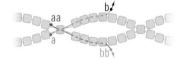

FIGURE 2

Stitch quick-and-easy netted bezels to encase rivolis, then add crystals, and snap! You have beautiful dangles for a pair of earrings.

stepbystep

Rivoli bezel

[1] Thread a needle on each end of 2 ft. (61 cm) of Fireline. With one needle, pick up a color B 15º seed bead and three color A 15º seed beads. Repeat 11 times.
[2] With the other needle, pick up three As, a B, and three As. Skip eight beads, and sew through the next B added in step 1 (figure 1, a–b).
[3] Pick up three As, a B, and three As. Skip seven beads, and sew through the next B (b–c). Repeat three times (c–d). Pick up three As, a B, and three As.
[4] With one needle, sew through the first B added in step 1 to form a ring, and step up through the next three As and a B (figure 2, a–b).
[5] With the other needle, sew through the first B added in step 1, and step up through the next three As and a B

opposite the beads you sewed through in step 4 (aa–bb).
[6] Designate one needle to work the top of the bezel and one to work the bottom. With the bottom needle, pick up two Bs, skip seven beads in the previous round, and sew through the next B. Repeat to complete the round, and snug up the beads. Sew through the ring of Bs, and end the thread (Basics, p. 13).
[7] With the top needle, pick up three As, a B, and three As, skip seven beads in the previous round, and sew through the next B. Repeat to complete the round, and step up through the next three As and a B.
[8] Insert the 14 mm rivoli, and hold it in place. Pick up two Bs, skip seven beads in the previous round, and sew through the next B. Repeat to complete the round, using firm tension. Sew through the final ring of Bs.

[9] Sew through the beadwork to exit a B along the edge of the rivoli (figure 3, point a). Pick up a B, a 3 mm bicone crystal, and a B, and sew through the next edge B (a–b). Repeat to complete the round (b–c). Retrace the thread path, tying a couple of half-hitch knots (Basics), but do not trim the thread.
[10] Make another rivoli bezel.

Assembly

[1] With the thread exiting an edge B, pick up a repeating pattern of an A and a B twice, then pick up an A, a 3 mm, a B, one side of a wire guard, and the loop of an earring finding.
[2] Center the loop of the earring finding on the wire guard, sew through the other side of the wire guard, and sew back through the last B, 3 mm, and A. Pick up a repeating pattern of a B and

FIGURE 3

materials
pair of earrings
- 2 14 mm rivolis
- 14 3 mm bicone crystals
- 1 g 15º seed beads in each of 2 colors: A, B
- pair of earring findings
- 2 wire guards
- Fireline 6 lb. test
- beading needles, #12

an A twice, skip a B, a 3 mm, and a B, and sew through the next edge B in the bezel. Retrace the thread path, and end the thread.
[3] Repeat steps 1 and 2 for the other rivoli bezel. •

Beaded BEAD CAPS

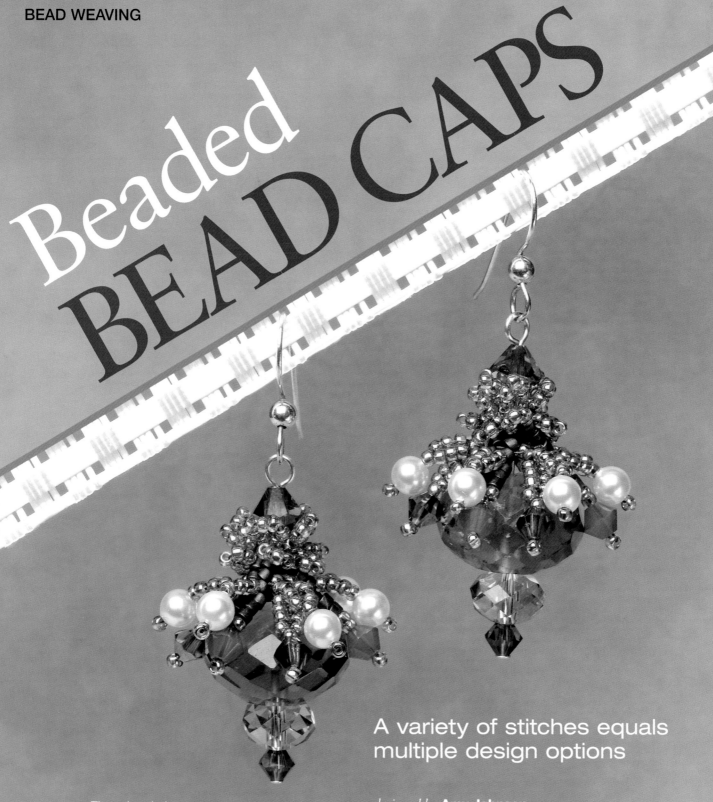

A variety of stitches equals multiple design options

designed by **Amy Johnson**

These beaded bead caps work well on coin-shaped, round, and oval beads.

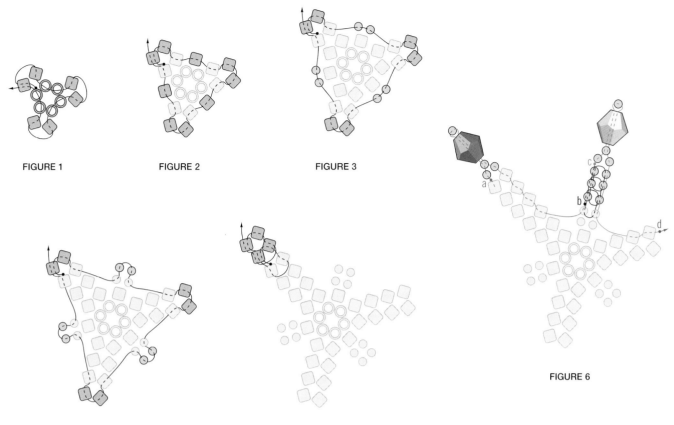

FIGURE 1

FIGURE 2

FIGURE 3

FIGURE 4

FIGURE 5

FIGURE 6

Combine ladder stitch, herringbone, and fringe to dress up any large art-glass, gemstone, or crystal bead. Mix and match the various techniques to achieve a different look for each pair you make.

stepbystep

Base

[1] On 2 yd. (1.8 m) of Fireline, stitch a six-bead ladder (Basics, p. 13) using 11º cylinder beads and leaving a 12-in. (30 cm) tail. Form the ladder into a ring (Basics) to create round 1.
[2] Work in herringbone stitch (Basics) as follows:
Round 2: Pick up two cylinders, and sew down through the next cylinder in the ring and up through the following cylinder. Repeat twice, and step up through the first cylinder added in this round (figure 1).
Round 3: Work an increase herringbone round: Pick up two cylinders, and sew down through the next cylinder in the previous round. Pick up a cylinder, and sew up through the next cylinder in the previous round. Repeat twice, and step up through the first cylinder added in this round (figure 2).
Round 4: Work an increase herringbone round: Pick up two cylinders, and sew down through the next cylinder in the previous round. Pick up two 15º seed beads, and sew up through the next cylinder in the previous round. Repeat twice, and step up through the first cylinder added in this round (figure 3).
Round 5: Pick up two cylinders, and sew down through the next cylinder in the previous round and up through the next 15º. Pick up two 15ºs, and sew down through the next 15º in the previous round and up through the next cylinder. Repeat twice, and step up through the first cylinder added in this round (figure 4).

Bottom fringe

[1] To make a cylinder fringe, pick up two cylinders, and sew down through the next cylinder, up through the cylinder your thread exited at the start of this step, and up through the first cylinder just added. Repeat once (figure 5).
[2] Add a crystal embellishment to the end of the cylinder fringe: Pick up two 15ºs, a color A 4 mm bicone crystal, and a 15º. Skip the last 15º, and sew back through the A and one 15º. Pick up a 15º, and sew through the next four cylinders in the fringe. Sew through the next 15º in the same round (figure 6, a–b).
[3] To make a 15º fringe: Pick up two 15ºs, and sew down through the next 15º, up through the 15º your thread exited at the start of this step, and up through the first 15º just added. Repeat twice (b–c).
[4] Add a crystal embellishment at the end of the 15º fringe: Pick up two 15ºs, a color B 4 mm bicone crystal, and a 15º. Skip the last 15º, and sew back through the B and one 15º. Pick up a 15º, and sew through the next four 15ºs in the fringe. Sew through two cylinders in the next column (c–d).
[5] Repeat steps 1–4 twice.

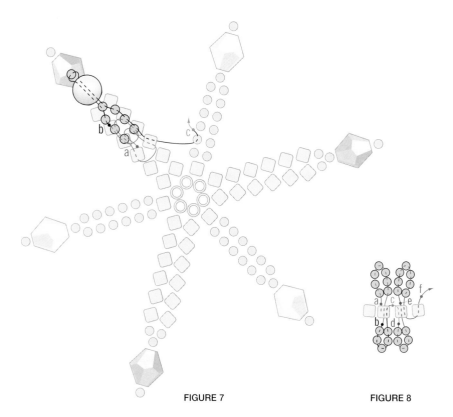

FIGURE 7   FIGURE 8

materials
pair of earrings
- **2** ¾-in. (1.9 cm) gemstone, crystal, or art-glass beads
- **2** 8 mm rondelles
- **2** 6 mm bicone crystals
- 4 mm bicone crystals
  8 color A
  6 color B
- **12** 4 mm crystal pearls
- **1–2** g 11º Japanese cylinder beads
- **2** g 15º seed beads
- **2** 2-in. (5 cm) 22-gauge head pins
- pair of earring findings
- Fireline 6 lb. test
- beading needles, #12 or #13
- chainnose pliers
- roundnose pliers
- wire cutters

Top fringe
The top round of fringe is worked in the same manner as the bottom fringe, off the pairs of cylinders and 15ºs established in the bottom fringe.
[1] Pick up two 15ºs, and sew down through the next cylinder in the previous round, up through the cylinder your thread exited at the start of this step, and up through the first 15º just added. Repeat once, but sew through the 15ºs just added instead of the cylinders (figure 7, a–b).
[2] Pick up two 15ºs, a 4 mm pearl, and a 15º. Skip the last 15º, and sew back through the pearl and one 15º. Pick up a 15º, and sew through the next two 15ºs and a cylinder in the next column. Sew through the next 15º in the same round (b–c).
[3] Repeat steps 1 and 2, but in step 2, sew through three 15ºs instead of two 15ºs and a cylinder, and sew through the next cylinder in the same round instead of a 15º.
[4] Repeat steps 1–3 until you have six top fringes. End the working thread (Basics).

Edge trim
[1] Thread a needle on the tail, and make sure the thread is exiting round 1

pointing away from the fringe (figure 8, point a). The edge trim will be added to the top and bottom of each cylinder in the original ladder.
[2] Pick up seven 15ºs, and sew back through the cylinder your thread exited at the start of this step (a–b). Pick up five 15ºs, and sew back through the same base cylinder (b–c). Sew through the next base cylinder (c–d). Pick up five 15ºs, and sew back through the cylinder your thread just exited (d–e). Pick up seven 15ºs, and sew back through the last cylinder your thread exited and the next cylinder in round 1 (e–f).
[3] Repeat step 2 until you have completed 12 loops off of round 1. End the tail.

Assembly
[1] On a head pin, string an A and an 8 mm rondelle; a ¾-in. (1.9 cm) gemstone, crystal, or art-glass bead; and the beaded bead cap and a 6 mm bicone crystal.
[2] Make a plain loop (Basics) above the 6 mm.
[3] Open the loop (Basics), and attach an earring finding.
[4] Make a second earring. ◉

DESIGNER'S NOTE:
For earrings with a little more sparkle (above), in step 2 of "Edge trim," instead of picking up seven 15ºs, pick up a 15º, a 3 mm pearl, a 3 mm Czech glass bead, and a 15º. Skip the last 15º, and sew back through the rest of the beads. Then, instead of picking up five 15ºs, pick up a 15º, a 4 mm crystal, and a 15º. Skip the last 15º, and sew back through the 4 mm and the 15º.

Regal presentation

The historically popular pairing of malachite and gold inspired the design of this necklace.

Create visual impact with symmetry and contrasting materials

designed by **Mark Avery**

Beaded beads are the focal point of this strung necklace. The availability of a variety of faceted and round gemstones widens your color options. Let this necklace inspire your own version.

step by step

Beaded beads

You will be working with two lengths of thread. These will be referred to as thread #1 and #2. At the start of each step, the instructions will tell you which needle to use.

[1] Thread a needle on each end of 24 in. (61 cm) of thread, and center six 5 mm spacers. Cross one of the needles through an end spacer to form a ring. This is thread #1.

[2] Cut a second 24-in. (61 cm) length of thread, thread a needle on each end, and sew through all the spacers, starting with the spacer opposite where thread #1 exits (figure 1). This is thread #2. Position the ring with thread #1 facing the top.

[3] On thread #1, with the left-hand needle, pick up two 4 mm gemstone beads, a spacer, and two 4 mms. With the right-hand needle, cross through the last 4 mm picked up (figure 2, a–b and e–f).

[4] With the left-hand needle, pick up a 4 mm, a spacer, and two 4 mms. With the right-hand needle, sew through the next spacer in the ring, and cross through the last 4 mm picked up (b–c and f–g).

[5] With the left-hand needle, pick up a 4 mm and a spacer. With the right-hand needle, sew through the next spacer in the ring, pick up two 4 mms, and cross through the last spacer picked up (c–d and g–h).

[6] On thread #2, with the left-hand needle, sew through the first 4 mm picked up with the right-hand needle in step 5, and pick up a 4 mm, a spacer, and two 4 mms. With the right-hand needle, cross through the last 4 mm picked up (i–j and m–n).

[7] With the left-hand needle, pick up a 4 mm, a spacer, and two 4 mms. With the right-hand needle, sew through the next spacer in the ring, and cross through the last 4 mm picked up (j–k and n–o).

[8] With the left-hand needle, pick up a 4 mm and a spacer. With the right-hand needle, sew through the next spacer in the ring and the first 4 mm picked up in step 3. Pick up a 4 mm, and cross through the last spacer picked up (k–l and o–p).

[9] With a needle from thread #1, pick up a spacer, and sew through the next spacer (figure 3, a–b). Repeat twice (b–c). With a needle from thread #2,

FIGURE 1

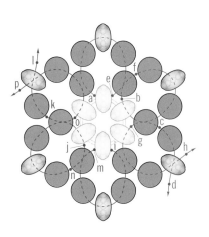

FIGURE 2

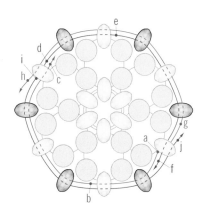

FIGURE 3

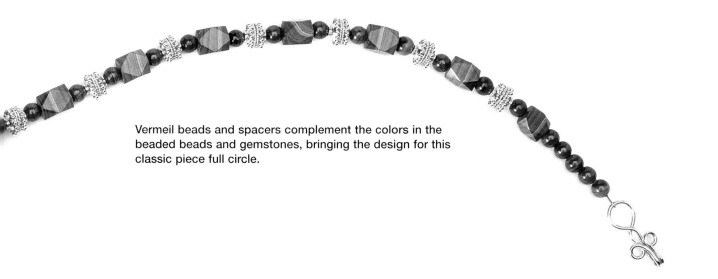

Vermeil beads and spacers complement the colors in the beaded beads and gemstones, bringing the design for this classic piece full circle.

working in the same direction, pick up a spacer, and sew through the next spacer (d–e). Repeat twice (e–f). With a thread that was not used to pick up a spacer, sew in the opposite direction through six spacers (g–h). Repeat with the other thread that was not used to pick up spacers (i–j). Snug up the spacers.

[10] Insert the 16 mm bead into the beadwork.

[11] To form the other half of the beaded bead, on thread #1, with the left-hand needle, pick up two 4 mms, a spacer, and a 4 mm. With the right-hand needle, pick up a 4 mm, and cross through the last 4 mm picked up with the left-hand needle (figure 4, a–b and e–f).

[12] With the left-hand needle, pick up a spacer and a 4 mm. With the right-hand needle, pick up a 4 mm, skip a spacer in the middle ring, sew through the next spacer, pick up a 4 mm, and cross through the last 4 mm picked up with the left-hand needle (b–c and f–g).

[13] With the left-hand needle, pick up a spacer. With the right-hand needle, pick up a 4 mm, skip a spacer, and sew through the next spacer in the middle ring. Pick up two 4 mms, and cross through the spacer just added (c–d and g–h).

[14] On thread #2, with the left-hand needle, pick up a 4 mm, and sew through the adjacent 4 mm of the previous stitch. Pick up a spacer and a 4 mm. With the right-hand needle, pick up a 4 mm, and cross through the last 4 mm picked up with the left-hand needle (i–j and m–n).

[15] With the left-hand needle, pick up a spacer and a 4 mm. With the right-hand needle, pick up a 4 mm, skip a spacer in the middle ring, sew through the next spacer, pick up a 4 mm, and cross through the last 4 mm picked up with the left-hand needle (j–k and n–o).

[16] With the left-hand needle, pick up a spacer. With the right-hand needle, pick up a 4 mm, skip a spacer, and sew through the next spacer in the middle ring. Pick up a 4 mm, sew through the adjacent 4 mm in the first stitch, and cross through the spacer picked up in this step (k–l and o–p).

[17] Sew through the end ring of spacers with each of the threads. End the threads (Basics, p. 13).

[18] Repeat steps 1–17 to make two more beads, but use 4 mm spacers instead of 5 mms and a 12 mm bead in step 10 instead of a 16 mm.

materials
necklace 23½ in. (59.7 cm)
- 16 mm faceted round glass bead
- 2 12 mm faceted round glass beads
- 14 12 x 8 mm faceted gemstone beads
- 16 8–10 mm Bali vermeil beads
- 42 6 mm round gemstone beads
- 108 4 mm round gemstone beads
- 24 5 mm Bali vermeil spacers
- 48 4 mm Bali vermeil spacers
- clasp
- 2 crimp beads
- bonded nylon thread, color to match beads
- flexible beading wire, .018–.024
- beading needles, #12
- crimping pliers
- wire cutters

Necklace
[1] Cut a 30-in. (76 cm) piece of beading wire, and center the largest beaded bead.

[2] On each end, string a 6 mm gemstone bead, an 8–10 mm Bali bead, a 6 mm, and a beaded bead.

[3] On each end, string a 6 mm, an 8–10 mm, a 6 mm, and a 12 x 8 mm faceted gemstone bead. Repeat six times.

[4] On each end, string five 6 mms, a crimp bead, and half of the clasp. Go back through the crimp beads and two or three beads, crimp the crimp beads (Basics), and trim the tails. ●

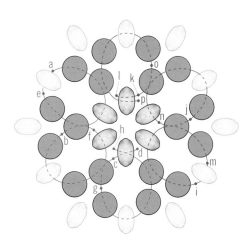

FIGURE 4

BEAD WEAVING

Treasured trellis

Stitch a beautiful band of flower components to create a lattice for your wrist

designed by **Juanita "Jaycee" Carlos**

The 4 x 6 mm oval pearls are only available in a few colors, but don't let that limit your overall color palette.

How does your garden grow? This ingenious bracelet is made by working one continuous band of motifs rather than stitching together individual components.

stepbystep

First component

[1] On a comfortable length of Fireline, attach a stop bead (Basics, p. 13), leaving a 6-in. (15 cm) tail. To make a ring around a pearl, pick up a 4 mm pearl, a 15° seed bead, four 11° seed beads, and a 15°, and sew through the 4 mm again (figure 1, a–b). Pick up a 15°, four 11°s, and a 15°, and sew through the 4 mm, an adjacent 15°, and the following 11° (b–c).

[2] Pick up a 15°, a 4 x 6 mm oval pearl, a 15°, a 3 mm pearl, a 15°, a 4 x 6 mm, and a 15°, and sew through the 11° your thread exited at the start of this step and the next 11° in the ring (figure 2, a–b).

[3] Pick up a 15°, a 4 x 6 mm, a 15°, a 3 mm, and a 15°, and sew through the previous 4 x 6 mm, the next 15°, the 11° your thread exited at the start of this step, and the next 11° in the ring (b–c).

[4] Repeat step 3 twice, but in the last repeat, sew through only one 11° in the ring instead of two (c–d), then sew through the end 15°, 4 x 6 mm, 15°, 3 mm, and next two 15°s (d–e).

[5] Pick up two 15°s, a 3 mm, and two 15°s, and sew through the two 15°s your thread exited at the start of this step (figure 3, a–b), the following 3 mm, and the next two 15°s (b–c). Repeat twice, but in the last repeat, sew through only one 15° after the 3 mm instead of two (c–d).

[6] Sew through the next 4 x 6 mm, 15°, and 11° in the ring; the next 15° and 4 x 6 mm; and the following three 15°s (figure 4, a–b).

[7] Pick up three 15°s, and sew through the next six 15°s (b–c). Pick up three 15°s, and sew through the next four 15°s (c–d).

[8] Sew through the next 3 mm, 15°, and 4 x 6 mm; the next three 15°s; and the following 11° in the ring (d–e).

[9] Repeat steps 2–7, ending and adding thread (Basics) as needed, but at the end of step 7, sew through the next three 15°s instead of four 15°s to exit at figure 5, point a.

materials

bracelet 7 in. (18 cm) without clasp

- **90** 4 x 6 mm oval pearls
- **9** 4 mm pearls
- **126** 3 mm pearls
- **1 g** 11° seed beads
- **5 g** 15° seed beads
- 4-strand slide clasp
- Fireline 4 lb. test
- beading needles, #12

EDITOR'S NOTE:

You can use 4 x 6 mm fire-polished beads in place of the 4 x 6 mm oval pearls, but keep in mind they do not taper as much at the ends. Either loosen your tension slightly or substitute 11°s for the 15°s to keep them from buckling.

FIGURE 1

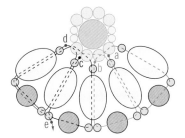

FIGURE 2

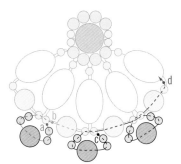

FIGURE 3

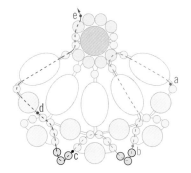

FIGURE 4

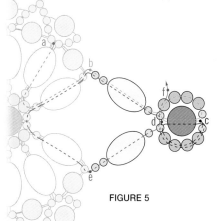

FIGURE 5

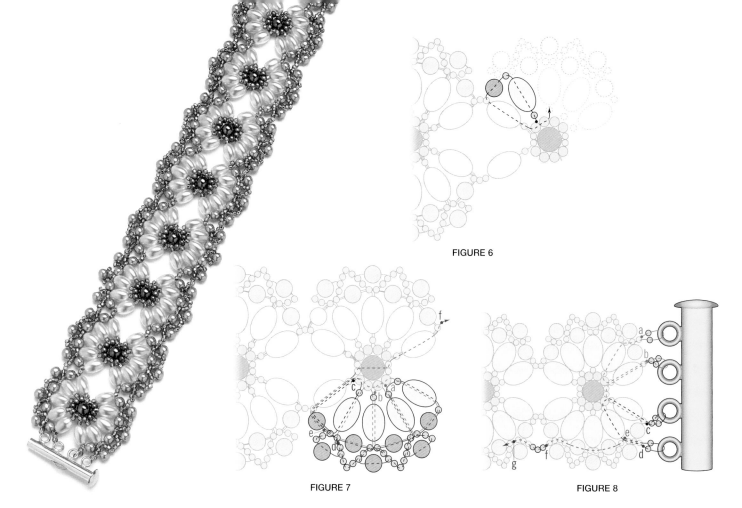

FIGURE 6

FIGURE 7

FIGURE 8

Subsequent components

[1] Sew through the next 4 x 6 mm, 15°s, 11° in the ring, 15°, 4 x 6 mm, and 15° (figure 5, a–b).

[2] Pick up two 15°s, a 4 x 6 mm, two 15°s, a 4 mm, a 15°, and four 11°s, and sew through the fourth 15° picked up at the start of this step and the 4 mm (b–c).

[3] Pick up a 15°, four 11°s, and a 15°, and sew through the 4 mm and the six beads just added to complete a ring around the 4 mm (c–d).

[4] Sew through the next two 15°s, 4 x 6 mm, and three 15°s; the following 4 x 6 mm in the previous component; the next four 15°s; and the following 4 x 6 mm and 15° (d–e). Pick up two 15°s, a 4 x 6 mm, and a 15°, and sew through the next two 15°s and 11° in the ring (e–f).

[5] Pick up a 15°, a 4 x 6 mm, a 15°, and a 3 mm, and sew through the adjacent 15°, 4 x 6 mm, and 15° and the next two 11°s in the ring of the new component (figure 6).

[6] Repeat steps 3–8 of "First component."

[7] Repeat step 2 of "First component" (figure 7, a–b).

[8] Repeat step 3 of "First component" twice (b–c).

[9] Sew through the next 15°, 4 x 6 mm, and 15°. Pick up a 3 mm and a 15°, and sew through the previous 4 x 6 mm, 15°, and 11° in the ring. Sew through the next six beads, exiting the bottom two 15°s (c–d).

[10] Repeat steps 5–7 of "First component" (d–e).

[11] Sew through the next 3 mm, 15°, and 4 x 6 mm; the following two 15°s; the 4 mm; the next two 15°s on the opposite side of the component; and the following 4 x 6 mm and 15° (e–f).

[12] Repeat steps 2–11 to make a total of nine components. End the working thread and tail.

Clasp and embellishment

[1] Add 1 yd. (.9 m) of Fireline to an end component, and exit an end three-bead column of 15°s (figure 8, point a). Pick up a 15°, an end loop of half of the clasp, and a 15°, and sew back through the three-bead column; the next 4 x 6 mm, 15°, and 11° in the ring; and the following 15°, 4 x 6 mm, and 15° (a–b).

[2] Pick up two 15°s, the next loop of the clasp, and a 15°, and sew back through the first 15° just picked up and the next 15°, 4 x 6 mm, four 15°s, 4 x 6 mm, and 15° (b–c).

[3] Pick up two 15°s, the next loop of the clasp, and a 15°, and sew back through the first 15° just picked up; the next 15°, 4 x 6 mm, and 15°; the next 11° in the ring; the following 15° and 4 x 6 mm; and the next three-bead column (c–d).

[4] Pick up a 15°, the other end loop of the clasp, and a 15°, and sew back through the three-bead column (d–e). Retrace the thread path to reinforce the clasp connection.

[5] Sew through the beadwork to exit a three-bead column on the other end of the component (e–f). Pick up three 15°s, and sew through the next three-bead column in the adjacent component (f–g). Continue adding three 15°s between the components for the length of the bracelet. End the thread.

[6] Repeat steps 1–5 at the other end of the bracelet. ●

Fuse box

Hang a fused-glass pendant from a chain of seed beads in coordinating colors

designed by **Anna Elizabeth Draeger**

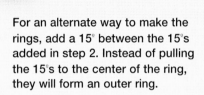

For an alternate way to make the rings, add a 15° between the 15°s added in step 2. Instead of pulling the 15°s to the center of the ring, they will form an outer ring.

materials
necklace 17 in. (43 cm)
- 1¼ x 1¹⁄₁₆-in. (3.2 x 2.7 cm) fused-glass pendant (James Daschbach, lilyrosebeads.com)
- 5–8 g 11° seed beads
- 4–7 g 15° seed beads
- clasp
- Fireline 6 lb. test, or nylon beading thread, size D
- beading needles, #12

Use circular square stitch to make a lightweight chain of seed bead links.

step by step

[1] On 1 yd. (.9 m) of Fireline or thread, pick up 30 11° seed beads, leaving a 4-in. (10 cm) tail. Sew through all the beads again, and continue through the first 11°. Gently pull the beads into a ring.

[2] Pick up a 15° seed bead, and sew through the 11° your thread exited at the start of this step and the next 11° in the ring **(photo a)**. Repeat until you've added a 15° to each 11° in the ring.

[3] Sew through the first five 15°s added. Pull gently to bring the 15°s to the center of the ring of 11°s **(photo b)**. Sew through the next few 15°s, and pull. Continue in this manner, and retrace the thread path through the 15°s.

[4] Sew through the ring of 11°s to exit next to the tail, and tie the threads together with a square knot (Basics, p. 13). Sew through the next few 11°s, and pull the knot into the adjacent 11°. Trim the working thread and tail.

[5] Repeat steps 1–4 to make the desired number of links.

[6] To connect the links, pick up 30 15°s on 12 in. (30 cm) of thread. Sew through two links, and tie a square knot to form the beads into a ring **(photo c)**. Retrace the thread path several times, and end the threads (Basics).

[7] Connect the pendant to the center link and the clasp halves to each end link as in step 6, but adjust the number of 15°s picked up to accommodate the pendant and clasp. ●

a

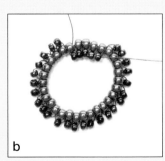

b

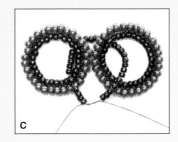

c

Crystal cluster brooch

Sparkling fringe arranged in a simple design makes for an arty pin

designed by **Leah Hanoud**

Arrange ovals of crystals symmetrically or asymmetrically on a mesh dome.

Sew crystals to a metal mesh dome finding to make this glittering accessory.

stepbystep

[1] On 2 yd. (1.8 m) of Fireline, pick up a color C 8º seed bead. Tie a square knot (Basics, p. 13) around it, leaving a ¼-in. (6 mm) tail.

[2] Determine where you'd like to stitch the inner oval of crystals on the mesh dome, estimating the center of the oval. Sew through the corresponding hole in the dome from back to front.

[3] Pick up an 8º, a color A 4 mm bicone crystal, and a color D 15º seed bead. Skip the D 15º, and sew back through the A 4 mm, the 8º, and the hole in the dome your thread is exiting (photo a). Snug up the beads, and sew through an adjacent hole in the dome.

[4] Repeat step 3, skipping holes in the dome as needed to keep the fringes close but not too crowded, to create the desired oval of color A crystal fringe (photo b).

[5] Continue working as in steps 3 and 4 to make a second oval of fringe around the first using 8ºs, color B 4 mm bicone crystals, and color C 15º seed beads (photo c).

[6] Cover the rest of the dome with fringe using 8ºs, color C 4 mm bicone crystals, and C 15ºs. As you add the outer fringes, set the dome on the pin-back finding to see where the prongs will attach to the dome. Avoid adding fringe to the holes the prongs will cover.

[7] Turn over the dome. Sew under a thread bridge between two adjacent holes, and tie a half-hitch knot (Basics). Repeat four or five times, and trim the thread.

[8] Place the dome on the pin-back finding. Grasp each prong with chainnose pliers, and bend it over the dome and into the beadwork (photo d). ●

materials

brooch 1½ x 1¼ in.
(3.8 x 3.2 cm)
- 4 mm bicone crystals
  15–20 color A
  30–35 color B
  75–80 color C
- 2 g 8º seed beads, color C
- 15º seed beads
  1 g color C
  1 g color D
- 1½ x 1¼-in. (3.8 x 3.2 cm) oval mesh dome with pin-back finding
- Fireline 6 lb. test
- beading needles, #10
- chainnose pliers

DESIGNER'S NOTE:
If you need a new length of Fireline at any point in the project, follow step 7 to end the thread, and follow step 1 to add a new thread.

EDITOR'S NOTE:
If desired, draw your ovals onto the mesh dome with a permanent marker in step 2. You can also draw where the prongs will attach to the dome.

Buttons

Loom a bracelet with large lampworked beads

designed by **Diane Baker**

Diane designed this bracelet for the first set of lampworked beads she made. You can use any lampworked beads that strike your fancy to create this quirky modified loomwork bracelet. Sew buttons to the ends of each row to add a new design element that eliminates edge warp threads.

stepbystep

Setup

[1] Cut a 10-in. (25 cm) piece of elastic cord. String one loop of the clasp, and tie a surgeon's knot (Basics, p. 13), leaving a 1–1½-in. (2.5–3.8 cm) tail.

Tie a second surgeon's knot to secure the elastic, and trim the tail. Dot with glue, if desired.
[2] Measure the desired length of the bracelet. String a loop of the other half of the clasp on the other end of the elastic, and tie a surgeon's knot. Tie a second

surgeon's knot to secure the elastic, and trim the tail. Dot with glue, if desired.
[3] Repeat steps 1 and 2 with a second piece of elastic and the remaining loops of the clasp.
[4] Cut an 18-in. (46 cm) piece of Fireline, and tie one end around half of the clasp. Set up the loom using the elastic cords as the warp threads, and tie the Fireline around the other half of the clasp to secure the frame of the bracelet **(photo a)**.

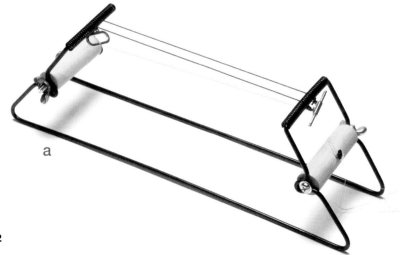

a

b

beads

This colorful bracelet is a great way to learn how to use a small loom for making jewelry.

materials

bracelet 7 in. (18 cm)

- **33** 12–14 mm lampworked beads*
- **22** 1/4–5/16-in. (6–8 mm) two-hole buttons
- 2-strand clasp
- Fireline 8–10 lb. test
- elastic cord, .019–.75 mm diameter
- beading needles, #10
- beading loom
- glue (optional)

* For this bracelet, Diane made her own beads, which are not for sale. For similar beads, contact artists through Pratt Fine Arts Center at pratt.org.

Modified loomwork

[1] Thread a needle at the center of 1 yd. (.9 m) of Fireline. Tie two overhand knots (Basics) next to each other, leaving a 2-in. (5 cm) tail.

[2] Sew through one button hole from back to front, then sew through the other hole. Pass the needle between the Fireline strands just below the first knot **(photo b)**, and snug the knot to the button.

[3] Pick up three 12–14 mm beads and a button. Place the stack of beads on top of the warp cords, positioning them so the middle bead has a warp cord on each side. Sew back through the other hole of the button, the three beads, and the remaining button with your needle and Fireline below the warp cords **(photo c)**. Sew back through the button, and snug up the beads. Tie a square knot (Basics) with the working thread and tail. Sew back through all the beads and buttons, and tie two square knots. Sew through the beads again, and trim. Thread a needle on the tail, sew through the beads, and trim.

[4] Repeat steps 1–3 for the length of the bracelet.

[5] Cut the Fireline added in step 4 of "Setup," and remove the bracelet from the loom. ⦿

EDITOR'S NOTES:

- **Try this technique with different types and sizes of beads. Use enough beads to span the desired length of your bracelet.**
- **If you're using smaller beads, use seed beads in place of the buttons for a more delicate look.**

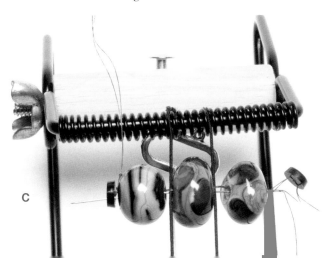

c

Multi-Stitch Projects

Subtle color changes
between rounds is a
nature-inspired detail.

Grand circles

Concentric rings expand in proportion to beads of different sizes and shapes

materials
necklace 30 in. (76 cm)

- 8 10–12 mm coin pearls
- 9 4–5 mm pearls
- 17 g 8º hex-cut beads, color A
- 14 g 8º seed beads, color B
- 11º seed beads
  50 g color C
  5 g color D
- 2 g 11º cylinder beads, color E
- 15º seed beads
  2 g color F
  1 g color G
- Fireline 6 lb. test
- beading needles, #12

designed by **Jonna Ellis Holston**

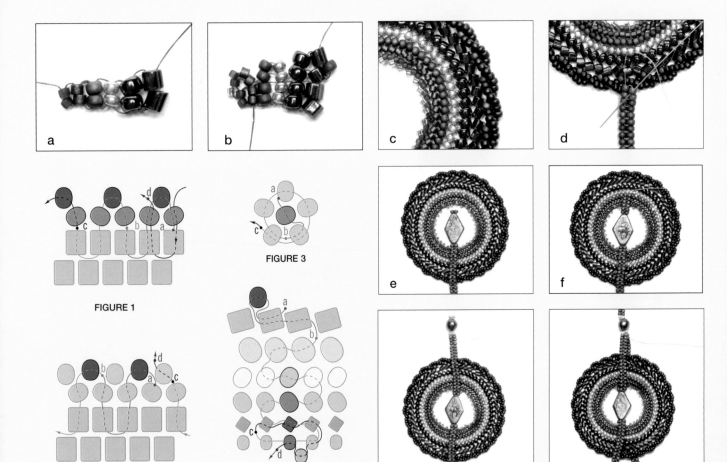

a

b

c

d

FIGURE 1

FIGURE 3

FIGURE 2

FIGURE 4

e

f

g

h

Ever expanding rings are seen wherever you look — tree rings, ripples on the surface of a pond, or the bands around the planet Saturn. Stitch a beaded version of this phenomenon to add a little nature to your wardrobe.

stepbystep

Toggle bar

[1] On 2 yd. (1.8 m) of Fireline, attach a stop bead (Basics, p. 13), leaving a 6-in. (15 cm) tail. Pick up 22 color A 8º hex-cut beads.
[2] Work eight rows of flat even-count peyote stitch (Basics) for a total of 10 rows, and zip up (Basics) the edges to form a tube.

[3] With your thread exiting an end A 8º, pick up a D 11º seed bead, a C 11º seed bead, and a D, and sew down through an adjacent A and up through the next A **(figure 1, a–b)**. Repeat once to form two picots **(b–c)**.
[4] Pick up a D and a C, and sew down through the adjacent D and A and up through the next A and D **(c–d)**.

[5] Pick up a C, and sew down through the next D and A and up through the adjacent A and D **(figure 2, a–b)**. Repeat once **(b–c)**. Step up through a C **(c–d)**.
[6] Pick up a D, and sew through an opposite C **(figure 3, a–b)**. Sew through the five Cs to secure the ring **(b–c)**.
[7] Sew through the beadwork to the other end, and repeat steps 3–6. End the thread (Basics).

Medallions

[1] On 3 yd. (2.7 m) of Fireline, pick up two color F 15º seed beads and two color E 11º cylinder beads, leaving a 24-in. (61 cm) tail. Sew

through the four beads again, and snug them up to form two columns of two beads each.
[2] Working in ladder stitch (Basics), pick up two beads per stitch: two Ds, two Cs, two color B 8º seed beads, and two As **(photo a)**. Do not reinforce the thread path. With the tail, sew through the adjacent Es.
[3] Work three stitches in herringbone stitch (Basics), following the bead order of the ladder.
[4] To make the turn, pick up a color G 15º seed bead, and sew up through the last F added.
[5] Repeat step 3.

[6] To make the turn, pick up a D, and sew up through the end A **(photo b)**.

[7] Repeat steps 3–6 to work a total of 56 rows.

[8] To join the ends to form a ring, sew through the A on the starting end, pick up a D, and sew back through the A your thread exited at the start of this step and the previous A **(figure 4, a–b)**. Snug up the beads.

[9] Sew across the edges, adding a bead appropriate to the row if needed to make the medallion lie flat **(b–c)**. Retrace the thread path between the last two rounds, and add a G to the inner edge of the medallion **(c–d)**. Sew through the beadwork, and exit an outer edge 11º.

[10] Pick up eight Cs or Ds, skip an edge 11º, and sew through the next edge 11º. Repeat around the medallion.

[11] Sew through the Bs to the next edge 11º without a loop. Pick up eight Cs or Ds, and sew from back to front through the next edge 11º without a loop. Repeat around the medallion **(photo c)**. End the threads.

[12] Make a total of nine medallions.

Connecting chains

[1] On 2 yd. (1.8 m) of Fireline, pick up four Cs, leaving a 24-in. (61 cm) tail. Sew through the beads again to form two columns of two beads each. Sew through the first two beads again.

[2] Working in modified herringbone stitch, pick up two Cs, and sew down through one C and up through two Cs. Repeat to make a chain 12 Cs long.

[3] Position a medallion on your work surface so that the seam is centered at the lower half of the circle.

[4] With the thread exiting the left C of the herringbone chain, sew through the D in the seam, and sew down through the C on the right edge of the chain **(photo d)**. Snug the chain to the medallion, and sew up through the left C your thread exited at the start of this step.

[5] Work five to eight more stitches to center the coin pearl within the herringbone medallion. Pick up a coin pearl and two Cs, and sew back through the coin pearl and two or three Cs in the right edge of the chain. Sew up through two or three Cs on the left edge of the chain, the coin pearl, and the C on the left of the pair picked up in this step **(photo e)**.

[6] Work the same number of stitches as the segment in step 5. Sew through the D across from the seam. Snug the chain to the medallion **(photo f)**, sew down through the C on the right edge of the chain, and sew up through the left C.

[7] Work 12 more stitches using Cs. Work one stitch using Ds.

[8] Pick up a 4–5 mm pearl and two Ds. Sew back through the 4–5 mm pearl, the D, and one or two Cs on the right edge of the chain **(photo g)**, and sew up through the Cs and D on the left edge of the chain, the pearl, and the D on the left of the pair picked up in this step.

[9] Repeat steps 2–8 seven times to connect seven of the remaining eight medallions. End and add thread (Basics) as needed.

[10] To work the chain on the reverse side of the medallion, repeat steps 1–7 but sew through the pearls previously stitched into the front chain and the D flanking the 4–5 mm pearls **(photo h)**.

[11] To connect the eighth medallion, repeat steps 2–4. Work seven stitches using Cs and one stitch using Ds. Pick up a C, and sew back through the adjacent D **(photo i)**. Do not end the thread.

[12] Repeat step 11 on the reverse side of the eighth medallion, but sew through the end pair of Ds to close the loop. End the threads.

[13] On the other end, use the tail to work a stitch using Ds. Pick up a 4–5 mm pearl and two Ds. Sew back through the 4–5 mm pearl and the D on the right edge of the chain, and sew up through the D on the left edge of the chain, the pearl, and the D on the left of the pair picked up in this step.

[14] Work 18 stitches using Cs and one stitch using Ds. Sew through the center point of the toggle bar. Pick up a B, a D, a C, and a D, and sew back through the B, the center point of the toggle bar, and the D on the right edge of the chain. Retrace the thread path a few times, and end the thread **(photo j)**.

[15] Attach the remaining chain on the reverse side of the end medallion to the toggle chain, sewing through the Ds and 4–5 mm pearl. Retrace the thread path, and end the thread. ●

Trillium ornament

Make a beaded flower that almost looks like the real thing

designed by **Diane Hertzler**

Use two sizes of seed beads to create a three-dimensional sculptural ornament.

materials

ornament 3 x 3½ in.
(7.6 x 8.9 cm)

- 11º seed beads
  5 g color A
  4 g color B
- 11º cylinder beads
  1–3 g color A
  2–3 g color B
  1 g color C
  1 g color D
- 1 g 15º seed beads,
  color B
- 4 ft. (1.2 m) 24-gauge
  craft wire
- Fireline 4 lb. test, or
  nylon beading thread,
  size B
- beading needles, #12
- chainnose pliers
- roundnose pliers
- wire cutters

stepbystep

Stem

[1] On a comfortable length of Fireline or thread, pick up two color A 11º seed beads, leaving a 6-in. (15 cm) tail. Working in ladder stitch (Basics, p. 13), make a six-bead ladder with A 11ºs. Form the ladder into a ring (Basics).

[2] Working in tubular herringbone stitch (Basics), make a tube 1¾ in. (4.4 cm) long, ending and adding thread (Basics) as needed.

[3] Work an increase between each stack: Pick up two A 11ºs, sew down through the next A 11º in the previous round, pick up an A 11º, and sew up through the following A 11º (figure 1, a–b). Repeat twice to complete the round, and step up

through the first A 11º added in this round (b–c).

[4] Repeat step 3, picking up two A 11ºs between the stacks instead of one and stepping up through the first A 11º added in this round (c–d).

[5] Working off all the A 11ºs in the previous round, work a round of six

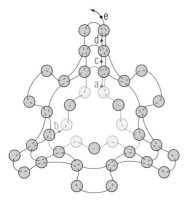

FIGURE 1

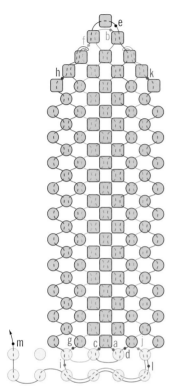

FIGURE 2

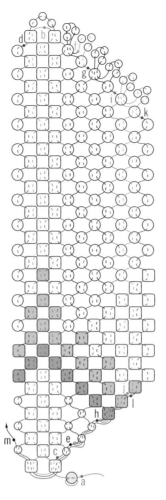

FIGURE 3

herringbone stitches using A 11ºs, and step up **(d–e)**.

[6] Work four more rounds of six stitches each using A 11ºs, stepping up after each round. To reinforce the final round, work a herringbone stitch thread path without adding any beads. End the tail but not the working thread.

Sepals

[1] Sew through the beadwork to exit an increase stack on the stem **(figure 2, point a)**. Pick up 24 color A 11º cylinder beads **(a–b)**, and work a row of flat even-count peyote stitch (Basics) using A cylinders **(b–c)**. To turn, sew down through the next A 11º in the stem and up through the A 11º your thread exited at the start of this step **(c–d)**.

[2] To add a row along one side of the center row of A cylinders, work 11 peyote stitches with A 11ºs and one stitch with an A cylinder **(d–e)**. Pick up an A cylinder, and sew through the adjacent A cylinder to position the thread on the other side of the center row of A cylinders **(e–f)**.

[3] Work a peyote stitch with an A cylinder and 11 stitches with A 11ºs, sewing through the A 11º in the stem for the last stitch. To turn, sew up through the next A 11º in the stem **(f–g)**.

[4] Step up through the last A 11º added, and work 10 stitches with A 11ºs and one stitch with an A cylinder. Work an odd-count decrease turn by sewing under the thread between the bead your thread is exiting and the next bead,

and then sew back through the last two cylinders **(g–h)**.

[5] Work a stitch with an A cylinder and 10 stitches with A 11ºs, sewing through the A 11º your thread exited at the start of step 4 **(h–i)**.

[6] Sew through the beadwork to exit the A 11º prior to the one your thread exited at the start of step 1 **(i–j)**.

[7] Step up through the next A 11º in the sepal, and work 10 stitches with A 11ºs and one stitch with an A cylinder. Work an odd-count decrease turn, exiting the last A cylinder added **(j–k)**.

[8] Work a stitch with an A cylinder and 10 stitches with A 11ºs, sewing through the A 11º your thread exited at the start of step 7 **(k–l)**. Sew through the beadwork, skipping an A 11º between the previous sepal and the next one **(l–m)**.

[9] Repeat steps 1–8 to make a total of three sepals, and end the thread.

Petals

[1] On 2 yd. (1.8 m) of Fireline or thread, attach a stop bead (Basics), leaving an 8-in. (20 cm) tail. Pick up eight color B 11º cylinder beads, two color C 11º cylinder beads, four color D

11º cylinder beads, a B cylinder, a D, and 19 B cylinders **(figure 3, a–b)**.

[2] Working in peyote stitch, work 11 stitches with B cylinders, two stitches with Ds, one stitch with a C, and four stitches with B cylinders. To turn, sew back through the first bead picked up in step 1 **(b–c)**.

[3] Work three stitches with color B 15º seed beads, one stitch with a C, one stitch with a D, and 12 stitches with color B 11º seed beads. To turn, pick up three B 15ºs, and sew through the adjacent end B cylinder in row 3 **(c–d)**.

[4] Work 12 stitches with B 11ºs, one stitch with a D, one stitch with a C, and three stitches with B 15ºs. To turn, sew through the beadwork to exit the first B cylinder picked up in step 1, and step up through the first B 15º added at the start of step 3 **(d–e)**.

[5] Work two stitches with B 15ºs, one stitch with a C, two stitches with Ds, and 11 stitches with B 11ºs. To turn, pick up three B 15ºs, and sew back through the B 11º your thread just exited, creating a picot **(e–f)**. Pick up three B 15ºs, and sew through the last B 11º added in this row **(f–g)**.

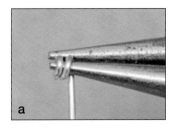

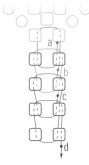

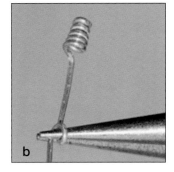

FIGURE 4

Process photos by Bob Hertzler

[6] Work 10 stitches with B 11ºs, two stitches with B cylinders, one stitch with a D, one stitch with a C, and one stitch with a B 15º. Work an odd-count decrease turn: Sew under the thread between the nearest two edge beads, and sew back through the last two beads your thread exited **(g–h)**.

[7] Work one stitch with a C, two stitches with Ds, two stitches with B cylinders, and nine stitches with B 11ºs. Turn as in step 5 **(h–i)**.

[8] Work eight stitches with B 11ºs, four stitches with B cylinders, and one stitch with a D, and work an odd-count decrease turn as in step 6 **(i–j)**.

[9] Work one stitch with a D, four stitches with B cylinders, and seven stitches with B 11ºs. Turn as in step 5 **(j–k)**.

[10] Work six stitches with B 11ºs and five stitches with B cylinders **(k–l)**.

[11] Sew through the beadwork to exit the end B 15º on the other side of the petal **(l–m)**. Work as in steps 5–10, and end the thread.

[12] Remove the stop bead, and thread a needle on the tail. Using the tail, pick up two B cylinders. Sew through

the two end B cylinders at the tip of the petal and the first B cylinder just picked up **(figure 4, a–b)**.

[13] Working in modified square stitch (Basics), pick up two B cylinders, and sew through the two B cylinders added in the previous step and the first B cylinder just picked up **(b–c)**.

[14] Repeat step 13 twice to work two more stitches **(c–d)**, and end the thread.

[15] Make a total of three petals.

Stamen

[1] Cut a 7-in. (18 cm) piece of craft wire. Grip the end of the wire with the tip of your roundnose pliers, and rotate the wire into a loop. Let go, then grip the loop at the same place on the pliers, and keep turning to make a second coil **(photo a)**. Repeat to make a total of five coils.

[2] Using chainnose pliers, make a 90-degree bend in the wire below the coils so the wire is in the same plane as the coils. Make a single coil about ¼ in. (6 mm) from the stack of five coils **(photo b)**.

[3] Repeat steps 1 and 2 to make a total of six stamens.

Assembly

[1] Thread two stamens through the five square stitch cylinders of each petal as shown in **photo c**.

[2] Thread all six stamens through the center of the stem so the petals are tucked in between the sepals.

[3] Cut each wire ¾ in. (1.9 cm) below the end of the stem, and make four or five coils at the end of each wire as in step 1 of "Stamen" **(photo d)**.

[4] To hang the flower, cut a 6-in. (15 cm) piece of Fireline or thread, and thread it through an A cylinder along the edge of a sepal. Tie the ends of the thread together with a square knot (Basics), and trim. **◉**

Choose colors that add to the lifelike quality of this flower.

PEYOTE STITCH / HERRINGBONE STITCH

Elizabethan
earrings

Create dimensional bezel settings for a pair of earrings

designed by **Laura McCabe**

Pearl accents add richness to the settings while a combination of stitches creates depth.

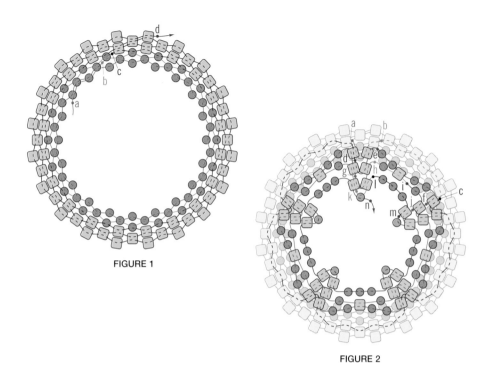

FIGURE 1

FIGURE 2

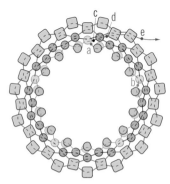

FIGURE 3

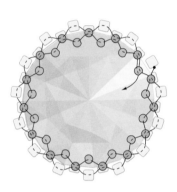

FIGURE 4

Combine modified herringbone stitch and peyote techniques to create a three-dimensional beaded form, raising rivolis to a whole new level.

step by step

Base ring
[1] On 2 yd. (1.8 m) of Fireline and using a #12 beading needle, pick up 40 color A 15° seed beads, leaving a 12-in. (30 cm) tail. Sew through the first few beads again to form a ring (**figure 1, a–b**).
[2] Work a round of tubular peyote stitch (Basics, p. 13) using As, and step up through the first A added at the start of this round (**b–c**).
[3] Work three rounds of peyote stitch using 11° cylinder beads, stepping up through the first cylinder added in each round (**c–d**).
[4] On the other side of the 15°s, use the tail to work two rounds of peyote stitch with cylinders. Zip up (Basics) the last round of cylinders added in this step and the last round of cylinders added in step 3, and end the tail (Basics).

Bezel support
[1] Using the working thread, sew through the beadwork to exit the first round of cylinders added in step 3 of "Base ring." Pick up two cylinders, and sew through the next cylinder in the

round (**figure 2, a–b**). Sew through the beadwork to exit the third cylinder in the round from the cylinder your thread just exited (**b–c**). Repeat to complete the round, and step up through the first cylinder added in this round (**c–d**).
[2] Pick up two cylinders, and sew through the next cylinder in the previous round to work a herringbone stitch (**d–e**). Pick up two As, a cylinder, and two As, and sew through the following cylinder (**e–f**). Repeat to complete the round, and step up through the first cylinder added in this round (**f–g**).
[3] Pick up two cylinders, and sew through the next cylinder in the previous round to work a herringbone stitch (**g–h**). Pick up an A, and sew through the next cylinder (**h–i**). Pick up an A, and sew through the next cylinder (**i–j**). Repeat to complete the round, and step up through the first cylinder added in this round (**j–k**).
[4] Pick up a color B 15° seed bead, and sew through the next cylinder (**k–l**). Pick up three As, and sew through the next cylinder (**l–m**). Repeat to complete the round, and step up through the first B added in this round (**m–n**).

Bezel
[1] Switch to a #13 needle. Pick up a 15° Czech Charlotte, a B, a Czech Charlotte, a B, and a Czech Charlotte, and sew through the next B (**figure 3, a–b**). Repeat to complete the round (**b–c**).
[2] Work a round of peyote stitch using Bs, sewing through a B in the bezel support every third stitch, and step up through the first B added in this round (**c–d**).
[3] Work two rounds of peyote stitch using cylinders, stepping up after each round (**d–e**).
[4] Place the rivoli in the bezel cup face up, and work one round with Bs and one round with Czech Charlottes, stepping up after each round (**figure 4**). If needed, work additional rounds with Czech Charlottes to secure the rivoli. Do not end the thread.

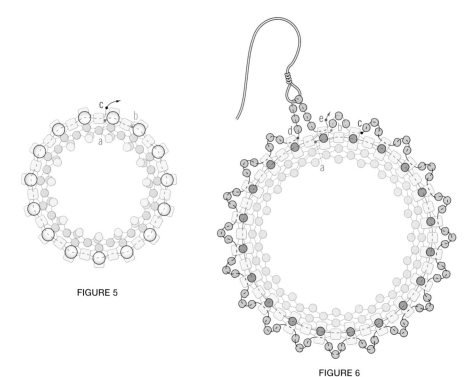

FIGURE 5

FIGURE 6

materials

pair of earrings 1 in. (2.5 cm)

- **2** 47SS Swarovski crystal rivolis, or **2** 10 mm rivolis
- **30** 1.6–2 mm freshwater seed pearls
- **5 g** 11º cylinder beads
- 15º Japanese seed beads
  4 g color A
  2 g color B
- **1 g** 15º Czech Charlottes
- **1 g** 15º Japanese Charlottes
- pair of earring findings
- Fireline 6 lb. test, conditioned with microcrystalline wax (optional)
- beading needles, #12 and #13

Embellishment

[1] Sew through the beadwork to exit a cylinder in the first round of cylinders in the "Bezel." Pick up a 1.6–2 mm seed pearl, and sew through the next cylinder in the round (**figure 5, a–b**). Repeat to complete the round (**b–c**).

[2] Sew through the beadwork to exit the second round of cylinders on the top of the "Base ring." Pick up a 15º Japanese Charlotte, and sew through the next cylinder in the round. Repeat to complete the round, and sew through the beadwork to exit the center round of cylinders (**figure 6, a–b**).

[3] Pick up three Czech Charlottes, and sew through the next cylinder in the round (**b–c**). Repeat to complete the round (**c–d**), but in the last repeat, pick up seven Czech Charlottes and the loop of an earring finding. Sew through the next cylinder in the round (**d–e**), and end the thread.

[4] Make a second earring. ●

DESIGNER'S NOTES:

- **To make a ring:** Work a band of peyote stitch to fit around your finger, and zip up the band to the "Base ring."
- **Link individual components together to create a bracelet or necklace.**

The back of the earring (right) is as interesting as the front (left).

TUBULAR HERRINGBONE STITCH /
PEYOTE STITCH

Floral *finery*

Bring together leaves,
petals, and vines for
two different looks

designed by **Mary Carroll**

Combine Russian leaves, petite petals, fringe. and a twisted tubular herringbone rope with bud-like increases to make one of two necklaces. Once you've mastered the techniques, there's no limit to the combinations.

stepbystep

Pink lariat
Inner petals
[1] Attach a stop bead (Basics, p. 13) to the center of 1 yd. (.9 m) of thread, and pick up 22 color B 11º cylinder beads. Turn, and begin working in flat even-count peyote stitch (Basics) until you have a total of five rows.

[2] Sew through the beadwork to exit the fourth up-bead from the end of the last row **(figure 1, a–b).**

[3] Work in peyote stitch, making a decrease turn at the end of each row for five rows: Stitch to the end of the row, exiting the last B **(b–c).** Sew under the thread bridge between the B your thread exited and the adjacent B, and sew back

through the B your thread exited and the last B added **(c–d).** Work four more decrease rows, ending with a three-bead row **(d–e).** End the thread (Basics).

[4] Remove the stop bead from the tail, and exit the fourth up-bead from the end on the other side of the petal. Repeat step 3 to complete the petal.

[5] Repeat steps 1–4 to make three more petals, but do not end one of the threads.

[6] With the remaining thread, sew through the beadwork to exit the narrow end of the petal. Use a ladder stitch (Basics) thread path to join the two Bs at the narrow end of each petal so the petals form a circle **(photo a).**

[7] Make a total of three inner petals.

materials
both projects
- nylon beading thread, size D
- flexible beading wire, .014
- beading needles, #12
- crimping pliers
- wire cutters

pink lariat 38 in. (97 cm)
- 10 8 mm round beads
- 3 6 mm round beads
- 21 3 mm bicone crystals
- 11º Japanese cylinder beads
  50 g color A
  8 g color B
- 8 g 15º or 11º seed beads for inside the herringbone rope (optional)
- 4 g 15º seed beads
- 4 crimp beads

green necklace 20 in. (51 cm)
- 25 mm art-glass bead
- 4 8 mm round beads
- 4 4 mm round beads
- 1–9 3 mm round beads
- 30 g 11º Japanese cylinder beads
- 11º seed bead
- clasp
- 4 crimp beads

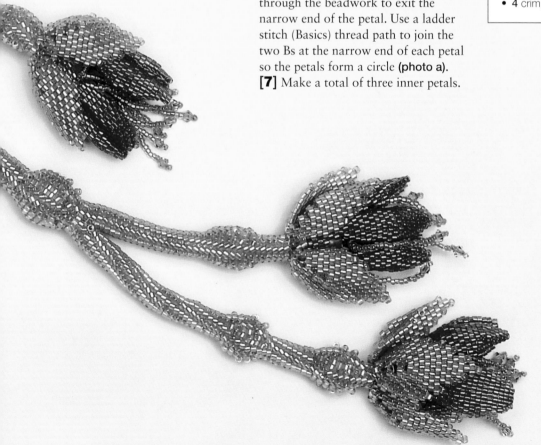

FIGURE 1

DESIGNER'S NOTE:
Mary gradated the colors in the ropes of the green necklace and used a second color for one of the outer leaves.

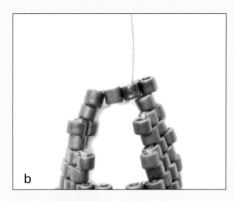

b

c

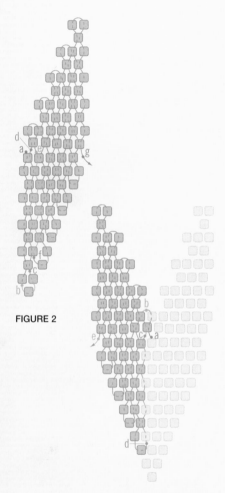

FIGURE 2

FIGURE 3

FIGURE 4

Outer leaves

[1] Attach a stop bead to the center of 1 yd. (.9 m) of thread, and pick up 10 color A cylinder beads **(figure 2, a–b)**.

[2] Pick up two As to make the turn **(b–c)**, and work across the row in peyote stitch using one A in each stitch **(c–d)**.

[3] Make an increase at the end of the row by picking up three As. Snug them up to the beadwork, then skip the last two As, and sew back through the first A just picked up **(d–e)**. Stitch back across the row in peyote stitch, stopping one stitch short of the end of the row **(e–f)**.

[4] Repeat steps 2 and 3 four times **(f–g)**.

[5] Remove the stop bead. Pick up an A, and sew up through the outer A of the first increase **(figure 3, a–b)**. Pick up an A, turn, and sew down through the first A picked up in this step **(b–c)**. Work across the row in peyote, stopping one stitch short of the end of the row **(c–d)**.

[6] Repeat steps 2 and 3 four times **(d–e)**.

[7] Sew through the beadwork to exit a top up-bead on the inside of the V. Work in ladder stitch to connect it to the corresponding up-bead on the other side of the V **(photo b)**. This will curve the leaf, giving it a cupped shape. Repeat to connect the other up-beads inside the V.

[8] Make a total of 12 outer leaves.

Rope

[1] Cut a piece of beading wire 6 in. (15 cm) longer than the desired finished length of your lariat. At one end, string a crimp bead, a 6 mm round bead, and a cylinder bead. Go back through the 6 mm and crimp bead, and crimp the crimp bead (Basics). String a set of inner petals so they cover the 6 mm **(photo c)**.

[2] If desired, string 11º or 15º seed beads along the length of the wire, interspersing 6 mm and 8 mm round beads where you would like to add bulges to the rope. Otherwise, leave the wire bare, and slip the 6 mms and 8 mms into place before starting the decreases for the bulges. This rope has bulges three rows from the flower, four rows after the first bulge, and 2½ in. (6.4 cm), 8¾ in. (22.2 cm), 9¾ in. (24.8 cm), and 24 in. (61 cm) from the flower.

[3] Using the ladder stitched beads that join the inner petals as a base, work two rounds of tubular herringbone stitch (Basics) using As.

[4] Work in twisted tubular herringbone (Basics) to the point where you would like a bulge to begin. Work the first stitch of the next round, and pick up an A before sewing up through the top bead in the next column. Repeat around, and step up **(figure 4, a–b)**.

[5] Work two rounds of tubular herringbone, but pick up two As after each regular stitch **(b–c)**.

[6] Work two rounds of tubular herringbone, picking up three As after each regular stitch **(c–d)**. If you are surrounding an 8 mm bead, work one more round with three As after each regular stitch. If you are adding the 6 mm or 8 mm beads as you stitch, place the bead in the cup of the bulge now.

[7] Work two rounds of tubular herringbone, but decrease by picking up two beads after each regular stitch.

[8] Work a round of tubular herringbone with one cylinder after each regular stitch. Step up, and resume working in twisted tubular herringbone until you reach the point where you'll add the next bulge.

[9] Work in twisted tubular herringbone using As until the rope is about 6 in. (15 cm) short of the desired finished length, ending and adding

d

thread (Basics) as needed and stitching bulges as desired. Do not end the thread.

Split end

[1] Repeat steps 1–8 of "Pink lariat: Rope" for each of the two remaining flowers, with these changes:
• Cut only a 7-in. (18 cm) piece of beading wire for each flower.
• Stitch one rope to 2 in. (5 cm) and the other to 3 in. (7.6 cm), adding bulges as desired.

[2] On one short rope, stitch two rounds of tubular herringbone, but do not add beads to one pair of stacks; stitch through the existing beads instead, leaving a notch in the round. You should have three pairs of stacks in the end round. End the thread.

[3] On the other short rope, stitch one round of tubular herringbone skipping a stack of beads, and two rounds skipping the same stack plus an adjacent stack. You should have two pairs of stacks in the end round.

[4] Join the two short ropes by stitching them together using a herringbone thread path: Position the two ropes so the notches are together, and stitch around both ropes using a herringbone thread path and skipping the short rows **(photo d)**.

[5] Slide an 8 mm bead over both wires, and stitch a bulge over it, as in steps 4–8 of "Rope."

[6] String a crimp bead over the two wires, and cross the wire from the long rope through it. Crimp the crimp bead, and trim the wires as necessary. Align the end rounds of the long rope and the split rope. Stitch the ropes together using a herringbone thread path. End the threads.

Finishing

[1] Attach a stop bead to a comfortable length of thread, leaving a 6-in. (15 cm) tail, and sew through a cylinder bead inside one of the flowers. Pick up 1 in. (2.5 cm) of 15º seed beads, a 3 mm bicone crystal, and a 15º. Skip the last 15º, and sew back through the 3 mm, the 15ºs, and the cylinder. Repeat to add six more fringes, and end the working thread and tail. Repeat to add fringe to the other flowers.

[2] Add a comfortable length of thread to the rope, exiting the beadwork where the rope meets a set of inner petals. Add one outer leaf at a time, sewing between the As on the leaf and the As on the rope using a herringbone thread path, until there are four leaves surrounding the rope. End the thread. Repeat to finish the remaining flowers.

Green necklace

[1] On a comfortable length of thread, leaving a 6-in. (15 cm) tail, work in ladder stitch (Basics) using 11º cylinder beads until your ladder is eight beads long. Join the ends to form a ring (Basics).

[2] Work in twisted tubular herringbone stitch (Basics) until the rope is 8½ in. (21.6 cm) long, ending and adding thread (Basics) as needed. End the tail, but do not end the working thread.

[3] Cut a 15-in. (38 cm) piece of beading wire, and string a crimp bead, a 4 mm round bead, and half of the clasp. Go back through the 4 mm and crimp bead, and crimp the crimp bead (Basics).

[4] String a 4 mm and an 8 mm round bead on the wire, then string the rope, ladder end first.

[5] Work the first half of an 8 mm bulge as in steps 4–6 of "Pink lariat: Rope." String an 8 mm on the wire, and work the second half of the bulge as in steps 7 and 8 of "Rope."

[6] String a crimp bead, the art-glass bead, an 8 mm, a 3 mm round bead, and an 11º seed bead. Skip the 11º, and go back through the other beads, pulling them up to the beadwork. Crimp the crimp bead, and trim the tail.

[7] Work in tubular herringbone until the crimp bead is covered and the beads meet the top of the art-glass bead. End the thread.

[8] Work steps 1–7 of "Pink lariat: Outer leaves" to make four outer leaves.

[9] To make the small leaves that decorate the herringone rope, follow the instructions for "Pink lariat: Outer leaves," but pick up six cylinders in step 1 instead of 10.

[10] Repeat steps 1–4 to begin the second half of the necklace.

[11] To taper the end of the necklace, work a round of twisted tubular herringbone, but for one stitch, pick up a single cylinder instead of two cylinders. Work the next round, and sew through the single cylinder instead of working the stitch. Work two rounds, skipping over the stitch with the single cylinder and sewing into the next stitch.

[12] Repeat step 11 to decrease the rope by another stitch. Continue working in two-stitch-per-round twisted tubular herringbone until the tail is long enough to wrap around the other rope several times.

[13] String a crimp bead on the beading wire so it sits inside the rope, and go through a cylinder inside the rope. Go back through the crimp bead, taking care that the rope is loose enough to coil, and crimp it.

[14] Work one more round of tubular herringbone, and sew through the beads in the last round to pull them tight together. End the thread.

[15] Attach the outer leaves to the rope above the art-glass bead as in step 2 of "Pink lariat: Finishing." Use the tails from the small leaves to tack them to the ropes as desired. Sew 3 mms to the top of the small leaves as desired.

[16] Wind the tapered rope around the other rope above the art-glass bead, and use the tail to tack it in place. End all the threads. ◗

PEYOTE STITCH /
HERRINGBONE STITCH

Star pendant

Alternate two favorite stitches to form a festive frame for a cabochon or rivoli

designed by **Smadar Grossman**

This intricate-looking pendant works up quickly. Combining peyote and herringbone stitch produces angles to make the shape of the star.

stepbystep

[1] On 3 yd. (2.7 m) of Fireline, center 88 11º cylinder beads. Tie the beads into a ring with a square knot (Basics, p. 13), and sew through the first 11º.

[2] Pick up two 11ºs, and work a herringbone stitch (Basics) by sewing through the next 11º in the ring (figure 1, a–b). Pick up an 11º, and work a peyote stitch (Basics) by skipping an 11º and sewing through the next 11º in the ring (b–c). Work a peyote stitch (c–d). Skip the next 11º in the ring, and sew through the following 11º, pulling the beadwork into a V shape (d–e). Work two more peyote stitches (e–f).

[3] Repeat step 2 around the ring, forming an eight-point star, and step up through the first 11º in the first stitch of the new round (f–g).

[4] Work a herringbone stitch and five peyote stitches using 11ºs (figure 2, a–b). Repeat around, and step up (b–c).

[5] Work a herringbone stitch and six peyote stitches using 11ºs (figure 3, a–b). Repeat around, and step up (b–c).

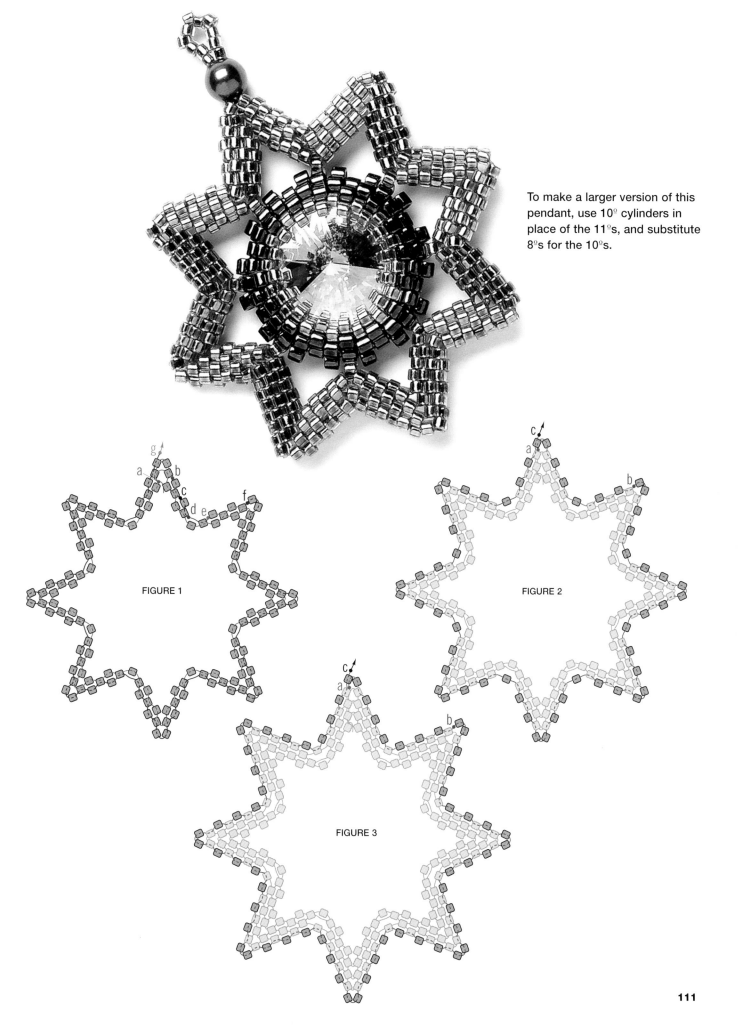

To make a larger version of this pendant, use 10° cylinders in place of the 11°s, and substitute 8°s for the 10°s.

FIGURE 1

FIGURE 2

FIGURE 3

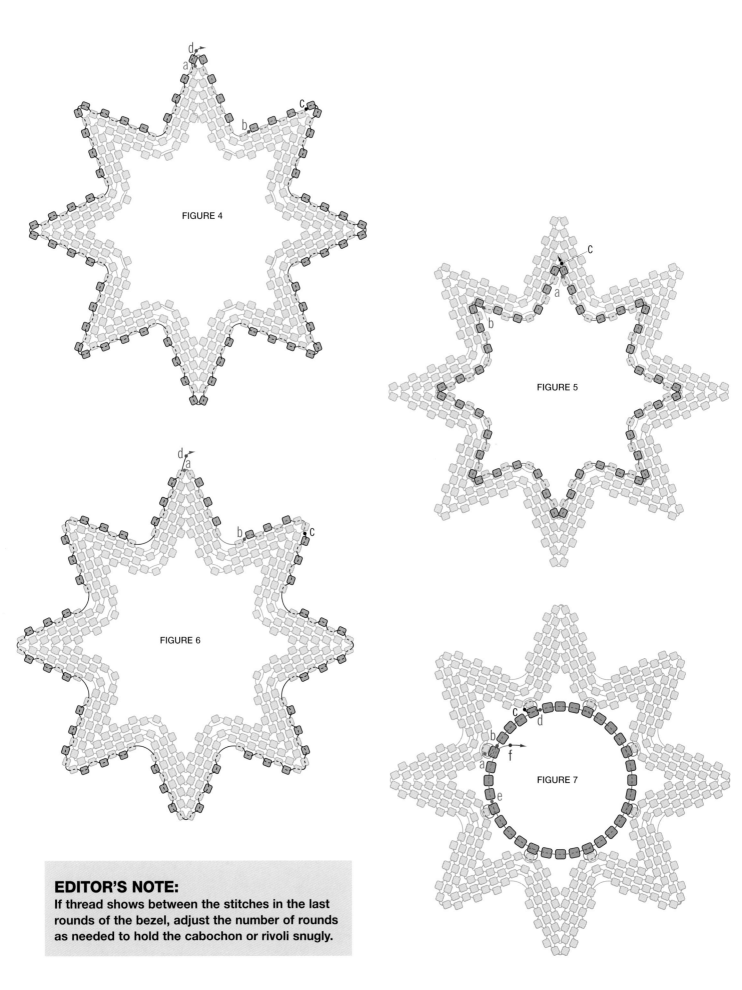

FIGURE 4

FIGURE 5

FIGURE 6

FIGURE 7

EDITOR'S NOTE:
If thread shows between the stitches in the last rounds of the bezel, adjust the number of rounds as needed to hold the cabochon or rivoli snugly.

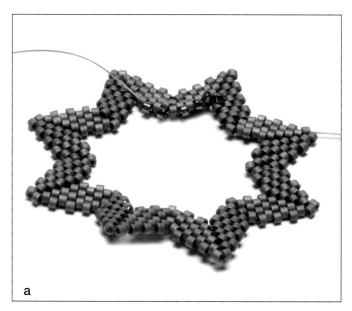

a

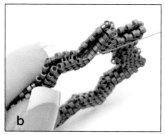

b

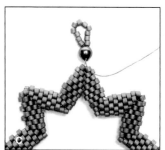

c

d

[6] Work a herringbone stitch and three peyote stitches using 11ºs, and sew through the next 11º **(figure 4, a–b)**. Work three peyote stitches using 11ºs **(b–c)**. Repeat around, and step up **(c–d)**.

[7] To begin the second layer, use the tail, and work a herringbone stitch and four peyote stitches using 11ºs **(figure 5, a–b** and **photo a)**. Repeat around, and step up **(b–c)**.

[8] Work a herringbone stitch and two peyote stitches using 11ºs. Skip an 11º, and sew through the next 11º. Work two peyote stitches using 11ºs. Repeat around, and step up.

[9] Repeat steps 4–6.

[10] Work a herringbone stitch thread path without beads, then work three peyote stitches using 11ºs, and sew through the next 11º **(figure 6, a–b)**. Work three peyote stitches using 11ºs **(b–c)**. Repeat around **(c–d)**.

[11] Zip up (Basics) the edges of the two layers **(photo b)**, sewing through the 11ºs at the inner and outer points. Exit an outer 11º of any point.

[12] Pick up a 4 mm round pearl and 11 11ºs. Sew back through the pearl and the adjacent 11º in the point to form a loop **(photo c)**. Retrace the thread path, and end the thread (Basics).

[13] Add 1 yd. (.9 m) of thread (Basics), and exit an inner point 11º **(figure 7, point a)**. Pick up a 10º cylinder bead, and sew through the point 11º and the 10º again **(a–b)**. Pick up four 10ºs, and sew back through the next

point 11º **(b–c)** and the last 10º **(c–d)**. Repeat around the inner points **(d–e)**. Pick up three 10ºs, and sew through the first 10º in the ring **(e–f)**.

[14] Work a round of circular peyote (Basics) using 10ºs, then work two rounds using 11ºs **(photo d)**.

[15] Sew back to the outer round of 10ºs, and work two rounds of circular peyote using 10ºs. Place the cabochon or rivoli face up in the bezel, then work two rounds of peyote using 11ºs. End the thread. ○

materials

pendant 2¼ x 1¹³⁄₁₆ in. (5.7 x 4.6 cm)

- 14–16 mm rivoli or flat-back cabochon
- 4 mm round pearl
- 6 g 11º cylinder beads
- 1 g 10º cylinder beads
- Fireline 6 lb. test
- beading needles, #12

Lily of the valley lariat

Suspend delicate blooms from a herringbone rope

designed by **Sylvia Sucipto**

15º seed beads are just the right size to create a matching pair of earrings. Tuck a tiny crystal instead of a pearl in each bloom for a bit of unexpected sparkle.

114

In Belgium, lily of the valley are called "meiklokjes" — little bells of May — due to their abundance of blooms around that time. It's said they bring happiness, so people present them as gifts to their loved ones. Since these darling flowers are only available once a year, I decided to capture them in beads so I can enjoy them all year long.

step by step

Flowers

[1] On 24 in. (61 cm) of thread, pick up 20 color A 11º seed beads, leaving a 12-in. (30 cm) tail. Tie the beads into a ring with a square knot (Basics, p. 13), and sew through the first A in the ring **(figure 1, a–b)**. The beads in this ring will shift to create the first two rounds of tubular peyote stitch (Basics) as the third round is added.

[2] Work five rounds of tubular peyote using As, stepping up after each round, for a total of seven rounds **(b–c)**.

[3] To make the petals, pick up five As, skip an A in the previous round, and sew through the next A. Repeat to complete the round **(c–d)**, and end the working thread (Basics).

[4] Make sure the tail is exiting an A in the first round, and use it to close the other end **(figure 2, point a)**: Pick up an A, and sew through the next two As in the previous round **(a–b)**. Repeat to complete the round, and step up through the first A added in this round **(b–c)**. Pick up an A, and sew through the next A in the previous round **(c–d)**. Repeat to complete the round, and step up through the first A added in this round **(d–e)**. Sew through the ring of five As added in the last round **(e–f)**, and end the tail.

[5] Make a total of 30 flowers.

Leaves

[1] Attach a stop bead (Basics) to the center of 4 yd. (3.7 m) of thread, wrap half of the thread around a piece of cardboard or a bobbin, and work with the other half of the thread. Pick up 62 color B 11º seed beads, skip the last three Bs, and sew back through the next B **(figure 3, a–b)**. Work 29 flat peyote stitches using Bs **(b–c)**.

[2] Work rows 4–15 using Bs as follows:
Row 4: Pick up two Bs, and sew back through the last B added in the previous row **(c–d)**. Work 28 stitches **(d–e)**.
Row 5: Work a decrease turn: Sew under the thread between the nearest two edge beads, and sew back through the last two beads your thread exited **(e–f)**. Work 27 stitches **(f–g)**.
Row 6: Pick up two Bs, and sew through the last B added in the previous row **(g–h)**. Work 26 stitches **(h–i)**.
Row 7: Work a decrease turn, and sew through the next two edge Bs **(i–j)**. Work 25 stitches **(j–k)**.
Row 8: Work a decrease turn, then sew through the next two edge Bs **(k–l)**. Work 23 stitches **(l–m)**.
Rows 9–14: Repeat row 8, decreasing two Bs per row **(m–n)**.
Row 15: Work a decrease turn, then sew through the next two edge Bs **(n–o)**. Work nine stitches **(o–p)**, then sew through the next 19 edge Bs, exiting a bottom B **(p–q)**.

[3] Unwind the tail from the cardboard or bobbin, and work as in rows 4–15 to finish the second half of the leaf as a mirror image of the first half. Do not end the threads.

[4] Make a second leaf.

Rope

[1] Make a tubular herringbone stitch rope (Basics) to the desired length, using six Bs per round, and ending and adding thread (Basics) as needed. You'll need at least 1 yd. (.9 m) of rope to wear this necklace as a lariat.

[2] To end the rope, work a round using only one B per stitch, and step up through the first B added in this round. Sew through the three Bs in the new round, and end the thread. Repeat on the other end of the rope.

Assembly

[1] Add 1 yd. (.9 m) of thread to one end of the herringbone rope. Exiting a B in the end round, pick up three Bs, a flower, a 4 mm pearl, and an A. Skip the A, and sew back through the rest of the beads and the B your thread exited in the rope. Sew through the next few Bs in the rope **(photo a)**, then sew through an adjacent B. Add a total of 15 flowers along the first 2½ in. (6.4 cm) of rope as desired, then end the thread. Repeat on the other end of the rope.

[2] Using the threads from a leaf, attach the leaf about 3 in. (7.6 cm) from the end of the rope by sewing through the existing thread path in the rope **(photo b)** and the two end rows of the leaf. Retrace the thread path several times, and end the threads. Repeat with the other leaf on the other end of the rope. ●

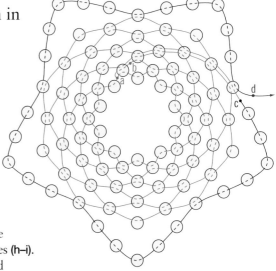

FIGURE 1

FIGURE 2

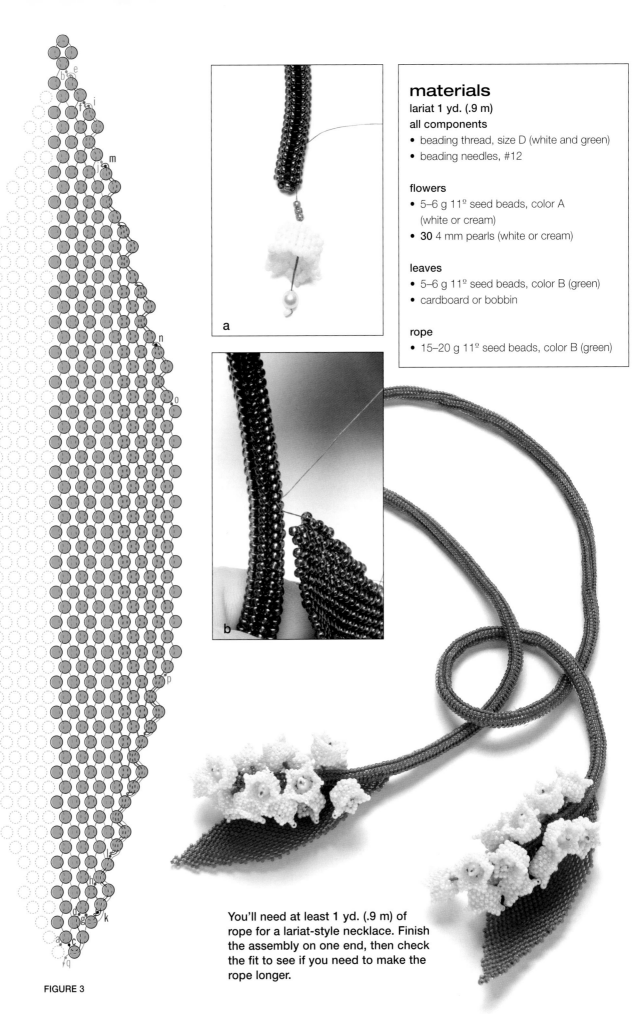

materials

lariat 1 yd. (.9 m)

all components
- beading thread, size D (white and green)
- beading needles, #12

flowers
- 5–6 g 11º seed beads, color A (white or cream)
- **30** 4 mm pearls (white or cream)

leaves
- 5–6 g 11º seed beads, color B (green)
- cardboard or bobbin

rope
- 15–20 g 11º seed beads, color B (green)

You'll need at least 1 yd. (.9 m) of rope for a lariat-style necklace. Finish the assembly on one end, then check the fit to see if you need to make the rope longer.

FIGURE 3

PEYOTE STITCH / HERRINGBONE STITCH

Bling-a-ling

Surround a rivoli with bicone crystal fringe and attach herringbone straps for a glamorous bracelet

designed by **Shirley Lim**

A crystal rivioli makes a stunning centerpiece for this eye-catching bracelet. Adjust the fit of the bracelet by increasing or decreasing the number of rows in the clasp.

stepbystep

Bezel

[1] On 2½ yd. (2.3 m) of nylon beading thread, center 46 11° cylinder beads. Sew through all the beads to form a ring, and sew through the first bead again. Work a round of tubular peyote stitch (Basics, p. 13) using cylinders. Step up through the first cylinder added.

[2] Continue working in tubular peyote using 15° seed beads for three rounds, keeping a firm tension. Tie a couple of half-hitch knots (Basics), but do not trim the working thread.

[3] With the tail, stitch a round of peyote using 15°s, and insert the rivoli face down in the bezel. Snug up the beadwork to secure the rivoli. Stitch two more rounds of peyote using 15°s. Tie a couple of half-hitch knots, but do not trim the tail.

Side bails

[1] With the tail, sew through the beadwork to exit the round of cylinders closest to the back of the rivoli. Pick up a cylinder, and sew through the next cylinder in the round. Repeat twice to add a total of three cylinders (**figure 1**).

[2] Work three peyote stitches off of the cylinders added in step 1 (**figure 2, a–b**). With your thread exiting the first cylinder added in step 1, pick up a cylinder, and sew under the thread between the nearest bezel cylinder and the adjacent 15° (**b–c**), then sew back through the cylinder just added (**c–d**).

[3] Work a total of 24 rows of flat odd-count peyote stitch (Basics), and zip up (Basics) the last row and the first row to complete the bail. End the tail (Basics).

[4] With the working thread, sew through the beadwork to exit the opposite side of the bezel, and make another bail.

Embellishment

[1] Using the working thread, sew through the beadwork to exit the middle round of cylinders. Pick up a 15°, a 4 mm bicone crystal, and three 15°s. Skip the three 15°s and sew back through the 4 mm, the 15°, and the next cylinder in the same round. Repeat to complete the round.

[2] Sew through the beadwork to exit the round of cylinders closest to the front of the rivoli, and repeat the embellishment in step 1. End the working thread.

Herringbone straps

[1] On 2 yd. (1.8 m) of nylon beading thread, pick up two 15°s, leaving a 6-in. (15 cm) tail. Sew through both beads again, and position them side by side. Working in ladder stitch (Basics), add two more stitches using 15°s. Form the ladder into a ring (Basics).

[2] Using 15°s, work in tubular herringbone stitch (Basics) to the desired length, ending and adding thread (Basics) as needed. Keep in mind that the strap will be folded in half. In my bracelet, each strap is 6½ in. (16.5 cm) long.

□ 11° Japanese cylinder beads

● 15° Japanese seed beads

FIGURE 1

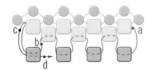

FIGURE 2

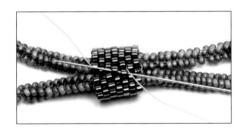

[3] Slide the herringbone strap through a side bail on the bezel, and check the fit of the strap. Making sure the strap is not twisted, join the ends by working a herringbone stitch thread path through the first and last rounds. End the working thread and tail.

[4] Make another strap on the other side of the bracelet.

Peyote bands

[1] On 1 yd. (.9 m) of nylon beading thread, attach a stop bead (Basics), leaving a 6-in. (15 cm) tail. Pick up seven cylinder beads, and work in flat odd-count peyote stitch for 26 rows. Wrap the peyote strip around the herringbone strap on one side of the bracelet, and zip up the ends **(photo)**. End the working thread and tail.

[2] Make another peyote band, and attach it to the other herringbone strap.

Clasp

[1] On 1½ yd. (1.4 m) of Fireline, attach a stop bead, leaving a 12-in. (30 cm) tail. Pick up five cylinders, and work a strip of square stitch (Basics) that is four cylinders wide and 10 rows long.

[2] Remove the stop bead, wrap the strip around one end loop of a herringbone strap, and work a square stitch thread path through the first and last rows to join the strip into a ring.

[3] Continue working in square stitch off of the ring using cylinders:

Rows 11–22: Work 12 rows with four cylinders per row.

Rows 23–29: To create an opening for the clasp bead, stitch seven rows with two stitches per row **(figure 3, a–b)**. Increase the last two rows to four cylinders per row: Pick up two cylinders, and sew through the first one again **(b–c)**. Repeat **(c–d)**, then sew through all four beads in row 28 **(d–e)**.

[4] Sew through row 29 to exit the other edge, and sew back through the last two beads added in row 28 **(figure 4, a–b)**. Stitch five rows with two stitches per row to make a second column. Join the last two stitches to the remaining beads in row 22 **(b–c)**. End the working Fireline.

[5] Determine where you want to attach the clasp bead, and with the tail, sew through the beadwork to exit at that point. Be sure you are working on the top of the bracelet (the rivoli is facing up). Pick up a 15°, a 6 mm margarita, and a 15°. Skip the 15°, and sew back through the margarita, the 15°, and the next cylinder in the strip. Retrace the thread path a few times to reinforce the join, and end the Fireline. **●**

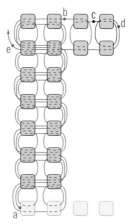

FIGURE 3

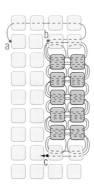

FIGURE 4

materials

mauve bracelet 7 in. (18 cm)

- 18 mm crystal rivoli (crystal AB)
- 6 mm margarita crystal (crystal transmission)
- **46** 4 mm bicone crystals (crystal AB 2X)
- 7–10 g 11° Japanese cylinder beads (Miyuki DB 875)
- 20 g 15° seed beads (metallic eggplant iris)
- nylon beading thread, size D
- Fireline 6 lb. test
- beading needles, #12

green bracelet colors:

- 18 mm rivoli (lagoon)
- 6 mm crystal margarita (fern green)
- 4 mm bicone crystals (olivine satin)
- 11° Japanese cylinder beads (Toho Treasures 508, metallic green/purple iris)
- 15° seed beads (mixture of Miyuki 2035 and Czech 463RF)

EDITOR'S NOTES:

- **Check the fit of the bracelet before joining the ends of the herring-bone straps so you can increase or decrease the length as necessary.**
- **Be careful to use an even, but not tight, tension when stitching the herringbone straps so they are flexible enough to bend in half.**

EDITOR'S NOTES:
• Consider repurposing an old locket, Girl Scout pins, or charms to personalize your key.
• Reuse an old faux pearl necklace in place of the chain, or use a satin or silk cord.

PEYOTE STITCH /
RIGHT-ANGLE WEAVE

Vintage skeleton key pendants

Create a modern-day talisman

designed by **Diane Hyde**

Everything old is new again in designer Diane Hyde's *Key to Happiness* necklace.

Give an antique key a modern look by embellishing it with beads, crystals, Lucite flowers, and leaves.

stepbystep

Key to Happiness necklace
Key pendant

[1] On 1 yd. (.9 m) of Fireline, attach a stop bead (Basics, p. 13), leaving a 6-in. (15 cm) tail. Pick up a repeating pattern of a color A 11º seed bead and a color B 11º seed bead until the beads equal the length of the stem of the key. Work in flat even- or odd-count peyote stitch (Basics), alternating a row of As with a row of Bs, for an even number of rows, until the strip is long enough to wrap around the stem.

[2] Remove the stop bead, wrap the strip around the stem of the key, and zip up (Basics) the ends to form a tube.

[3] With the thread exiting an end bead pointing toward the bottom of the key, pick up a color D 3 mm bicone crystal, a 15º seed bead, and a D, and sew back through the adjacent 11º in the end of the tube. Sew through the next 11º in the tube **(photo a)**. Repeat around the end of the tube. End the threads (Basics).

Flowers

[1] Cut a small circle of Ultrasuede approximately 10 mm in diameter to fit inside the back of the 18 mm filigree. On 18 in. (46 cm) of Fireline, sew the Ultrasuede to the back of the filigree. Exit through the center hole of the filigree on the front.

[2] Pick up a Lucite leaf, and sew down through the filigree and the Ultrasuede. Retrace the thread path to reinforce the stitch **(photo b)**. Repeat with the other leaf.

[3] With the filigree facing up and the thread exiting the center hole, pick up the Lucite flower and a 3 mm pearl. Sew down through the flower, the filigree, and the Ultrasuede. Retrace the thread path to secure.

[4] Sew up through the Ultrasuede and the filigree, exiting between the leaves just below the center of the flower. Pick up six color C 3 mm bicone crystals and a 15º, and sew back through the Cs just added, the filigree, and the Ultrasuede. Repeat twice to make a total of three crystal stems.

[5] Attach the filigree to the key by sewing through the loop of the key and the filigree. Retrace the thread path, and end the thread.

Necklace

[1] Cut two 10¼-in. (26 cm) pieces of oval-link chain.

[2] Open a 6–9 mm jump ring (Basics), attach a loop of the channel link and the loop of the key, and close the jump ring. Repeat with another channel link.

[3] Open a 3 x 4 mm jump ring, attach the remaining loop of a channel link and an end link of chain, and close the jump ring. Repeat with the other channel link and chain.

[4] Open a 3 x 4 jump ring, attach half of the clasp and a remaining end link of chain, and close the jump ring. Repeat with the other half of the clasp and the other chain.

---

materials

all projects
- Fireline 6 lb. test
- beading needles, #12
- chainnose pliers
- roundnose pliers
- wire cutters

Key to Happiness
necklace 22 in. (56 cm)
- 3¼-in. (8.3 cm) vintage skeleton key
- 18 mm round filigree finding
- 16 mm Lucite flower
- **2** 16 x 17 mm Lucite leaves
- **2** 6 mm crystal channel links
- **18** 3 mm bicone crystals, color C
- **11–12** 3 mm bicone crystals, color D
- 3 mm pearl
- **2** g 11º seed beads in each of **2** colors: A, B
- **12–15** 15º seed beads
- clasp

- 20½ in. (52.1 cm) oval-link chain
- **2** 6–9 mm jump rings
- **4** 3 x 4 mm oval jump rings
- Ultrasuede

I'll Fly Away
necklace 18 in. (46 cm)
- 2½-in. (6.4 cm) vintage skeleton key
- **2** 18 x 25 mm left and right metal wings (drilled) (Designer's Findings, designersfindings.net)
- 10 mm pearl
- **2** 8 mm pearls
- **8** 4 mm bicone crystals
- **46** 3 mm bicone crystals
- **2** g 11º seed beads
- **3** g 15º seed beads
- clasp
- 18 in. (46 cm) round-link chain
- 1-in. (2.5 cm) head pin
- **2** 2-in. (5 cm) eye pins

- **2** 6 mm round jump rings
- **6** 3 x 4 mm oval jump rings

Swags and Sparkles
necklace 24 in. (61 cm)
- 3-in. (7.6 cm) vintage skeleton key
- **8–10** 4–10 mm accent beads
- **8** 4 mm pearls
- **42** 3 mm pearls
- **50** 4 mm bicone crystals
- **7** 3 mm bicone crystals
- **3** g 11º seed beads
- clasp
- 24 in. (61 cm) oval-link chain
- **7** 1½-in. (3.8 cm) eye pins
- **2** 9 mm round jump rings
- **2** 4 x 7 mm jump rings
- **2** 3 x 4 mm oval jump rings

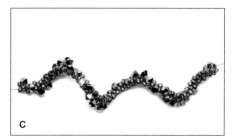

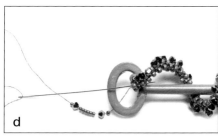

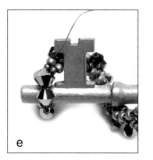

I'll Fly Away necklace
Key pendant

[1] On 2 yd. (1.8 m) of Fireline, attach a stop bead (Basics, p. 13), leaving a 9-in. (23 cm) tail. Pick up an alternating pattern of an 11º seed bead and a 15º seed bead until you have a strand that is 1½ times the length of the stem of the key and contains an even number of beads. Work in flat even-count peyote stitch (Basics), alternating a row of 15ºs with a row of 11ºs for a total of six rows.

[2] Roll the strip into a tube, and zip up (Basics) the first and last rows. Exit an end 11º with your needle pointing toward the beadwork.

[3] Pick up a 3 mm bicone crystal, and sew through the next 11º in the row. Repeat for the length of the row to create a ridge of crystals. Keep a firm tension, and allow the tube to twist **(photo c)**. At the end of the row, tie a few half-hitch knots (Basics), but don't trim the thread.

[4] Place one end of the peyote tube against the loop of the key so the crystal ridge is on top of the key. Pick up a 15º, a 3 mm, six to nine 15ºs, a 3 mm, and a 15º, and sew through the loop of the key and the last 11º your thread exited in the tube to form a ring **(photo d)**. Sew through the beads just added to reinforce the ring. End the thread (Basics).

[5] Gently wind the tube around the stem of the key, and adjust as necessary to keep the crystal ridge as visible as possible and to align the unattached end of the tube with the end of the key.

[6] Using the tail, pick up a repeating pattern of a 3 mm crystal and an 11º to create a ring of beads that fits snugly around the bottom of the key **(photo e)**. Sew through the last 11º your thread exited in the tube, and sew through the beads just added to reinforce the ring. To prevent the ring of beads from slipping off the end of the key, sew through the beadwork to the back of the key. Pick up a 15º, a 4 mm bicone crystal, five 3 mms, and a 15º, and sew through the ninth 11º from the end in the tube **(photo f)**. Sew back through the beads just added, and tie a few half-hitch knots, but do not trim.

[7] On a head pin, string a 10 mm pearl and a 4 mm bicone crystal. Make a wrapped loop (Basics) to make a pearl dangle.

[8] Sew through the beadwork to exit a bead in the ring around the bottom of the key. Pick up a 15º, a 4 mm, the loop of the dangle, a 4 mm, and a 3 mm, and sew through a bead on the opposite side of the ring **(photo g)**. Retrace the thread path, and end the thread.

Necklace

[1] Cut a 9-in. (23 cm) piece of round-link chain.

[2] On an eye pin, string an 8 mm pearl and a 4 mm, and make a plain loop (Basics) to create a link.

[3] Open a 3 x 4 mm jump ring (Basics), attach a loop of the link and one end of the chain, and close the jump ring.

[4] Open a 3 x 4 mm jump ring, attach the remaining loop of the link and the top of an 18 x 25 mm wing, and close the jump ring.

[5] Open a 6 mm jump ring, attach the bottom of a wing and the loop of the key, and close the jump ring.

[6] Open a 3 x 4 mm jump ring, attach half of the clasp and the remaining end of the chain, and close the jump ring.

[7] Repeat steps 1–6 for the other side of the necklace.

Swags and Sparkles necklace
Key pendant

[1] On 2 yd. (1.8 m) of Fireline, pick up 12 11º seed beads, leaving a 6-in. (15 cm) tail. Sew through all the beads again, and continue through the next six beads. Form the ring into a square; each side will have three 11ºs **(figure 1)**.

[2] Pick up nine 11ºs, sew through the last three 11ºs your thread exited in the previous stitch, and continue through the first six 11ºs just added **(figure 2)**.

[3] Working in modified right-angle weave (Basics, p. 13), repeat step 2 until you have a total of seven stitches.

[4] Working off the first row, stitch another row of right-angle weave (Basics).

[5] Wrap the strip of right-angle weave around the stem of the key, and work a row of right-angle weave to connect both sides of the strip **(figure 3)**.

[6] To add the embellishment beads, sew through the beadwork to exit an 11° at the corner of a stitch. Pick up an 11°, a 4 mm bicone crystal, and an 11°. Cross the stitch diagonally, and sew through the opposite side of the stitch (figure 4, a–b). Repeat (b–c) to add an 11°, a 4 mm bicone, and an 11° in each stitch.

Swag

[1] With the thread exiting an end bead in the tube (figure 5, point a), pick up an 11°, 11 3 mm pearls, an 11°, a 4 mm bicone, a 4 mm pearl, a 4 mm bicone, an 11°, 11 3 mm pearls, and an 11°. Sew through three 11°s at the tube's opposite end (a–b).
[2] Pick up an 11°, seven 3 mm pearls, an 11°, a 4 mm bicone, a 4 mm pearl, a 4 mm bicone, an 11°, seven 3 mm pearls, and an 11°. Sew through three 11°s in the second-to-last stitch on the opposite end of the tube (b–c).
[3] Pick up an 11°, three 3 mm pearls, an 11°, a 4 mm bicone, a 4 mm pearl, a 4 mm bicone, an 11°, three 3 mm pearls, and an 11°. Sew through the three 11°s in the third-from-last stitch on the opposite end of the tube (c–d).
[4] Pick up an 11°, a 4 mm pearl, and an 11°, and sew back through the 4 mm pearl (d–e). Pick up an 11°, skip three 11°s, and sew through the next 11° in the tube (e–f). End the thread (Basics).

Necklace

[1] Cut two 12-in. (30 cm) pieces of oval-link chain.
[2] On an eye pin, string a 4 mm pearl, a 4–10 mm accent bead, and a 3 mm bicone crystal, and make a plain loop (Basics) to create a link. Make a total of seven links using any combination of beads.
[3] Open a 9 mm jump ring (Basics), attach one loop of a link to the stem of the key next to the right-angle weave tube, and close the jump ring. Open a 4 x 7 mm jump ring, attach another link to the loop of the key, and close the jump ring.
[4] Open the remaining loop of a link, and attach the end of a chain. Close the loop. Repeat with the other link and chain.
[5] Decide where you want to position the other five links along the chain, and cut the chain at each spot. Attach a link at each cut. Cut chain from either side if necessary to keep the chains even.
[6] Open a 3 x 4 mm jump ring, attach the end of a chain and half of the clasp, and close the jump ring. Repeat with the other half of the clasp and the other chain. ○

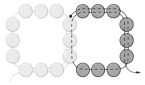

FIGURE 1

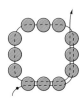

FIGURE 2

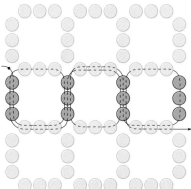

FIGURE 3

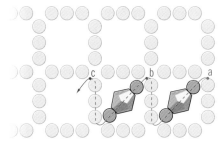

FIGURE 4

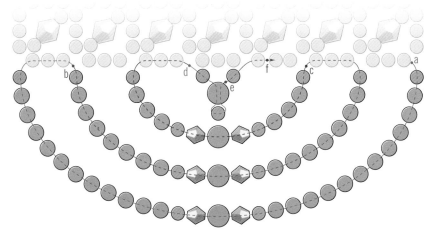

FIGURE 5

The right connection

Interspersed rows of right-angle weave connect four peyote tubes

designed by **Eileen Spitz**

The center of this bracelet gets all the attention when you embellish it with layers of bicones and margarita crystals. Enjoy the time-saving design that uses 10º cylinders for faster stitching.

stepbystep

Bands

[1] On a comfortable length of Fireline and leaving a 12-in. (30 cm) tail, follow the **pattern** on p. 126 to work in flat odd-count peyote stitch (Basics, p. 13) using color A, B, and C 10º cylinder beads. End and add thread (Basics) as needed. Add or omit rows to adjust the length of the band. Repeat to make a second band.

[2] Using the working thread from a band, exit an end edge 10º, pick up a 2 mm round crystal, skip the adjacent 10º, sew down through the next 10º **(figure 1, a–b)**, and sew up through the following 10º **(b–c)**. Repeat across the edge. Sew through the beadwork to exit the 10º directly below the last 2 mm added.

[3] Repeat step 2 to add a 2 mm above every other unembellished 10º. Repeat once more to fill in the remaining spaces.

Two peyote stitch panels are joined with a unique beadwork centerpiece.

[4] Sew through the beadwork to exit the other edge of the band, and repeat steps 2 and 3 to complete the crystal embellishment along this edge. Exit an end up-bead with the thread exiting toward the center of the band. Do not end the working thread or tail.

[5] Repeat steps 2–4 on the other band.

Tubes

[1] On a comfortable length of Fireline, pick up 17 10ºs in the color of your choice, leaving a 6-in. (15 cm) tail. Work in flat odd-count peyote stitch for a total of 12 rows. Zip up (Basics) the ends to form a tube. Exit an end 10º.

[2] Pick up a 2 mm, skip a 10º, sew down through the next 10º, and sew up through the following 10º. Repeat around the end

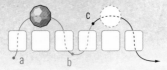

FIGURE 1

materials
bracelet 6½ in. (16.5 cm)

- **2** 6 mm margarita crystals
- **20** 3 mm round fire-polished beads
- 3 mm bicone crystals
  50 color A
  18 color B
- **178** 2 mm round crystals
- **3** g 10º cylinder beads, in each of **3** colors: A, B, C
- 5-loop slide clasp
- Fireline 6 lb. test
- beading needles, #12

to add a 2 mm above every 10º. Sew through the beadwork to exit the other end of the tube, and add the crystal embellishment. Do not end the working thread or tail.

[3] Repeat steps 1 and 2 three times to make a total of four tubes.

Assembly

[1] Place a tube next to a band, and using the working thread from the band, sew through a corresponding 10º in the tube and through the 10º in the band again (**figure 2, a–b**). Retrace the thread path (**b–c**), and sew through the next two 10ºs in the band (**c–d**). Repeat along the end of the band. Do not end the working thread.

[2] Using the tail from the band, exit the third up-bead on the end with the thread exiting toward the center of the band. Pick up a 3 mm round fire-polished bead, sew through a clasp loop, pick up a 3 mm, and sew through the 10º your thread exited at the start

of this step. Retrace the thread path. Sew through the next two 10ºs. Repeat to attach the band to the remaining four clasp loops. End the tail.

[3] Repeat steps 1 and 2 to attach a tube and the other half of the clasp to the other band.

[4] Using the working thread from a tube attached to a band, sew through an end 10º with the thread exiting toward the center of the tube. Work a row of peyote stitch using color A 3 mm bicone crystals (**figure 3**). End the working thread.

[5] Using the working thread from an unattached tube, repeat step 4. Sew through the beadwork to exit the last A 3 mm added (**figure 4, point a**). Place the unattached tube next to a tube attached to a band.

[6] Following a right-angle weave (Basics) thread path, pick up a 2 mm, sew through the last A 3 mm added in step 4 (**a–b**), pick up a 2 mm, and sew through the last A 3 mm added in step 5

(**b–c**). Snug up the beads. Sew through the first 2 mm added in this step and the next A 3 mm on the opposite tube (**c–d**).

[7] Pick up a 2 mm, and sew through the opposite A 3 mm, the first 2 mm picked up in step 6, the opposite A 3 mm, the 2 mm picked up in this step, and the next A 3 mm (**d–e**). Snug up the beads.

[8] Continue in right-angle weave to the end of the row, connecting the remaining A 3 mms.

[9] Repeat steps 4–8 to attach the remaining tube to the other band.

[10] To connect the two segments, repeat steps 4–8, but replace the A 3 mms and 2 mms with 10ºs in the color of your choice.

[11] To embellish the top of a center tube, sew through an end 10º with the thread exiting toward the center of the tube. Work a row of peyote stitch using 2 mms (**figure 5, a–b**). Sew up through the next end 10º in the direction of the center of the bracelet. Work another row of peyote stitch in the opposite

- ■ DBM011 Transparent Amber
- ■ DBM709 Metallic Olive
- ☐ DBM101 Transparent Light Topaz Luster

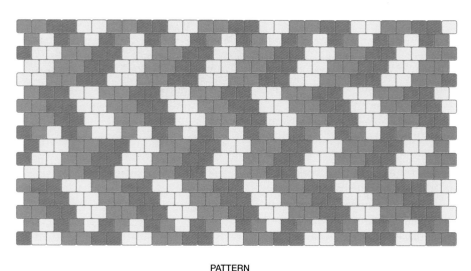

PATTERN

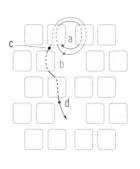

FIGURE 2

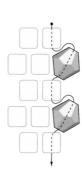

FIGURE 3

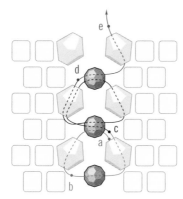

FIGURE 4

direction using 2 mms **(b–c)**. Sew through the beadwork to exit the last 2 mm added in this step **(c–d)**.

[12] Following a right-angle weave thread path, pick up a color B 3 mm bicone crystal, sew through the first 2 mm picked up in step 11 **(figure 6, a–b)**, pick up a B 3 mm, and sew through the last 2 mm added in step 11 **(b–c)**. Snug up the beads. Sew through the first B 3 mm added in this step, the 2 mm on the opposite tube, the second B 3 mm added in this step, and the next 2 mm **(c–d)**.

[13] Pick up a B 3 mm, and sew through the opposite 2 mm, the previous B 3 mm, the next 2 mm, the B 3 mm picked up in this step, and the next 2 mm **(d–e)**. Snug up the beads.

[14] Continue in right-angle weave to the end of the row, adding B 3 mms between the remaining 2 mms.

[15] Repeat steps 11–14 to embellish the other center tube.

[16] Sew through the beadwork between the center tubes, exiting a 10° at a point just off of center. Pick up a 6 mm margarita crystal and a 2 mm. Skip the 2 mm, and sew back through the 6 mm and the 10° your thread just exited. Retrace the thread path. Sew through the beadwork to a similar position on the other side of center. Repeat to add another margarita. End the working threads and tails. ●

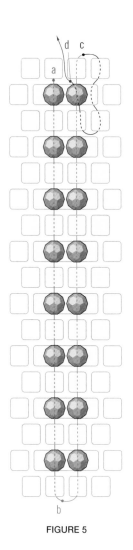

FIGURE 5

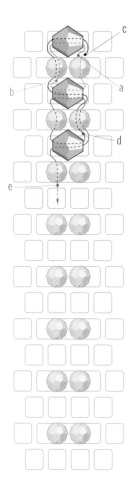

FIGURE 6

127

Paisley

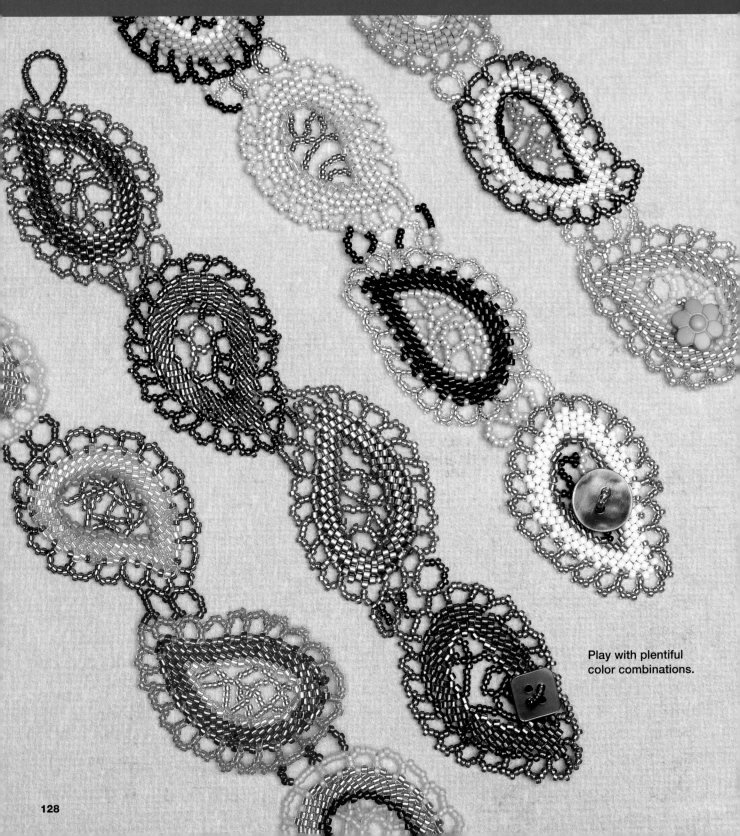

Play with plentiful
color combinations.

parade

Each paisley in this design has a unique interior. Go wild with a variety of colors, or rein it in with a simple palette.

stepbystep

Paisley components
Base

[1] Attach a color A 11º cylinder bead as a stop bead (Basics, p. 13) to the center of 2 yd. (1.8 m) of conditioned thread (Basics), and wind one half of the thread around a bobbin if desired. Use the other half to work steps 2–8.

[2] Pick up five color B 11º cylinder beads, a color C 15º seed bead, and a B. Skip the last three beads, and sew back through the fourth B picked up (figure 1, a–b).

[3] Work two peyote stitches (Basics) with Bs, exiting the stop bead A at the end of the second stitch (b–c).

[4] Turn, and work two stitches with Bs (c–d).

[5] Pick up a C and a B, and sew back through the last B added in the previous row, then work a stitch with a B (d–e).

[6] Pick up a B, an A, and a B. Sew back through the first B just picked up, and work a stitch with a B (e–f).

[7] Repeat steps 5 and 6 (f–g) until you have nine As along the edge, including the stop bead, then work step 5 again.

[8] Pick up a B, and sew back through the last B added in the previous row. Pick up a C and a B, and sew back through the B picked up at the start of this step (figure 2).

[9] Undo the thread loop around the stop bead, and use the second half of the thread to work steps 4–8, but work step 7 until you have 12 As along the edge, including the stop bead.

[10] To connect the ends of both halves, exit a B on one end, pick up a B, and sew through the corresponding B on the other end (figure 3, a–b).

[11] Sew through the next B on the end, pick up a B, and sew through the corresponding B on the other end (b–c).

[12] Sew through the next A on the end, pick up a B, and sew through the corresponding A on the other end (c–d).

[13] Sew through the previous B, the last B added, and the corresponding B on the other end (d–e).

[14] Sew through the next B, the middle B added in step 11, and the corresponding B on the other end (e–f).

Shaping

[1] Using the longer working thread, sew through the beadwork to exit the C at the point of the paisley component in the direction of the shorter edge, and sew through the next B (figure 4, a–b). Sew through the next four edge pairs of Cs and Bs (b–c). Pull the thread taut to create a curve along the short edge.

[2] Pick up a C or a B, and sew through the next C and B (c–d). Repeat around, picking up Bs or Cs to smooth the outer edge.

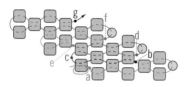

FIGURE 1

FIGURE 2

FIGURE 3

FIGURE 4

[gray bar at top of page]

materials

bracelet 6½–7 in. (16.5–18 cm)

- 2–5 g 11º cylinder beads in each of **2 colors: A, B***
- 1–4 g 15º seed beads in each of **2 colors: C, D***
- 8–12 mm button with shank
- nylon beading thread, size D, conditioned with beeswax or Thread Heaven
- beading needles, #10 or #12
- bobbin (optional)

* The directions are written for a single paisley component using colors A–D. Use as many colors as you like to make additional components.

FIGURE 5

FIGURE 6

Embellishments

Outer trim

[1] With your thread exiting the C at the point, pick up nine Cs, skip two beads along the edge, and sew through the following bead **(figure 5, a–b)**.

[2] Sew back through the last two Cs added **(b–c)**. Pick up seven Cs, skip the next few beads along the edge, and sew through the following bead **(c–d)**.

[3] Repeat step 2 around the paisley. When you reach the final repeat, pick up five Cs, and sew through the first two Cs added in step 1 and the C at the point **(figure 6)**. End this thread (Basics).

Center decoration

[1] Using the remaining thread, sew through the beadwork to exit an A along the inner edge. Pick up an A, and sew through the next inner edge A. Repeat around, exiting any A along the inner edge.

[2] Pick up the desired number of color D 15º seed beads, and sew through an inner edge A. Continue in this manner, sewing through As or Ds just added to create the desired pattern. While you work, lay the paisley component on your work surface to check that the added beads lie flat.

[3] Make a total of four embellished paisley components in the same colors, or designate new bead colors for A–D.

Assembly

[1] Lay the paisley components on your work surface in a pleasing arrangement, leaving spaces between them so that the finished bracelet is the desired length.

[2] With the remaining thread, sew through the beadwork to exit a C on the outer trim that is near where you want to connect the adjacent paisley component. Pick up enough 15ºs to span the space between the paisley components, and sew through a C on the outer trim of the adjacent component. Repeat three or four times as desired, creating lacy links as in "Center decoration."

[3] Connect the remaining paisley components as in step 2.

[4] On an end component, sew through the beadwork, exiting the top surface near the end, and pick up a button. Sew back through the beadwork, and retrace the thread path a few times to reinforce the connection.

[5] Wrap the bracelet around your wrist to determine the placement of the loop closure, and sew through the beadwork at the other end to exit the outer trim at the desired spot. Pick up enough 15ºs to fit around the button. Sew back through the beadwork to create a loop, and check the fit of the loop around the button. Retrace the thread path a few times to reinforce the connection. End all remaining threads. ●

Flowers of valor

A floral motif evokes an emblem of service

designed by **Aurelio Castaño**

Aurelio always liked the look of military medals from the Elizabethan period, and wanted to create a piece that resembled one — only softer. Shapely seed bead petals surrounding a peyote bezel with a crystal center fit the bill beautifully.

step by step

[1] On 2 yd. (1.8 m) of thread or Fireline, pick up 20 color A 11º seed beads. Tie the beads into a ring with a square knot (Basics, p. 13), leaving a 6-in. (15 cm) tail. Sew through the first bead in the ring.

[2] Working in tubular peyote stitch (Basics), pick up an A, skip an A in the ring, and sew through the next A. Repeat around the ring, and step up through the first A added in this round. Work a total of five rounds of tubular peyote using As.

materials

pair of earrings

- **2** 8 mm cube crystals
- 2 g 11º seed beads in each of **2** colors: A, B
- 1 g 15º seed beads, color B
- pair of earring findings
- nylon beading thread or Fireline 6 lb. test
- beading needles, #10
- **2** pairs of pliers

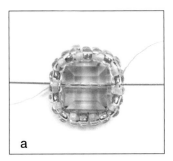

a

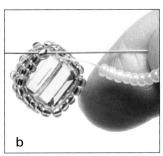

b

EDITOR'S NOTE:
Gold or silver seed beads paired with a single color make for a regal look. For a playful version, stitch the bezel in an organic shade of green, alternate the color of the petals, and embellish every other petal.

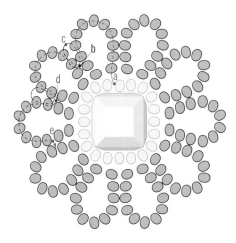

FIGURE 1

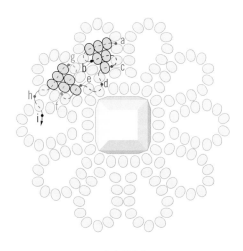

FIGURE 2

Insert an 8 mm cube crystal into the bezel. Work a round using color B 15º seed beads, and sew through the last round again to snug up the beads.

[3] Sew through the beadwork to exit an A in round 3 aligned with the hole of the cube. Sew through the cube **(photo a)** and an A in round 3 aligned with the other side of the hole. Retrace the thread path to secure the cube in the bezel.

[4] Sew through the beadwork to exit an A in round 1. To make a petal, pick up 12 color B 11º seed beads, and sew through the next up-bead **(photo b)**. Repeat around the bezel, adding a total of 10 petals, then sew through the first 10 B 11ºs of the first petal **(figure 1, a–b)**.

[5] To join the petals, sew up through the third and fourth B 11ºs of the next petal **(b–c)**. Sew down through the ninth and 10th B 11ºs of the previous petal, sew up through the third and fourth B 11ºs of the next petal again, and continue through the following six B 11ºs **(c–d)**.

[6] Repeat step 5 **(d–e)** eight times. To join the last petal to the first, sew up through the third and fourth B 11ºs of the first petal, sew down through the ninth and 10th B 11ºs of

the last petal, and sew up through the third B 11º of the first petal.

[7] Pick up three As, and sew down through the 10th B 11º of the petal **(figure 2, a–b)**. Pick up two As, and sew down through the second B 11º of the petal **(b–c)**. Pick up an A, and sew down through the 12th B 11º of the petal **(c–d)**. Sew through the next up-bead in the bezel then up through the first B in the next petal **(d–e)**.

[8] Pick up an A, and sew up through the 11th B 11º of the petal **(e–f)**. Pick up two As, and sew up through the third B 11º of the petal **(f–g)**. Pick up three As, and sew up through the ninth B 11º of the petal **(g–h)**. Sew down through the fourth A of the next petal **(h–i)**.

[9] Repeat steps 7 and 8 around the flower. End the working thread and tail (Basics).

[10] Open the loop (Basics) of an earring finding, attach a petal, and close the loop.

[11] Make a second earring. ●

Black
&GOLD

This dramatic cuff is classy and comfortable. Wear it with jeans or for a night out on the town!

Make a bold statement with contrasting colors

designed by **Cathy Lampole**

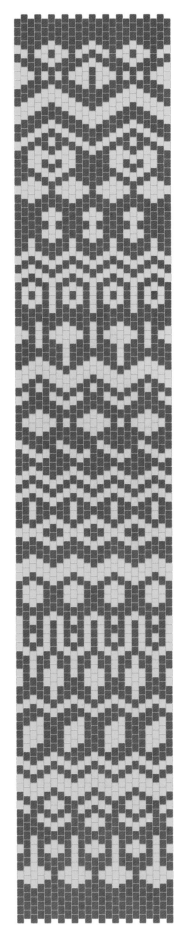

FIGURE 1

Watch the interesting patterns in this bracelet emerge as you work in flat odd-count peyote stitch. Capture a few rounds of glittering crystals in netting to serve as a toggle loop with a coordinating peyote tube toggle bar.

step by step

Peyote band

[1] Using color A and B 11º cylinder beads, and leaving a 6-in. (15 cm) tail, work the pattern (figure 1) in flat odd-count peyote stitch (Basics, p. 13). End and add thread (Basics) as needed.

[2] At the center of one end of the band, stitch a strip of flat odd-count peyote five As wide and 31 rows long. Work one decrease row at the end of the strip (figure 2): Sew through the two end As, pick up an A, and sew through the next two As. End the working thread and tail.

[3] Add 2 yd. (1.8 m) of thread to the band, and exit an end edge bead. Pick up three 15º seed beads, and sew through the next two cylinders along the edge, making a picot (photo a). Repeat to add picots all along the edge. Sew through the beadwork to add picots to the edges of the strip added in

step 2. Sew through the beadwork to exit the other edge of the band, and complete the picot embellishment along this edge. End the thread.

Toggle clasp
Toggle ring

[1] On 2 yd. (1.8 m) of thread, center a repeating pattern of a 15º and a color A 4 mm bicone crystal 12 times. Sew through the first 15º again to form a ring (figure 3, a–b). Retrace the thread path through the ring twice, and exit a 15º.

[2] Pick up five 15ºs, and sew through the next 15º in the ring (b–c). Repeat around the ring, and step up through the first three 15ºs in the first stitch (c–d).

[3] Pick up a color B 4 mm bicone crystal, and sew through the center 15º in the next stitch of the previous round (figure 4, a–b). Repeat around the ring (b–c).

[4] Pick up seven 15ºs, and sew through the center 15º in the next stitch in the previous round (c–d). Repeat around the ring, and step up through the first four 15ºs in the first stitch (d–e).

[5] Pick up a 15º, a 6 mm bicone crystal, and a 15º. Sew through the center 15º in the next stitch of the previous round (e–f). Repeat around the ring, and end the working thread.

[6] With the tail, repeat steps 2 and 3 off of the original ring, and exit a 15º between two 4 mms.

[7] Pick up three 15ºs, and sew through the center 15º between two 6 mms from step 5. Pick up three 15ºs, and sew

materials
bracelet 8 in. (20 cm)
- bicone crystals
  17 6 mm, color A or B
  12 4 mm, color A
  24 4 mm, color B
- **9 g** 11º cylinder beads in each of **2** colors: A, B
- **4 g** 15º Japanese seed beads, color A or B
- nylon beading thread, size D
- beading needles, #12

EDITOR'S NOTE:
Make a copy of the pattern in black and white. You can use colored pencils to fill in your own color palette.

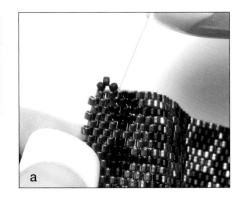

a

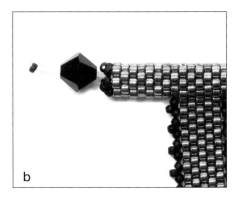

b

c

d

FIGURE 2

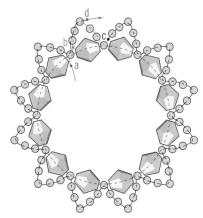

FIGURE 3

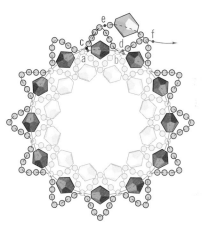

FIGURE 4

FIGURE 5

through the next 15° between the next two 4 mms from the previous round. Repeat to complete the round (figure 5).
[8] Retrace the thread path around the outer ring of 15°s and 6 mms, and end the thread.

Toggle bar

[1] On 1 yd. (.9 m) of thread, use As to make an flat odd-count peyote strip 21 beads wide and 12 rows long, leaving a 12-in. (30 cm) tail.
[2] Roll the strip into a tube, and zip up the first and last rows (Basics). Exit the eighth cylinder in the tube, and work a strip of flat odd-count peyote five beads wide and 28 rows long off the center beads.
[3] Use the working thread to work a picot embellishment of 15°s along both edges of the strip as in the peyote band.
[4] Using the tail, work a picot embellishment of 15°s around one end of the tube. Sew through the tube, and add a picot embellishment around the other end. Do not end this thread.
[5] Using the other thread, sew through the tube, and pick up a 6 mm and a 15°. Sew back through the 6 mm and the peyote tube (photo b). Repeat to add a 6 mm and 15° on the remaining end. Retrace the thread path several times, and end the thread.

Assembly

[1] Using the thread from step 4 of "Toggle bar," stitch the toggle bar to the peyote band 12 rows from the end without the peyote strip (photo c). Retrace the thread path to secure the join, and end the thread.
[2] Position the toggle ring at the other end, and thread the strip through the center of the ring. Zip up the strip to the band (photo d), retrace the thread path, and exit an end A at the base of the strip.
[3] Pick up a 6 mm and a 15°. Skip the 15°, and sew back through the 6 mm and the next A in the strip. Repeat twice, and end the thread. ○

Net some glamour

Adorn a netted
rope with rounds
of graduated
gemstones, pearls,
or crystals

designed by **Cynthia Poh**

See the Editor's Notes
on p. 139 to add a spiral
of crystals around any
portion of the piece.

Round beads from size 3 mm to 8 mm sit atop gradually increasing netted stitches in this necklace and bracelet. Gemstones are a great option (if you can find them in each size) because of their variegated color. Crystal pearls work equally well, especially when accented with a few crystals.

step by step

Necklace
Netted rope
[1] On a comfortable length of Fireline, pick up a repeating pattern of a color A 11º seed bead and a color B 11º seed bead three times, leaving a 10-in. (25 cm) tail. Tie the beads into a ring with a square knot (Basics, p. 13), then sew through the first A and B again (figure 1, a–b).

[2] Pick up an A, a B, and an A. Skip the next A in the ring, and sew through the following B (b–c). Repeat twice, and step up through the first A and B added in this round (c–d).

[3] Work in netting as follows, ending and adding thread (Basics) as needed:

Rounds 3–16: Work the following stitches for each round: Pick up an A, a B, and an A, and sew through the next B in the previous round (d–e). Repeat twice, and step up through the first A and B added in the round (e–f).

Rounds 17–32: For each round, work three stitches using two As, a B, and two As per stitch, stepping up through two As and a B at the end of each round (figure 2).

Rounds 33–42: For each round, work three stitches using three As, a B, and three As per stitch, stepping up through three As and a B at the end of each round.

Rounds 43–58: For each round, work three stitches using four As, a B, and four As per stitch, stepping up through four As and a B at the end of each round.

Rounds 59–68: Work as in rounds 33–42.

Rounds 69–84: Work as in rounds 17–32.

Rounds 85–99: Work as in rounds 3–16.

Round 100: To end the rope: Pick up an A, and sew through the next B in the previous round. Repeat twice, then sew through all six beads you sewed through in this round again. Do not end the working thread or tail.

⬤	11º seed bead, color A
◯	11º seed bead, color B
◐	15º seed bead

materials

all projects
• Fireline 6 lb. test
• beading needles, #10 and #12

aqua necklace 15–16 in. (38–41 cm)*
• round gemstone beads (amazonite)
  48 8 mm
  60 6 mm
  96 4 mm
  97 3 mm
• 11º seed beads
  20 g color A (silver)
  10 g color B (cream)
• 5 g 15º seed beads (silver)

red bracelet 7½ in. (19.1 cm)
• Swarovski round beads
  8 8 mm crystal pearls (bordeaux)
  4 8 mm round crystals (dark red coral)
  24 6 mm crystal pearls (bordeaux)
  24 4 mm crystal pearls (bordeaux)
• 11º seed beads
  10 g color A (silver)
  5 g color B (silver)
• 2 g 15º seed beads (silver)
• clasp

purple necklace and bracelet colors:
• Swarovski round beads
  8 mm crystal pearls (dark purple)
  8 mm round crystals (purple velvet)
  6 mm crystal pearls (dark purple)
  4 mm crystal pearls (dark purple)
• 11º seed beads
  10 g color A (Miyuki 4201, Duracoat galvanized silver)
  5 g color B (Miyuki 591, ivory pearl Ceylon)
• 2 g 13º Charlottes (silver)

*A note on length:
Your necklace will be longer than 15–16 in. (38–41 cm) as you work "Necklace: Netted rope," but it will shrink to this length as you add "Embellishments." For a longer necklace, work additional rounds as in rounds 3–16 and 85–99 of "Necklace: Netted rope." Embellish these extra rounds as in rounds 4–16 and 85–98 of "Embellishment." You will need three 3 mm round beads to embellish each additional round.

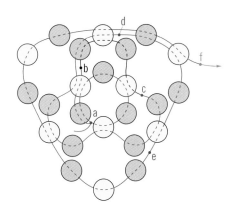

FIGURE 1

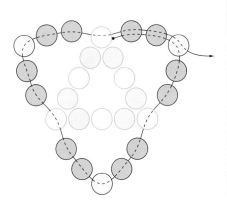

FIGURE 2

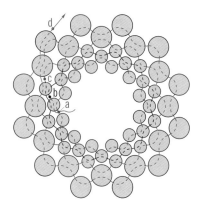

FIGURE 3

a

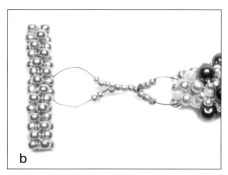

b

c

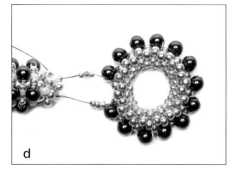

d

Embellishment

[1] Add a comfortable length of Fireline to the starting end of the rope, and exit a B in round 3. Pick up a 15° seed bead, a 3 mm round bead, and a 15°, and sew through the next B in the round **(photo a)**. Repeat twice, and step up through the next A and B in round 4.

[2] Sewing through the Bs in each round, embellish the netted rope as follows, ending and adding thread as needed:

Rounds 4–16: For each round, work three stitches using a 15°, a 3 mm, and a 15° per stitch, stepping up through an A and a B at the end of each round. In the last round of this section, step up through two As and a B.

Rounds 17–32: For each round, work three stitches using two 15°s, a 4 mm round bead, and two 15°s per stitch, stepping up through two As and a B at the end of each round. In the last round of this section, step up through three As and a B.

Rounds 33–42: For each round, work three stitches using three 15°s, a 6 mm round bead, and three 15°s per stitch, stepping up through three As and a B at the end of each round. In the last round of this section, step up through four As and a B.

Rounds 43–58: For each round, work three stitches using four 15°s, an 8 mm round bead, and four 15°s per stitch, stepping up through four As and a B at the end of each round. In the last round of this section, step up through three As and a B.

Rounds 59–68: Work as in rounds

33–42, but in the last round of this section, step up through two As and a B.

Rounds 69–84: Work as in rounds 17–32, but in the last round of this section, step up through one A and a B.

Rounds 85–98: Work as in rounds 4–16, but in the last round of this section, step up through one A and a B. End the working thread.

Toggle bar

[1] On 1 yd. (.9 m) of Fireline, pick up 14 As, leaving a 6-in. (15 cm) tail. Work a total of eight rows in flat even-count peyote stitch (Basics), making a strip with four As on each straight edge. Zip up (Basics) the first and last rows to form a tube, and end the working thread and tail.

[2] Using the thread on one end of the netted rope, exit an A or a B in the end ring of beads. Pick up 10 15°s, and sew through two beads at the center of the toggle bar. Pick up three 15°s, skip the last three 15°s of the 10 added at the start of this step, and sew back through the next four 15°s. Pick up three 15°s, and sew through the A or B in the end ring opposite the bead your thread exited at the start of this step **(photo b)**. Retrace the thread path through the clasp connection, and end the thread.

Toggle ring

[1] On 1 yd. (.9 m) of Fireline, center an even number of 15°s to fit around

the toggle bar (about 24). Tie the beads into a ring with a square knot. With one end of the thread, sew through the next 15° in the ring **(figure 3, a–b)**.

[2] Working in circular peyote stitch (Basics), work a round with one 15° per stitch, and step up through the first 15° added in this round **(b–c)**.

[3] Work two rounds with one A per stitch, stepping up through the first A added in each round **(c–d)**.

[4] With the other end of the thread, work two rounds with 15°s and one round with As. Zip up the As in the outer rounds.

[5] Exit an A in an outer round. Pick up a 3 mm, and sew through the next A in the round. Repeat around, stopping short of the last stitch, and end the threads **(photo c)**.

[6] Using the thread on the remaining end of the netted rope, exit an A or a B in the end ring of beads. Pick up three 15°s, and sew through three 11°s in the toggle ring not embellished with 3 mms. Pick up three 15°s, and sew through the A or B opposite the bead your thread exited at the start of this step **(photo d)**. Retrace the thread path through the clasp connection, and end the thread.

Bracelet
Netted rope

Since much of the netting is exposed in the bracelet, you may choose to work

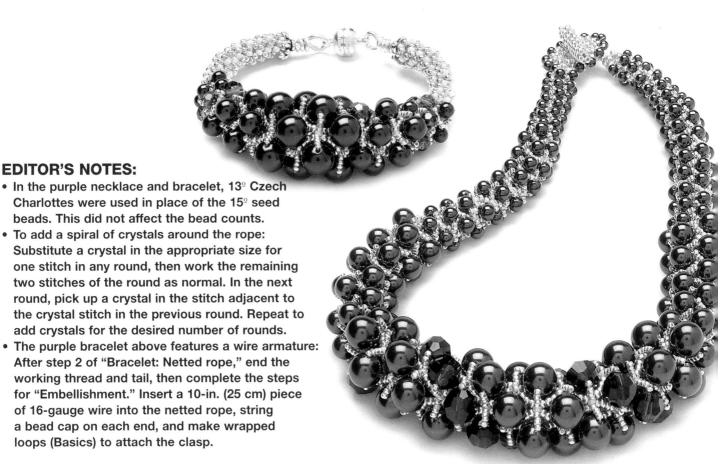

EDITOR'S NOTES:

- In the purple necklace and bracelet, 13° Czech Charlottes were used in place of the 15° seed beads. This did not affect the bead counts.
- To add a spiral of crystals around the rope: Substitute a crystal in the appropriate size for one stitch in any round, then work the remaining two stitches of the round as normal. In the next round, pick up a crystal in the stitch adjacent to the crystal stitch in the previous round. Repeat to add crystals for the desired number of rounds.
- The purple bracelet above features a wire armature: After step 2 of "Bracelet: Netted rope," end the working thread and tail, then complete the steps for "Embellishment." Insert a 10-in. (25 cm) piece of 16-gauge wire into the netted rope, string a bead cap on each end, and make wrapped loops (Basics) to attach the clasp.

with 11° seed beads in one color. However, using two colors makes it easier to see which 11° to sew through in each stitch. The following instructions use two colors of 11°s.

[1] Work steps 1 and 2 of "Necklace: Netted rope."

[2] Work in netting as follows, ending and adding thread (Basics, p. 13) as needed:

Rounds 3–20: For each round, work three stitches using an A, a B, and an A per stitch, stepping up through an A and a B at the end of each round.

Rounds 21–24: For each round, work three stitches using two As, a B, and two As per stitch, stepping up through two As and a B at the end of each round.

Rounds 25–28: For each round, work three stitches using three As, a B, and three As per stitch, stepping up through three As and a B at the end of each round.

Rounds 29–32: For each round, work three stitches using four As, a B, and four As per stitch, stepping up through four As and a B at the end of each round.

Rounds 33–36: Work as in rounds 25–28.

Rounds 37–40: Work as in rounds 21–24.

Rounds 41–59: Work as in rounds 3–20.

Round 60: To end the rope: Pick up an A, and sew through the next B in the previous round. Repeat twice, then sew through all six beads you sewed through in this round again.

[3] Pick up six 11°s and half of the clasp, and sew through the 11° opposite the 11° your thread exited at the start of this step. Retrace the thread path through the clasp connection, and end the working thread.

[4] Using the tail, attach the other half of the clasp.

Embellishment

[1] Add a comfortable length of Fireline to the netted rope, exiting a B in round 21. Pick up two 15° seed beads, a 4 mm round bead, and two 15°s, and sew through the next B in the round. Repeat twice, and step up through the next two As and a B in round 22.

[2] Sewing through the Bs in each round, embellish the netted rounds as follows, ending and adding thread as needed:

Rounds 22–24: For each round, work three stitches with two 15°s, a 4 mm round bead, and two 15°s per stitch, stepping up through two As and a B at the end of each round. In the last round of this section, step up through three As and a B.

Rounds 25–28: For each round, work three stitches with three 15°s, a 6 mm round bead, and three 15°s per stitch, stepping up through three As and a B at the end of each round. In the last round of this section, step up through four As and a B.

Rounds 29–32: For each round, work three stitches with four 15°s, an 8 mm round bead, and four 15°s per stitch, stepping up through four As and a B at the end of each round. In the last round of this section, step up through three As and a B.

Rounds 33–36: Work as in rounds 25–28, but in the last round of this section, step up through two As and a B.

Rounds 37–40: Work as in rounds 21–24, but in the last round of this section, step up through one A and a B. End the thread. ●

European motif

Dress up a pretty peyote pattern with netting and fringe for a traditional holiday decoration

designed by **Deb Moffett-Hall**

Larger beads used in the fringe allow for faster embellishing than seed bead fringe and provide endless accent bead options.

Outlined in gold, the bold colors in this peyote ribbon create a dramatic ornament. If you prefer more delicate décor, choose a palette of pastel beads instead.

step by step

Peyote strip
[1] On a comfortable length of thread, attach a stop bead (Basics, p. 13), leaving a 6-in. (15 cm) tail. Using 11º cylinder beads, pick up the beads for the first two rows: an A, two Bs, an E, an F, a D, four Bs, an A, five Bs, a C, four Bs, and an A. These beads are faded in the **pattern**.

[2] Work rows 3–32 in flat even-count peyote stitch (Basics) using cylinder beads in colors A–I. Referring to the **figure**, start on row 3, and pick up one cylinder per stitch. End and add thread (Basics) as needed:

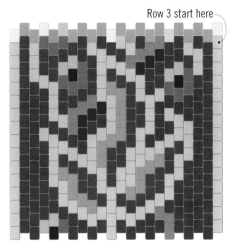

Row 3 start here

11º Delica bead colors
- A (DB1832, Duracoat galvanized gold)
- B (DB001, black opaque)
- C (DB0727, opaque vermillion red)
- D (DB0760, matte opaque light sapphire)
- E (DB0167, opaque light sapphire AB)
- F (DB0880, matte opaque dark blue AB)
- G (DB0791, dyed matte opaque red)
- H (DB0797, dyed matte opaque olive)
- I (DB0877, matte opaque green AB)

Row 3: A, B, B, C, B, A, B, B, D, D, B
Row 4: A, A, D, B, A, B, A, C, B, A, B
Row 5: A, A, B, G, C, B, A, B, B, B, B
Row 6: A, A, B, E, B, A, C, G, B, B, B
Row 7: A, A, E, B, G, A, A, D, E, B, B
Row 8: A, A, B, F, B, H, A, B, E, D, B
Row 9: A, B, F, B, A, H, A, D, D, A, B
Row 10: A, B, A, D, B, I, H, B, D, D, B
Row 11: A, B, D, A, A, I, A, B, B, B, B
Row 12: A, B, A, B, C, A, H, A, B, B, B
Row 13: A, B, B, B, H, I, G, C, B, B, B
Row 14: A, B, A, C, G, A, H, A, A, B, B
Row 15: A, B, A, B, H, I, B, G, A, B, B
Row 16: A, B, B, C, B, A, H, A, B, A, B
Row 17: A, B, A, B, A, I, A, G, B, A, B
Row 18: A, B, A, B, A, I, H, B, A, A, B
Row 19: A, B, H, A, A, H, I, B, A, B, B
Row 20: A, B, A, A, A, H, A, A, H, A, B
Row 21: A, B, A, I, A, H, I, A, H, B, B
Row 22: A, B, A, H, A, H, A, I, H, B, B
Row 23: A, B, A, H, I, A, A, H, I, B, B
Row 24: A, B, A, I, H, H, A, H, A, B, B
Row 25: A, B, B, H, I, A, A, H, A, B, B
Row 26: A, B, B, I, H, A, I, H, A, B, B
Row 27: A, B, B, A, H, H, H, I, A, B, B
Row 28: A, B, B, A, I, A, H, A, B, B, B
Row 29: A, B, B, C, A, A, A, A, B, B, B
Row 30: A, B, E, B, A, A, A, B, C, B, B
Row 31: A, B, B, B, B, B, B, B, D, E, B
Row 32: A, B, F, B, B, A, B, B, C, B, B

[3] Repeat rows 3–32 for a total of eight leaf motifs, and end the working thread and tail.

Fringe
[1] Add 2 yd. (1.8 m) of thread to the peyote strip, exiting the edge A in row 1.
[2] Pick up a color C 4 mm round bead, an A cylinder, a 5 x 8 mm drop bead (small end first), a 6 mm disk bead, a 6 mm round bead, a 6 mm disk, a 5 x 8 mm drop (large end first), an A cylinder, a C 4 mm, a color A 4 mm fire-polished bead, a C 4 mm, a 5 x 10 mm cone (small end first), a 7 x 10 mm drop bead (small end first), a 6 mm disk, a 5 x 8 mm drop (large end first), and an A cylinder. Skip the

materials
gold ornament
- 2½-in. (6.4 cm) diameter ornament
- 8 7 x 10 mm drop beads, color C (red)
- 40 5 x 8 mm drop beads, color E (light blue AB)
- 32 6 mm bugle beads, color A (gold)
- 40 6 mm glass disk beads, color I (green)
- 16 6 mm round glass beads, color C (red)
- 64 4 mm round glass beads, color C (red)
- 8 4 mm fire-polished beads, color A (gold)
- 11º cylinder beads (see color key below figure)
  5–6 g colors A, B
  2–3 g colors C, D, H, I
  1–2 g colors E, F, G
- 8 5 x 10 mm gold-plated metal cones
- nylon beading thread, size D
- beading needles, #12

red ornament accent bead colors:
- 5 x 10 mm drops and 5 x 8 mm drops, color B (black)
- 6 mm disk beads, color C (red)
- 6 mm round crystals, 6 mm bugle beads, and 4 mm fire-polished beads, color A (gold)
- 4 mm fire-polished beads (in place of 4 mm round glass beads), color I (green)

a

b

c

d

e

f

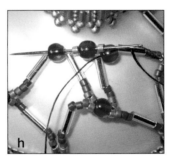

g

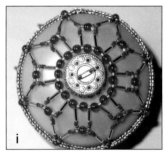

h

i

last cylinder picked up, and sew back through the next six beads (photo a).

[3] Pick up a C 4 mm, an A cylinder, a 5 x 8 mm drop (small end first), a 6 mm disk, a 6 mm round, a 6 mm disk, a 5 x 8 mm drop (large end first), an A cylinder, and a C 4 mm. Skip 13 A cylinders along the edge of the peyote strip, and sew up through the next A cylinder. Sew down through the following A cylinder along the edge and back through the last C 4 mm picked up (photo b).

[4] Repeat steps 2 and 3 to add a total of seven fringes, but omit the first C 4 mm picked up in step 2.

[5] To work the last fringe, repeat step 2, but omit the first C 4 mm. Repeat step 3, but omit the last C 4 mm, and sew through the first C 4 mm picked up in the first fringe instead (photo c).

[6] Zip up (Basics and photo d) the end rows of the peyote strip. Retrace the join, and then exit an A cylinder

EDITOR'S NOTE:
Make a matching bracelet by repeating steps 1 and 2 of "Peyote strip" until you reach the desired length.

along the edge opposite the fringe, directly across from a C 4 mm. Place the beadwork over the ornament to work the netted rounds.

Netting

[1] To begin the first round of netting, pick up a C 4 mm, an A cylinder, an E cylinder, an I cylinder, a C cylinder, a 6 mm bugle bead, a C cylinder, an I cylinder, an E cylinder, an A cylinder, a C 4 mm, an A cylinder, an E cylinder, an I cylinder, a C cylinder, a 6 mm bugle, a C cylinder, an I cylinder, an E cylinder, an A cylinder, and a C 4 mm. Skip 13 A cylinders along the edge of the peyote strip, and sew down through

the next A cylinder. Sew up through the following A cylinder along the edge and back through the last C 4 mm picked up (photo e).

[2] Repeat step 1, but omit the first C 4 mm picked up (photo f) for a total of seven stitches.

[3] To work the last netted stitch, repeat step 1, but omit the first C 4 mm. Omit the last C 4 mm, sewing through the first C 4 mm picked up in the first stitch instead. Step up by sewing through the next 10 beads, exiting the center C 4 mm of the first stitch in this round.

[4] To begin the second round of netting, pick up an A cylinder, an E cylinder, an

I cylinder, a C cylinder, a 6 mm bugle, a C 4 mm, a 6 mm bugle, a C cylinder, an I cylinder, an E cylinder, and an A cylinder. Sew through the center C 4 mm of the next stitch in the previous round (photo g). Repeat around, and step up through the first six beads, exiting the center C 4 mm of the first stitch in this round.

[5] Pick up an A cylinder, a C 4 mm, and an A cylinder. Sew through the center C 4 mm of the next stitch in the previous round (photo h). Repeat around, and retrace the ring of A cylinders and C 4 mms to snug them up to the ornament top (photo i). End the working thread. ●

CAPTIVE cabochons

Surround round or
oval cabochons
with peyote stitch,
and dress them up
with loads of fringe

designed by **Maggie Roschyk**

Any round or oval cabochon
will work with this design,
so if you can't find the exact
ones shown here, feel free
to substitute size and style
to suit your individual taste.

materials

bracelet 7 in. (18 cm)

- ¾ x 1-in. (1.9 x 2.5 cm) oval or 1-in. (2.5 cm) round cabochon
- **45–75** assorted pearls, crystals, and glass accent beads
- 18–25 g 8º hex-cut beads
- 1 g 11º seed beads
- 1 g 11º cylinder beads
- 3–5 g 15º seed beads
- 4-strand slide clasp
- Fireline 6 lb. test
- beading needles, #12

EDITOR'S NOTE:
For a cabochon with a low profile, you may only need two rounds of 11º seed beads, one round of 11º cylinders, and one round of 15º seed beads. If you have a hard time holding the cab in place while you're stitching it to the peyote base, work a round of 15ºs on the other side of the first round of 11ºs. This will hold the cabochon in place better without affecting the instructions.

Soft draping peyote stitch makes up a thick cuff-style band that just begs to be embellished. Attaching an interesting cabochon surrounded by just the right accent beads creates an elegant and substantial bracelet.

stepbystep

Peyote band

[1] On 2 yd. (1.8 m) of Fireline, pick up 14 8º hex-cut beads, leaving a 6-in. (15 cm) tail. Working in flat even-count peyote stitch (Basics, p. 13), make a band that is 14 beads wide and 132 rows long, ending and adding thread (Basics) as needed. Each straight edge will have 66 beads. Test the fit, and add or remove rows as needed. End the working thread and tail.

[2] Add 2 yd. (1.8 m) of Fireline at one end of the band, and exit the edge bead in the second-to-last row **(figure 1, point a)**. Pick up two 15º seed beads, and sew through the next hex-cut **(a–b)**. Repeat across the row **(b–c)**.

[3] Pick up three 15ºs, and sew through the next two edge hex-cuts **(c–d)**, creating a picot. Repeat along the edge. Fill in the stitches at the other end, as in step 2, and then repeat the picot embellishment along the remaining edge.

[4] Center the clasp at one end of the band. Sew through the first few hex-cuts and 15ºs until you reach the beads that line up with the first loop of half of the clasp **(figure 2, point a)**. Pick up two 15ºs, the first loop of the clasp, and two 15ºs, and sew through the same hex-cut or 15ºs your thread exited and the next few beads. Exit near the next loop of the clasp **(a–b)**. Repeat across the row **(b–c)**, and retrace the thread path. Zigzag through the peyote band to exit the opposite end, and repeat to attach the other half of the clasp.

Cabochon bezel

[1] On 1 yd. (.9 m) of Fireline, leave a 12-in. (30 cm) tail, and pick up enough 11º seed beads to surround the bottom edge of your cabochon, making sure to pick up an even number. Work one to four rounds of tubular peyote stitch (Basics) using 11ºs, depending on the height of your cabochon. The taller the cab, the more rounds you'll need. Work two rounds of tubular peyote using 11º cylinder beads. Work one round using 15ºs. End the working thread.

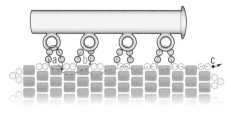

FIGURE 1

FIGURE 2

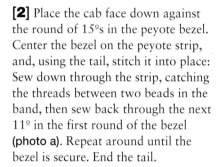

[2] Place the cab face down against the round of 15ºs in the peyote bezel. Center the bezel on the peyote strip, and, using the tail, stitch it into place: Sew down through the strip, catching the threads between two beads in the band, then sew back through the next 11º in the first round of the bezel **(photo a)**. Repeat around until the bezel is secure. End the tail.

Embellishments

[1] Add 2 yd. (1.8 m) of Fireline to the band, and exit an edge bead in the second-to-last row with the needle

pointing toward the center of the band. Pick up an accent bead and a 15º. Skip the 15º, and sew back through the accent bead and the next hex-cut in the row **(photo b)**. Repeat to add accent embellishment to the last two rows of the band.

[2] Sew through the beadwork to exit several rows away from the cabochon. Embellish several rows as in step 1, but only embellish partial rows, moving closer to the bezel. Add embellishments to the bezel if desired.

[3] Sew through the beadwork to embellish the other end of the bracelet as in step 1, and end the thread. ●

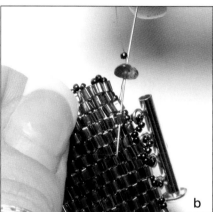

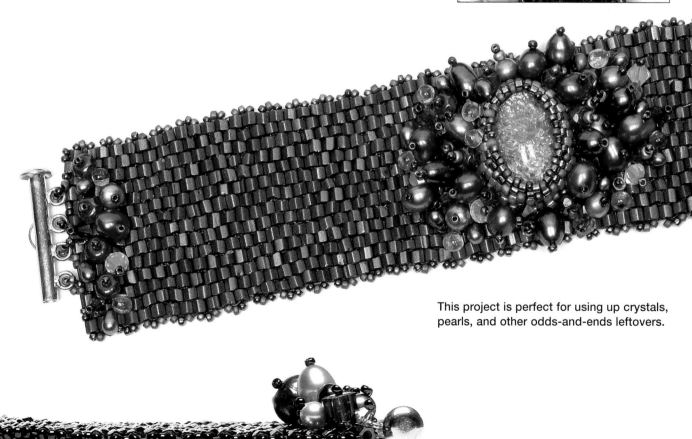

This project is perfect for using up crystals, pearls, and other odds-and-ends leftovers.

PEYOTE STITCH / FRINGE

Haut monde
hexagons

Flat odd-count peyote medallions flow from one to another via strands of seed beads in this statement necklace

Experiment with a monochromatic or contrasting color scheme.

designed by **Jimmie Boatright**

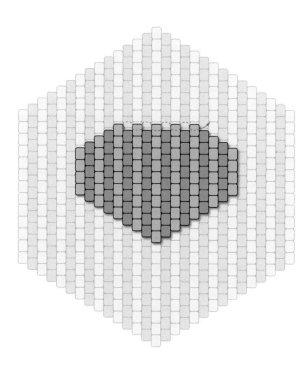

FIGURE 1

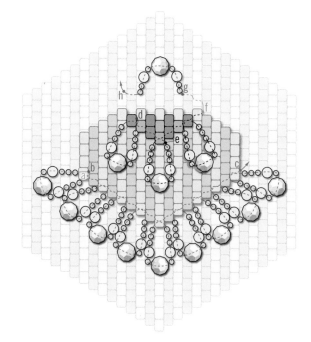

FIGURE 2

A large, peyote stitch hexagon provides the canvas for a small hexagon, fringe, and fire-polished beads, which add texture and dimension.

stepbystep

Large hexagon
[1] Attach a stop bead (Basics, p. 13), to the center of 3 yd. (2.7 m) of Fireline, and wrap half of the Fireline around a bobbin or piece of cardboard. With the other half of the Fireline, pick up 29 11º cylinder beads, and work in flat odd-count peyote stitch (Basics) until you have a total of 25 rows, ending with an odd-count turn (Editor's Notes, p. 149). You will have 13 beads on each straight edge.
[2] Taper the next 14 rows to a point: Decrease one bead per row by working an even-count decrease (Editor's Notes) at the end of each row until you have one bead in the final row. End the working Fireline (Basics).
[3] Unwind the other half of the Fireline, and remove the stop bead. Repeat step 2 to taper the other side, and end the Fireline.

Medium hexagons
[1] Attach a stop bead to the center of 2 yd. (1.8 m) of Fireline, and wrap half of the Fireline around a bobbin or piece of cardboard. With the other half of the Fireline, pick up 19 cylinders, and work in flat odd-count peyote for 19 rows, ending with an odd-count turn. You will have 10 beads on each straight edge.
[2] Taper the next nine rows to a point as in step 2 of "Large hexagon." End the working Fireline.
[3] Unwind the other half of the Fireline, and remove the stop bead. Repeat step 2, and end the Fireline.
[4] Make a second medium hexagon.

Small hexagon
[1] Attach a stop bead to the center of 1 yd. (.9 m) of Fireline, and wrap half of the Fireline around a bobbin or piece of cardboard. With the other half of the Fireline, pick up 17 cylinders, and work in flat odd-count peyote for seven rows, ending with an odd-count turn. You will have four beads on each straight edge.
[2] Taper the next eight rows as in step 2 of "Large hexagon." Tie a couple of half-hitch knots (Basics), but do not trim the working Fireline.

[3] Unwind the other half of the Fireline, and remove the stop bead. Taper the next four rows until you have five up-beads in the final row.
[4] Center the unfinished edge of the small hexagon at the center of the 17th row from the top of the large hexagon. Zip up (Basics) the two pieces (figure 1).
[5] Continue to taper the small hexagon until you have one bead in the final row. The last four rows will fold over the front of the small hexagon. Do not end the Fireline.

Embellishment
[1] With the Fireline from the bottom half of the small hexagon, sew through the beadwork to exit the bottom cylinder of a straight edge, with your needle pointing toward the point of the small hexagon. Pick up three 15º seed beads, a 3 mm round bead, a 15º, a 4 mm fire-polished bead, a 15º, a 3 mm, and three 15ºs, and sew through the cylinder your thread is exiting (figure 2, a–b). Sew through the next two edge cylinders along the tapered end. Repeat the embellishment for a total of nine loops (b–c). End the Fireline.
[2] With the Fireline from the top half of the small hexagon, sew through the beadwork to exit the fourth edge cylinder from the top point (point d).

147

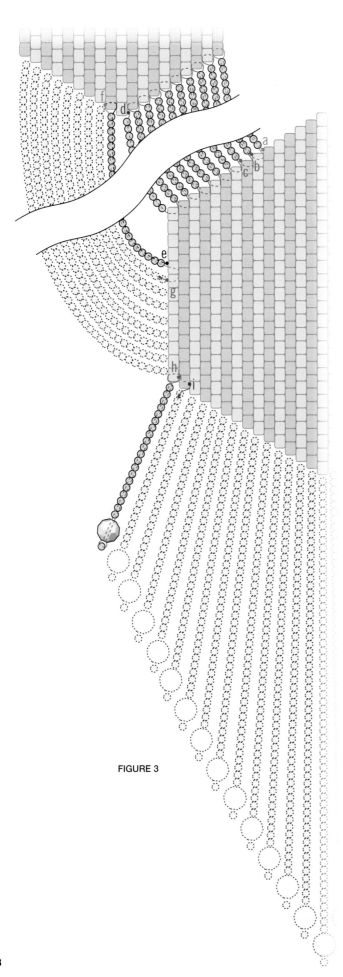

FIGURE 3

Pick up three 15⁰s, a 3 mm, a 15⁰, a 4 mm, a 15⁰, a 3 mm, and three 15⁰s, and sew through the cylinder your Fireline is exiting and the next three cylinders along the edge (**d–e**). Repeat, then repeat again but sew through only one cylinder (**e–f**).

[3] Sew through the beadwork to exit a cylinder in the large hexagon two rows above the row connecting the small hexagon to the large hexagon (**point g**). Pick up two 15⁰s, a 3 mm, a 15⁰, a 4 mm, a 15⁰, a 3 mm, and two 15⁰s, skip two cylinders in the row, and sew through the next cylinder, centering the loop over the small hexagon (**g–h**). End the Fireline.

Connecting the hexagons

[1] Add 3 yd. (2.7 m) of beading thread (Basics) to the top of the large hexagon, and exit the sixth edge cylinder from the center point (**figure 3, point a**). Pick up 50 15⁰s, sew through the first cylinder on a tapered end of a medium hexagon, and sew back through the 15⁰s just added and the next cylinder in the large hexagon (**a–b**).

[2] Pick up 51 15⁰s, sew through the next cylinder on the tapered end of the medium hexagon, and sew back through the 15⁰s just added and the next cylinder in the large hexagon (**b–c**).

[3] Continue to connect the medium hexagon to the large hexagon by increasing one 15⁰ per strand for a total of 10 connecting strands (**c–d**). End and add thread as needed.

[4] Sew through the beadwork to exit the fifth cylinder on the straight edge of the large hexagon (**point e**). Pick up 75 15⁰s, and sew through the next cylinder along the tapered end of the medium hexagon (**e–f**). Sew back through the 15⁰s just added, the cylinder your thread exited at the start of this step, and the next cylinder on the straight edge of the large hexagon (**f–g**).

[5] Continue to connect the medium hexagon to the large hexagon as in step 4, but increase five 15⁰s per strand for a total of nine connecting strands with 115 15⁰s in the ninth strand. End the thread.

[6] Repeat steps 1–5 on the other side of the large hexagon to connect the other medium hexagon.

Fringe

[1] Add a comfortable length of beading thread to the large hexagon, and exit the first cylinder on the bottom (**figure 3, point h**). Pick up 20 15ºs, a 4 mm, and a 15º. Skip the last 15º, and sew back through the rest of the beads just added, the cylinder your thread exited at the start of this step, and the next cylinder in the hexagon (**h–i**).

[2] Continue adding fringe to the bottom of the large hexagon, increasing each fringe by three 15ºs until you reach the center point. You will have 62 15ºs in the center fringe.

[3] Continue adding fringe, but decrease each fringe by three 15ºs so you have 20 15ºs in the final fringe. End the thread.

Neck straps

[1] Attach a split ring to each half of the clasp.

[2] Determine the finished length of the necklace, and add 2 yd. (1.8 m) to that number. Cut a piece of Fireline to that length, and center it in the remaining point of a medium hexagon (**figure 4, points a and aa**). Over both ends of the Fireline, pick up 25 15ºs and a 6 mm fire-polished bead (**a–b and aa–bb**).

[3] On one end of the Fireline, pick up an alternating pattern of 20 15ºs and a 6 mm to the desired length, ending with a 6 mm. Pick up two 15ºs, a split ring, and two 15ºs, and sew back through the last 6 mm added (**b–c**).

[4] With the same end of Fireline, pick up 20 15ºs, and sew back through the next 6 mm added in the previous step. Repeat until you sew through the last 6 mm before the medium hexagon (**c–d**).

[5] Pick up 28 15ºs, skip the cylinder adjacent to the center cylinder, and sew through the following cylinder along the tapered edge of the hexagon (**d–e**).

[6] Pick up 31 15ºs, and sew through the 6 mm and a 15º. Sew back through the 6 mm (**e–f**).

[7] Pick up 34 15ºs, skip two cylinders in the hexagon, and sew through the following two cylinders.

[8] Pick up 37 15ºs, sew through the 6 mm and a 15º, and sew back through the 6 mm.

[9] Pick up 40 15ºs, skip the next two cylinders in the hexagon, and sew

through the last cylinder along the edge. Sew through the 15ºs just added, and end the Fireline.

[10] Repeat steps 3–9 with the other end of Fireline, but in step 3, sew through the 6 mms added with the other end of Fireline rather than picking up new 6 mms.

[11] Repeat steps 1–10 for the other neck strap. ⊙

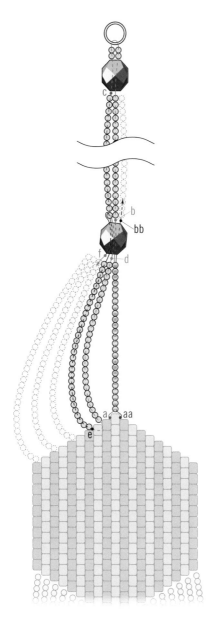

FIGURE 4

materials

necklace 17–24 in. (43–61 cm)

- **6–14** 6 mm fire-polished beads
- **42** 4 mm fire-polished beads
- **26** 3 mm round beads
- 24 g 11º Japanese cylinder beads
- 10 g 15º seed beads
- clasp
- **2** 4 mm split rings
- Fireline 6 lb. test
- Nymo or nylon beading thread, size D
- beading needles, #12
- bobbin or cardboard
- split-ring pliers (optional)

EDITOR'S NOTES:

- **Odd-count turn: Pick up a cylinder, sew under the thread bridge between the two adjacent cylinders along the edge, and sew back through the cylinder just added.**
- **Even-count decrease: After working the last stitch in the row, sew under the thread bridge between the two adjacent cylinders along the edge, and sew back through the last two cylinders.**
- **Mix two or three colors of cylinder beads to create hexagons with a mosaic look.**
- **Using nylon beading thread for the connecting strands and the fringe will allow your work to drape properly.**

Garden *of* daisies

designed by **Kimie Suto**

Vining daisy chains artfully adorn peyote components

The delicacy of daisy chain is bolstered by strong lines and playful colors in a powerfully feminine necklace.

Teardrop-shaped peyote stitch components join together to form the centerpiece of this classic Y-necklace. A leafy daisy chain meanders through it, adding bursts of color in all the right places.

step by step

Teardrop components

[1] On 1½ yd. (1.4 m) of thread, pick up a color C 8º seed bead and 45 color A 11º seed beads, leaving a 24-in. (61 cm) tail. Tie the beads into a ring with a square knot (Basics, p. 13), and sew through the C again **(figure 1, a–b)**. These beads form the first two rounds of a peyote stitch component.

[2] Work in tubular peyote stitch (Basics):
Round 3: Pick up an A, skip the next A in the ring, and sew through the following A **(b–c)**. Repeat six times **(c–d)**. Work nine stitches using color B 9º or 10º seed beads **(d–e)**. Work seven more stitches with As, sewing through the first C to complete the final stitch **(e–f)**. Step up through the first A added in this round **(f–g)**.
Round 4: Work six stitches using As **(g–h)**, 10 stitches using Bs **(h–i)**, and six stitches using As **(i–j)**. Step up through the next C and the first A in each of the last two rounds **(j–k)**.
Round 5: Work six stitches using As, nine stitches using Cs, and six stitches using As. Sew through the next A and C **(k–l)**.
Round 6: Pick up an A, and sew through the first A in round 2 **(figure 2, a–b)**. Continue adding a round of beads between the round 2 beads, working six

more stitches with As, nine with Bs, and seven with As. Step up through the first A added in this round **(b–c)**.
Round 7: Work six stitches with As, 10 stitches with Bs, and six stitches with As. Step up through the top C and the first A in each of the last two rounds **(c–d)**.

[3] Zip up (Basics) rounds 5 and 7 to form the beadwork into a teardrop-shaped tube, exiting the top C **(d–e)**.

[4] Pick up about eight color E 11º seed beads, a 7 x 10 mm bead cap, and a 10 mm glass pearl. Check that this line of beads fits within the teardrop, and add or remove Es if necessary. Sew through the center 11º in round 1 of the component, then sew back through the beads just added. Sew through the top C again **(figure 3)**. Sew through the first A in round 1, and flip the component over.

[5] Pick up an A, and sew through the next A in round 1 **(figure 4, a–b)**. Pulling the top edges together, sew through the corresponding A on the opposite side of round 1 **(b–c)**, sew back through the bead just added, and continue through the last A in round 1 and the top C **(c–d)**. End the working thread (Basics) but not the tail. The component now has both a front and a back surface — the front shows the line of beads added in step 4, and the back shows the join created in this step.

materials
necklace 17 in. (43 cm)
- **7** 10 mm glass pearls
- **16** 6 mm glass pearls
- **10–12** 3 mm bugle beads
- **25–30** 2 mm glass pearls, color I
- **10–12** 2 mm glass pearls, color J
- **4 g** 8º seed beads, color C
- **3 g** 8º seed beads, color D
- **6 g** 9º or 10º seed beads, color B
- **13 g** 11º seed beads, color A
- **6 g** 11º seed beads, color E
- **2 g** 11º seed beads in each of **3** colors: F, G, H
- **6** 7 x 10 mm bead caps
- 15 mm five-petal metal flower stamping
- 10 mm metal flower component
- nylon beading thread, size D
- beading needles, #12
- Bead Stopper

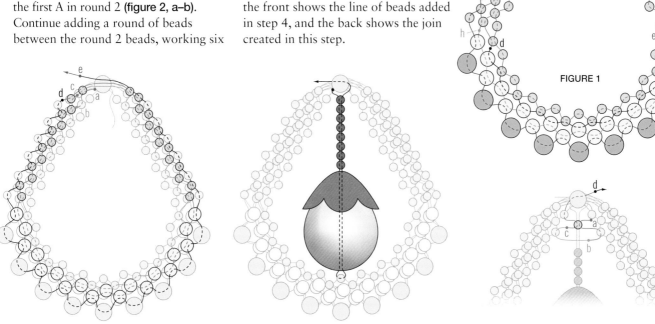

FIGURE 1

FIGURE 2

FIGURE 3

FIGURE 4

151

[6] Add a new 1½-yd. (1.4 m) thread (Basics) to the first component, exiting the bottom middle C. Work as in steps 1–5 to create another component, with the following changes:
• Treat the C your thread is exiting as if it were the first C in step 1.
• Begin with only 41 As, and adjust the number of As stitched in rounds 3–7 accordingly **(figure 5)**.

[7] To begin the vine embellishment, use the tail of the first component to pick up four Es, a color D 8º seed bead, an E, four Cs, and a D. Sew back through the first C picked up in this step **(figure 6, a–b)**. Pick up three Cs, and sew through the fourth C added in the previous stitch **(b–c)**. This completes the first daisy.

[8] Pick up 15 Es and three color I 2 mm glass pearls. Skip the pearls, and sew back through the last three Es picked up **(c–d)**. Sew through the beadwork as shown, and pick up two Es, a 3 mm bugle bead, a color F 11º seed bead, a C, and an F, and sew back through the bugle and two Es **(d–e)**. Pick up three Es, skip the next E in the vine, and sew through the next two Es **(e–f)**.

[9] Refer to **figure 7** to add more embellishment using color F, G, and H 11º seed beads; color I and J 2 mm glass pearls; bugles; and D 8ºs. End the thread.

[10] Using the tail from the second component, repeat steps 7–9, but work around the component in the opposite direction from the first so the embellishment appears to continue from the first component to the next. Vary the embellishment colors as desired, and tack it to the teardrop component as needed.

[11] Repeat steps 1–10 to create two more double-teardrop components.

Assembly

[1] Add a new 12-in. (30 cm) thread to a double-teardrop component, and exit the top C. Sew through the top C of each of the other two double-teardrop components, sew through all three again to form them into a ring, and tie a square knot **(figure 8)**.

[2] Pick up the 15 mm flower stamping, the 10 mm flower component, and an 11º. Sew back through the flower component and stamping and the next two Cs in the ring **(figure 9, a–b)**. Retrace the thread path through the components

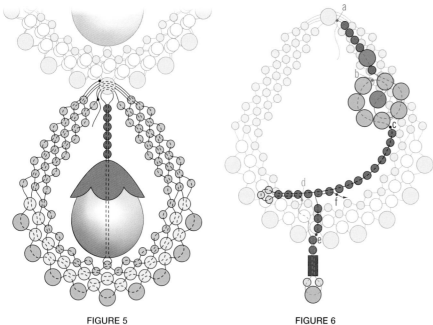

FIGURE 5

FIGURE 6

FIGURE 7

FIGURE 8

FIGURE 9

and the 11º, exiting the 8º your thread just exited **(b–c)**. End the thread.

[3] Attach a Bead Stopper to the center of 2 yd. (1.8 m) of thread. With one end of the thread, sew through the fourth C from the outer edge of a component.

[4] Pick up 20 As, a 6 mm glass pearl, five As, a C, 20 As, a 6 mm, and five As, and sew through the C your thread exited at the start of this step. Continue through the beads to exit the next C **(figure 10, a–b)**.

[5] Work as in step 4 three times, alternating bead counts as shown **(b–c)**.

[6] Pick up two As, a 10 mm, and an A. Sew back through the 10 mm. Pick up two As, and sew through the end C again **(figure 11)**. Retrace the thread path, and end the thread.

[7] Remove the Bead Stopper from the tail, and use **figure 12** as a guide to stitch a daisy chain vine that is about the same length as the beadwork stitched in steps 4 and 5. Weave the vine through the openings between the strands, and sew through the last C. Sew back into the vine, and end the thread.

[8] Repeat steps 3–5 to stitch the other neck strap. Pick up enough As (about 23) to make a loop around the 10 mm, and sew through the end C again **(figure 13)**. Retrace the thread path through the loop, and end the thread. Repeat step 7 to complete the second neck strap. **○**

Sunny yellow accented with fuchsia, orange, and green is a cheerful color alternative.

FIGURE 10 FIGURE 11 FIGURE 12 FIGURE 13

Kaleidoscope connection

designed by **Julie Olah**

Revisit a childhood favorite with bright colors and patterns

Connect a collection of kaleidoscopic components for a brick stitch bracelet that works up quickly.

materials

bracelet 7 in. (18 cm)
- 8 6º seed beads
- 4–6 g 11º seed beads in each of **4–6** colors: A, B, C, D, E, F
- clasp
- 3 9 mm split rings or soldered jump rings
- Fireline 6 lb. test, or nylon beading thread, size D
- beading needles, #10 or #12

step by step

Open circle

[1] Tie 1 yd. (.9 m) of Fireline or thread to a 9 mm split ring or soldered jump ring, leaving a 6-in. (15 cm) tail. Pick up two color A 11º seed beads. Position the As side by side around the outside of the ring, sew through the ring, and sew back through the second A **(figure 1, a–b)**.
[2] Working in brick stitch (Basics, p. 13), pick up an A, sew through the split ring or soldered jump ring as if it is a thread bridge, and sew back through the A just added **(b–c)**.
[3] Repeat step 2 around the split ring or soldered jump ring to add about 14 As.
[4] When you reach the first A added, sew down through it, through the split ring or soldered jump ring, and back through the A **(figure 2)**.
[5] Pick up two color B 11º seed beads, sew under the thread bridge connecting the first two As in the previous round, and sew back through the second B **(figure 3, a–b)**.
[6] Pick up a B, and sew under the next thread bridge and back through the B **(b–c)**.
[7] Continue working in brick stitch, adding one or two Bs per thread bridge to make the second round of Bs fit snugly around the first round of As. Tie a few half-hitch knots (Basics), but do not trim the working thread. End the tail (Basics).
[8] Make a total of three open circles, using colors A–C or A–F as desired.

FIGURE 1

FIGURE 2

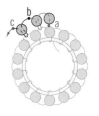

FIGURE 3

FIGURE 4

FIGURE 5

Patterned circles

[1] On 1 yd. (.9 m) of Fireline or thread, pick up five As, and tie them into a ring with a square knot (Basics), leaving a 6-in. (15 cm) tail. Sew through the first A again **(figure 4, a–b)**.

[2] Pick up a B, and sew through the next A in the ring **(b–c)**. Repeat around, and step up through the first B added **(c–d)**.

[3] Working in circular peyote stitch (Basics), pick up two color C 11º seed beads, and sew through the next B **(figure 5, a–b)**. Repeat around, and step up through the first C added **(b–c)**.

[4] Pick up a color D 11º seed bead, and sew through the next C **(figure 6, a–b)**. Pick up a B, and sew through the next C **(b–c)**. Repeat around, alternating Ds and Bs, and step up through the first D added **(c–d)**.

[5] Work a round of circular peyote stitch, adding a C for each stitch, and step up through the first C added **(figure 7)**.

[6] Pick up two Bs, and sew through the next C **(figure 8, a–b)**. Pick up two Cs, and sew through the next C **(b–c)**. Repeat around, alternating between two Bs and two Cs, and step up through the first pair of Bs added **(c–d)**. Tie a few half-hitch knots, but do not trim the working thread. End the tail.

[7] Make a total of four patterned circles, using colors A–D or A–F as desired.

Assembly

Connecting the circles

[1] With your working thread exiting a pair of 11ºs in a patterned circle, pick up an 11º in the color of your choice, a 6º seed bead, and an 11º in the color of your choice. Sew through two 11º in round 2 of an open circle **(figure 9, a–b)**. Pick up an 11ºs in the color of your choice, and sew back through the 6º. Pick up an 11º in the color of your choice, and sew through the pair of 11ºs your thread exited at the start of this step **(b–c)**. Retrace the thread path to reinforce the connection, and end the thread.

[2] Using the working thread from the open circle, sew through the beadwork to exit an 11º opposite the pair of 11ºs in the connection made in the previous step. Pick up an 11º, a 6º, and an 11º, and sew through a pair of 11ºs in a patterned circle. Pick up an 11º, sew back through the 6º, pick up an 11º, and sew through the 11º adjacent to the one your thread exited at the start of this step. Retrace the thread path to reinforce the connection, and end the thread.

[3] Connect the remaining circles as in steps 1 and 2, alternating between a patterned circle and an open circle. Do not end the thread on the last patterned circle.

Clasp

[1] Using the working thread from the end patterned circle,

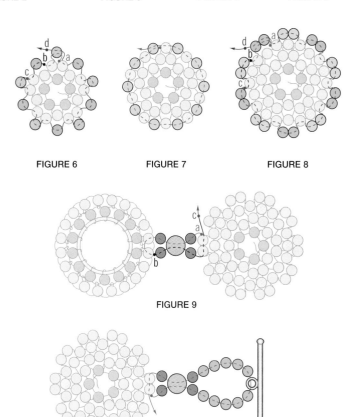

FIGURE 6

FIGURE 7

FIGURE 8

FIGURE 9

FIGURE 10

exit a pair of 11ºs opposite the last connection. Pick up an A, a 6º, an A, five Bs, half of a clasp, five Bs, and an A. Sew back through the 6º, pick up an A, and sew through the pair of 11ºs your thread exited at the start of this step **(figure 10)**. Retrace the thread path to reinforce the connection, and end the thread.

[2] Add thread (Basics) to the patterned circle at the remaining end of the bracelet, and repeat step 1 to add the second half of the clasp. ●

DESIGNER'S NOTE:

For earrings, make an open circle and a patterned circle, and connect them as in "Assembly." Attach an earring finding as in "Clasp," but use just four 11ºs.

Nebula

Concentric rings of crystals and seed beads orbit a pearl center

designed by **Grace Nehls**

materials

bracelet 7½ in. (19.1 cm)

- round crystal pearls
  8 mm
  6 6 mm
  2 4 mm
  16 3 mm
- **126** 3 mm bicone crystals
- **102** 2 mm round crystals
- 11º seed beads
  5 g color A
  3 g color B
- 5 g 15º seed beads
- Fireline 6 and 8 lb. test
- beading needles, #12

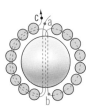

FIGURE 1

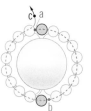

FIGURE 2

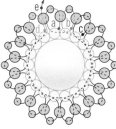

FIGURE 3

The elegant rings in this showstopping bracelet can dress up a casual look or accent an elegant outfit.

stepbystep

Band

Center component

[1] On 1½ yd. (1.4 m) of 8 lb. Fireline, pick up an 8 mm pearl, leaving a 6-in. (15 cm) tail.

[2] Pick up eight color A 11º seed beads, and sew through the pearl again (figure 1, a–b). Repeat, and sew through the first eight A 11ºs (b–c).

[3] Pick up an A 11º, and sew through the next eight A 11ºs (figure 2, a–b). Repeat (b–c).

[4] Pick up an A 11º, a 15º seed bead, and an A 11º. Sew through the A 11º your thread exited at the start of this step and the next A 11º in the ring (figure 3, a–b).

[5] Pick up an A 11º and a 15º, and sew through the adjacent 11º from the

FIGURE 4

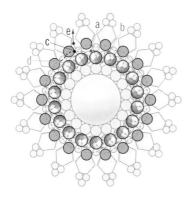

FIGURE 5

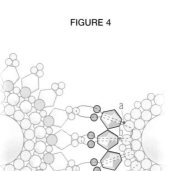

FIGURE 6

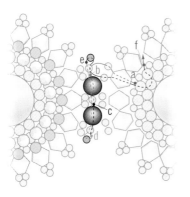

FIGURE 7

previous stitch, the A 11º your thread exited at the start of this step, and the next A 11º in the ring (b–c). Repeat around the ring until you sew through the last unembellished 11º in the ring (c–d). Sew through the next A 11º in the first stitch, pick up a 15º, and sew through the adjacent A 11º in the last stitch, the A 11º in the ring, and the next A 11º in the first stitch again (d–e).
[6] Pick up a 3 mm bicone crystal and three 15ºs. Skip the last three 15ºs, and sew back through the 3 mm bicone, the A 11º your thread exited at the start of this step, the next A 11º in the ring, and the adjacent A 11º in the next stitch (figure 4, a–b). Repeat around the ring (b–c).
[7] Pick up a 2 mm round crystal, and sew through the next A 11º in the second

round (figure 5, a–b). Repeat around the ring, and exit a 15º in the second round (b–c).
[8] Pick up a color B 11º seed bead, and sew through the next 15º in the round (c–d). Repeat around the ring (d–e). Retrace the thread path through the 15ºs and Bs, and end the thread (Basics, p. 13).

Side components
[1] To create the side components, repeat steps 1–5 of "Center component" with the following changes:
• In step 1, pick up a 6 mm pearl instead of an 8 mm pearl.
• In step 2, pick up six A 11ºs instead of eight.
[2] Work as in step 6, but adjust the first three fringes as follows: Pick up a 3 mm bicone and a 15º. Sew through the center 15º from a fringe on the center

component, pick up a 15º, and sew back through the 3 mm, the A 11º your thread exited at the start of this step, the next A 11º in the ring, and the adjacent A 11º in the next stitch (figure 6, a–b). Repeat twice (b–c), then continue the round of fringe as in step 6.
To add 3 mm pearl embellishments to the connection, sew through the first 3 mm bicone and two 15ºs connecting the side component to the center component (figure 7, a–b). Pick up a 3 mm pearl, and sew through the next center 15º (b–c). Repeat (c–d). Pick up a 15º, and sew back through the last 15º, 3 mm pearl, 15º, 3 mm pearl, and 15º (d–e). Pick up a 15º, and sew through the beadwork to exit an A 11º in the second round (e–f).

MORE PROJECT IDEAS:
Let the versatile components inspire additional projects:
• Make one center and two side components to use as a necklace focal piece, then use beading wire to string the neck chain.
• Connect one or more components for a pair of earrings.
• Skip step 6 to omit the 3 mm crystal fringe, making a more casual component.

Adding fringe to
the clasp loop
completes
the design.

FIGURE 8

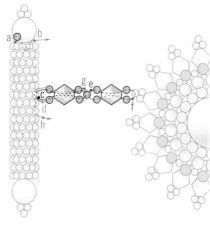

FIGURE 9

[3] Repeat steps 7 and 8 of "Center component."

[4] Repeat steps 1–3 for a total of six side components. Connect three on each side of the center component. Make sure to connect the three corresponding fringes on each component.

Clasp

Toggle bar

[1] On 1 yd. (.9 m) of 6 lb. Fireline, attach a stop bead (Basics), leaving an 8-in. (20 cm) tail. Pick up 17 15°s. Working in flat odd-count peyote stitch (Basics), work a total of 10 rows **(figure 8)**. Roll the strip into a tube, and zip up (Basics) the ends.

[2] Sew through the center of the tube, and pick up a 4 mm pearl and three 15°s. Skip the three 15°s, and sew

back through the 4 mm pearl. Repeat on the other end of the tube. Sew through the beadwork to exit an edge 15° at one end of the tube.

[3] Pick up a 15°, and sew through the next two 15°s on the end **(figure 9, a–b)**. Repeat, adding a 15° between all the 15°s on the end of the tube. Step up through a 15° in the new round, pick up a 15°, and sew through the next 15° in the round. Repeat around the end. Sew through the tube, and repeat on the other end. Sew through the tube, and exit a 15° in the seventh round of the tube at **point c**.

[4] Pick up a 15°, a 3 mm bicone, and three 15°s. Sew back through the 3 mm bicone, pick up a 15°, and sew through the 15° your

thread exited at the start of this step **(c–d)**. Sew through the 15°, 3 mm bicone, and two 15°s just added **(d–e)**. Pick up a 15°, a 3 mm bicone, and a 15°, and sew through the center 15° on the corresponding fringe of an end side component **(e–f)**. Pick up a 15°, and sew back through the last 3 mm bicone added. Pick up a 15°, and sew through the center 15° **(f–g)**. Sew through the beadwork to exit the next 15° in the same row on the tube **(g–h)**. Repeat this step twice to add a total of three connectors between the toggle bar and the side component.

[5] Add 3 mm pearl embellishments to the connection as in step 2 of "Side components."

Toggle ring

[1] On 1 yd. (.9 m) of 8 lb. Fireline, pick up a repeating pattern of a 15° and an A 11° 18 times. Sew through the first 15° again to form a ring, leaving a 6-in. (15 cm) tail.

[2] Pick up a 3 mm bicone and three 15°s. Skip the three 15°s, and sew back through the 3 mm bicone and the next 15° and 11° in the ring. Repeat around the ring, but attach three of the fringes from the remaining end side component to attach the loop. Add the 3 mm pearl embellishment as in step 2 of "Side components." End the working thread and tail. ●

The back of this bracelet is just as lovely as the front, doubling your design options.

NETTING / RIGHT-ANGLE WEAVE

Star power

Use this charming star component four different ways to create eye-catching accessories

designed by **Glorianne Ljubich**

materials

all projects
- Fireline 6 lb. test
- beading needles, #12

pair of earrings
- **36** 4 mm fire-polished beads
- 2 g 2 x 4 mm peanut beads
- 2 g 11º seed beads
- 2 g 15º seed beads
- pair of earring findings

bracelet 7 in. (18 cm)
- **24** 4 mm bicone crystals
- 2 g 2 x 4 mm peanut beads
- 2 g 11º seed beads
- 3 g 15º seed beads
- clasp
- **2** 4 mm jump rings
- **2** pairs of pliers

pendant 1½ in. (3.8 cm)
- **6** 6 mm gemstone beads
- **6** 6º seed beads
- 1 g 2 x 4 mm peanut beads
- 1 g 11º seed beads
- 6 mm brass bead cage

ring
- **6** 4 mm pearls
- 1 g 2 x 4 mm peanut beads
- 1 g 11º seed beads
- 1 g 15º seed beads

EDITOR'S NOTES:
- Peanut beads may also be called butterfly beads dogbones, berry beads, farfalle, or barbells.
- Use a contrasting color for the center ring of beads to emphasize the floral look of the component.
- Substitute 4 mm pearls, bicone crystals, or gemstone beads for the fire-polished beads.

stepbystep

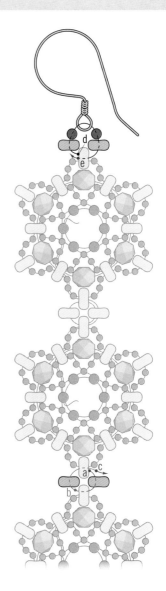

Small star component

[1] On 18 in. (46 cm) of Fireline, pick up six 11º seed beads, and tie them into a ring with a square knot (Basics, p. 13), leaving a 6-in. (15 cm) tail. Sew through the first 11º.

[2] Pick up a 15º seed bead, and sew through the next 11º in the ring **(figure 1, a–b)**. Repeat around the ring, and step up through the first 15º added in this round **(b–c)**.

[3] Pick up two 15ºs, a 2 x 4 mm peanut bead, and two 15ºs, and sew through the next 15º in the previous round **(c–d)**. Repeat to complete the round, and step up through the first two 15ºs and peanut bead added in this round **(d–e)**.

[4] Retrace the thread path, and tie a couple of half-hitch knots (Basics), but do not trim the working thread or tail.

Large star component

[1] On 30 in. (76 cm) of Fireline, follow steps 1–3 of "Small star component."

[2] Pick up a 4 mm fire-polished bead, and sew through the next peanut bead in the previous round **(figure 2, a–b)**. Repeat to complete the round, exiting the peanut bead your thread exited at the start of this step **(b–c)**.

[3] Pick up three 15ºs, a peanut bead, and three 15ºs, and sew through the next peanut bead in the previous round **(c–d)**. Repeat to complete the round, and step up through the first three 15ºs and peanut bead added in this round **(d–e)**.

[4] Retrace the thread path, and tie a couple of half-hitch knots, but do not trim the working thread or tail.

Earrings

[1] Make a total of six large star components.

[2] With the working thread exiting a peanut bead in the outer round of one component, pick up a peanut bead, sew through the corresponding peanut bead on another component **(figure 3, a–b)**, pick up a peanut bead, and sew through the peanut bead your thread exited at the start of this step **(b–c)**. Retrace the thread path several times, and end the working thread and tail (Basics).

[3] Repeat step 2 to join the second component to a third component, being sure to make this connection opposite the first one.

[4] Using the working thread of the third component, sew through the beadwork to exit a peanut bead opposite the joining peanut beads **(point d)**. Pick up a peanut bead, an 11º, the loop of an earring finding, an 11º, and a peanut bead, and sew through the peanut bead your thread exited at the start of this step **(d–e)**. Retrace the thread path, and end the working thread and tail.

[5] Make a second earring.

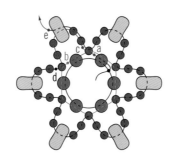

FIGURE 1

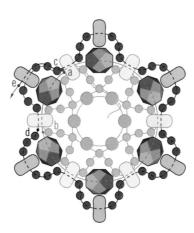

FIGURE 2

FIGURE 3

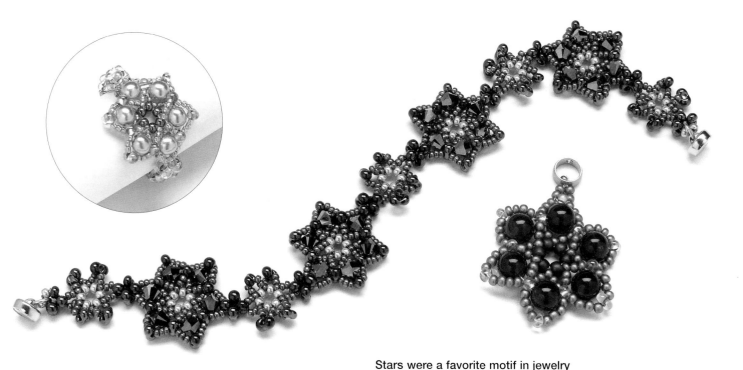

Stars were a favorite motif in jewelry designs during the Victorian era.

Bracelet

[1] Make a total of four large star components using 4 mm bicone crystals instead of 4 mm fire-polished beads.

[2] Make a total of five small star components.

[3] Arrange the star components on your work surface, alternating between a large star and a small star, with a small star on each end. With the working thread exiting a peanut bead in the outer round of an end component, pick up a peanut bead, sew through the corresponding peanut bead on another component, pick up a peanut bead, and sew through the peanut bead your thread exited at the start of this step. Retrace the thread path. Repeat to join the remaining components. End all threads except the tail on each end component.

[4] Open a 4 mm jump ring (Basics), and attach half of the clasp. Repeat with another 4 mm jump ring and the other half of the clasp.

[5] With the tail of an end component, sew through the beadwork to exit a peanut bead opposite the joining peanut beads. Pick up a peanut bead, an 11º, a 4 mm jump ring, an 11º, and a peanut bead, and sew through the peanut bead your thread exited at the start of this step. Retrace the thread path, and end the thread.

[6] Repeat step 5 at the other end of the bracelet.

Pendant

[1] Make a large star component using 6º seed beads in place of the 11ºs, 6 mm gemstone beads instead of the 4 mm fire-polished beads, and 11º seed beads in place of the 15ºs. The peanut beads remain the same. In step 3, increase to four 11ºs between the peanut beads.

[2] With the thread exiting a peanut bead, pick up two 11ºs, and sew through one hole in the bead cage. Pick up an 11º, and sew back through the bead cage. Pick up two 11ºs, and sew through the peanut bead your thread exited at the start of this step. Retrace the thread path, and end the working thread and tail.

Ring

[1] Make a large star component substituting 4 mm pearls for the 4 mm fire-polished beads in step 2.

[2] With the working thread exiting a peanut bead in the outer round of the component, pick up three peanut beads, and sew through the peanut bead your thread exited at the start of this step. Continue working in right-angle weave (Basics) by adding three peanut beads for each stitch until you have a strip of right-angle weave long enough to fit around your finger.

[3] To join the strip to the other side of the component, pick up a peanut bead, and sew through the corresponding peanut bead on the opposite side of the component. Pick up a peanut bead, and sew through the peanut bead your thread exited at the start of this step. Retrace the thread path, and end the working thread and tail. ○

Crystal compass

Crystals take a vintage finding in a new direction

designed by **Marcia DeCoster**

These vintage mesh bangle findings will vary slightly in size and color.

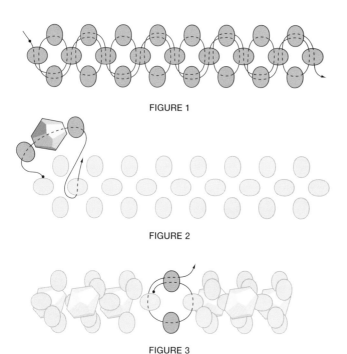

FIGURE 1

FIGURE 2

FIGURE 3

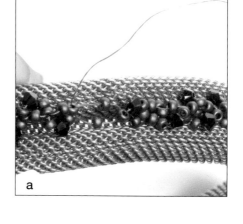

a

Marcia tries to recycle or reuse pieces from the past when designing jewelry. In this quick and clever project, she infused a slinky brass finding with just the right glint of crystals, creating a fun fashion accessory.

stepby**step**

Embellished strip

[1] On 3 yd. (2.7 m) of Fireline, pick up four color A 11º seed beads, leaving a 6-in. (15 cm) tail. Working in right-angle weave (Basics, p. 13, and **figure 1**), make a strip 65 stitches long using As.

[2] Wrap the strip around the bangle finding to check the fit, and add or remove stitches as needed. Make sure to end with an odd number of stitches, and exit an end A in the strip.

[3] Pick up an A, a 3 mm bicone crystal, and an A, and sew through the opposite A in the stitch (**figure 2**). Flip over the strip and repeat, adding an A, a 3 mm crystal, and an A, to the back of the next stitch. Repeat along the strip until you've added an A, a 3 mm crystal, and an A to the front and back of every other stitch.

[4] Wrap the strip around the bangle finding, join the strip into a ring (**photo a** and **figure 3**), and add a crystal embellishment to the join. End the working thread and tail (Basics).

materials
bangle 2½ in. (6.4 cm) inner diameter
- approximately **70** 3 mm bicone crystals
- **12** 3 mm pearls
- 11º seed beads
  4 g color A
  1 g color B
- 1 g 15º seed beads
- brass bangle finding (beadsofcolour.com)
- Fireline 6 lb. test
- beading needles, #12

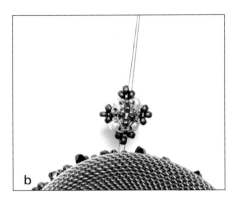

b

c

EDITOR'S NOTE:
Use a medallion to add a splash of
color to this mesh necklace.

Medallions

[1] On 1 yd. (.9 m) of Fireline, pick up a repeating pattern of three As and a 3 mm pearl four times, leaving a 12-in. (30 cm) tail. Sew through the first three As and 3 mm pearl again to form a ring (figure 4, a–b).

[2] Pick up an A, and sew through the next 3 mm pearl. Repeat three times, and step up through the first A in the new round (b–c).

[3] Pick up three 15º seed beads, and sew through the next A in the previous round. Repeat three times, and step up through the center 15º in the first stitch of the new round (c–d).

[4] Pick up a color B 11º seed bead, and sew through the center 15º in the next stitch. Repeat three times (d–e), then sew through the beadwork to exit a center A in the first round, opposite the tail.

[5] Stitch the medallion to the bangle finding: Center it over the embellished strip, sew through the bangle finding, and sew back through the center A (photo b). Retrace the thread path, and sew through the beadwork to exit the next center A in the first round.

[6] Stitch the center A of the medallion to an A in the strip (photo c), retrace the thread path, and end the thread.

[7] Repeat steps 5 and 6 with the remaining two center As using the tail.

[8] Repeat steps 1–7 three times, stitching the medallions at equal distances around the bangle finding. ●

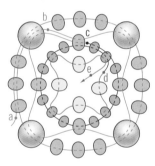

FIGURE 4

Pearl parlay

A series of repeating motifs woven together results in an elegant pathway of pearls

designed by
Juanita "Jaycee" Carlos

Try experimenting with contrasting colors of 3 mm bicone crystals to emphasize the center embellishment.

materials
bracelet 7 in. (18 cm)
- **111** 4 mm glass pearls
- 3 mm bicone crystals
  36 color A
  36 color B
  21 color C
- 4 g 11º seed beads
- 3-strand clasp
- Fireline 6 lb. test
- beading needles, #12

Start with a triangle of pearls, add a border of seed beads, and embellish with crystals. Before you know it, this beautiful bracelet will emerge.

stepbystep

Pearl motif

[1] On a comfortable length of Fireline, pick up an alternating pattern of an 11º seed bead and a 4 mm pearl three times, and sew through the first three beads again to form a ring (**figure 1, a–b**).

[2] Pick up five 11ºs, and sew through the next 11º in the ring (**b–c**). Repeat twice to complete the triangle unit. Sew through the next seven 11ºs (**c–d**), and snug up the beads so the pearls sit up slightly in the triangle.

[3] Pick up a color A 3 mm bicone crystal, three 11ºs, and a color B 3 mm bicone crystal, and sew through the last three 11ºs your thread exited in the previous step (**figure 2, a–b**). Sew through the A and the next two 11ºs (**b–c**). Pick up a 4 mm, an 11º, a 4 mm, an 11º, and a 4 mm. Sew through the 11º your thread is exiting and the next 11º (**c–d**).

[4] Pick up four 11ºs, skip the 4 mm, and sew through the next 11º (**d–e**). Pick up five 11ºs, skip the 4 mm, and sew through the next 11º (**e–f**). Pick up four 11ºs, and sew through the next eight 11ºs, the next 4 mm, and the following two 11ºs (**f–g**).

[5] Repeat steps 3 and 4 four times to make and connect a total of six triangle units.

[6] To connect the first and last triangle units, pick up an A, and sew through the corresponding 11º and the next two 11ºs in the first triangle (**figure 3, a–b**). Pick up a B, and sew through the corresponding 11º in the previous triangle (**b–c**). Sew through the next two 11ºs, and retrace the thread path. Sew through the beadwork to the center of the ring of triangles, exiting the center 11º in a five-bead stitch added in step 2 (**c–d**).

EDITOR'S NOTES:
- Be sure to keep a fairly firm tension so the pearls "pop" up above the other beads.
- Retracing the thread paths gives the bracelet stability.

Center embellishment

[1] Pick up two 11ºs, a 4 mm, and two 11ºs, skip the next triangle in the ring, and sew through the center 11º of the following triangle (**d–e**). Repeat twice, and exit the first two beads added in this round (**e–f**).

[2] Pick up two 11ºs, and sew through the center 11º in the adjacent triangle (**figure 4, a–b**). Pick up two 11ºs, and sew through the 11º after the 4 mm in the new ring (**b–c**). Pick up a color C 3 mm bicone crystal, and sew through the 11º before the next 4 mm in the new ring (**c–d**). Repeat this step twice to embellish the center of the ring of triangles (**d–e**).

[3] Sew through the beadwork to exit at **point f**.

Assembly

[1] Repeat steps 3 and 4 of "Pearl motif" four times, then connect the last triangle unit to the adjacent triangle in the previous ring of triangles as in step 6.

[2] Sew through the beadwork to exit the center 11º of the second-to-last triangle unit just made (**figure 5**), and repeat steps 1–3 of "Center embellishment."

[3] Make a total of seven linked pearl motifs, alternating the placement of the As and Bs. For the center embellishment of the fourth and sixth motifs, sew through the beadwork to exit the center 11º in the last triangle unit made (**figure 3, point d**). For the third, fifth, and seventh motifs, sew through the

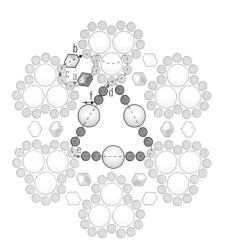

FIGURE 1

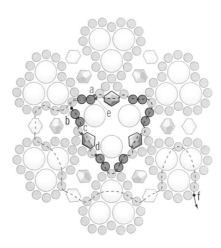

FIGURE 2

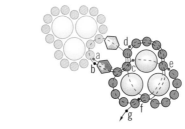

FIGURE 3

FIGURE 4

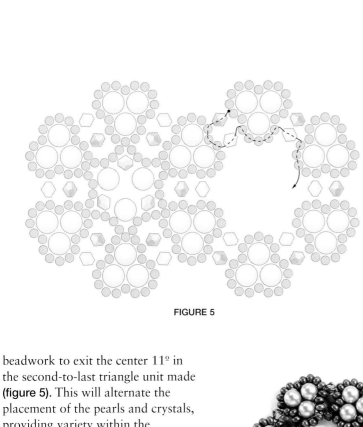

FIGURE 5

beadwork to exit the center 11º in the second-to-last triangle unit made **(figure 5)**. This will alternate the placement of the pearls and crystals, providing variety within the components.

Clasp

[1] Sew through the beadwork to exit an end 11º on one end of the bracelet **(figure 6, point a)**. Pick up an 11º, and sew through the first loop of half of the clasp, the 11º just added, and the next two 11ºs in the bracelet **(a–b)**.

[2] Pick up two 11ºs, and sew through the second loop of the clasp, the two 11ºs just added, the next four 11ºs, the next 3 mm, and the following four 11ºs **(b–c)**.

[3] Pick up two 11ºs, and sew through the second loop of the clasp again, the two 11ºs just added, and the next two 11ºs **(c–d)**.

[4] Pick up an 11º, and sew through the remaining loop of the clasp, the 11º just added, the next seven 11ºs, and the next 4 mm **(d–e)**. Retrace the thread path, and end the thread (Basics, p. 13).

[5] Repeat steps 1–4 on the other end of the bracelet. ●

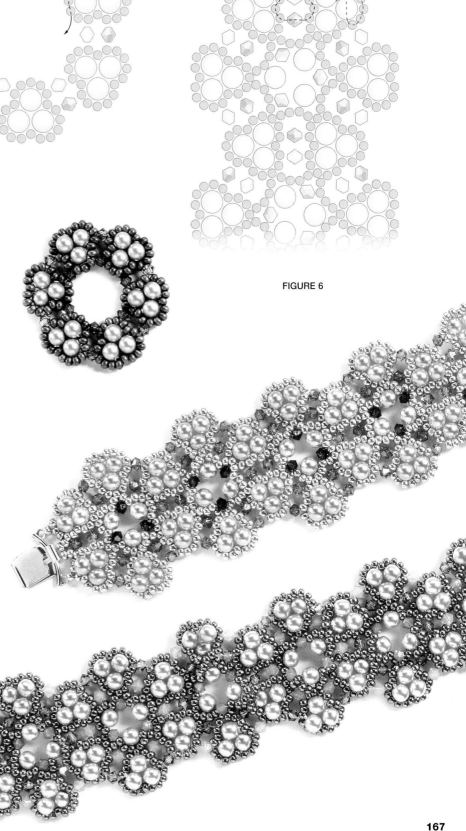

FIGURE 6

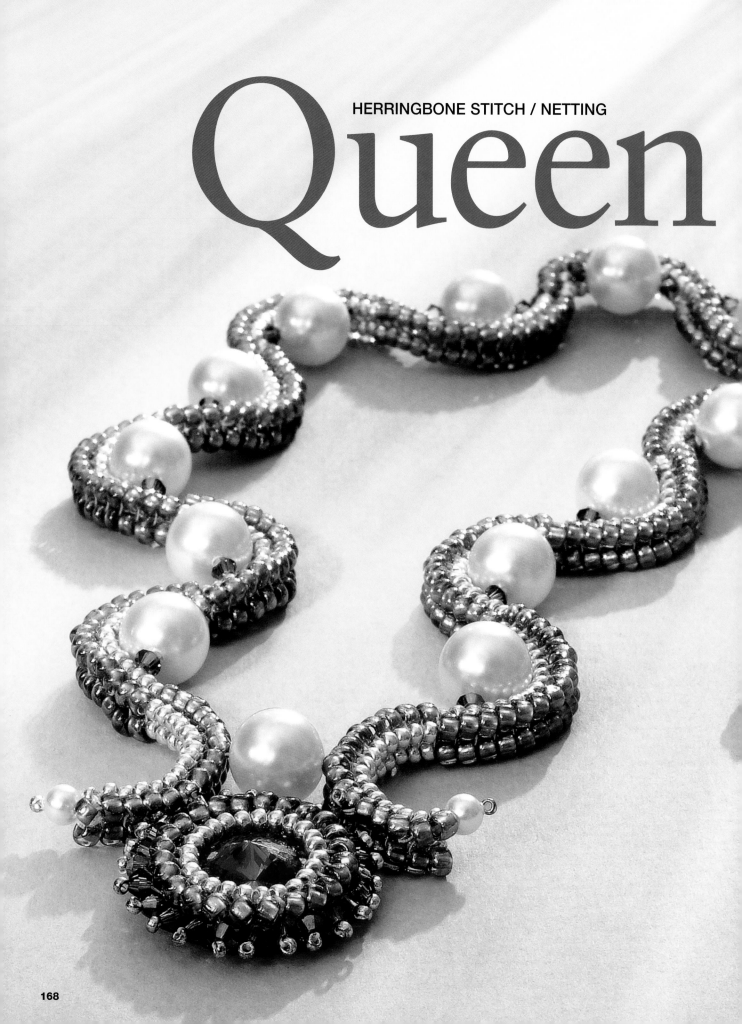

Queen

of the sea

Nestle pearls in an undulating wave of herringbone rope

designed by **Jenny Van**

Turn the centerpiece into a sparkly stand-alone pendant by adding a soldered jump ring to one of the fringes in step 5 of "Centerpiece."

Simple modifications of stitches can produce the most stunning results. Placing smaller beads opposite larger ones in tubular herringbone produces a gentle curve, and switching the beads sends the curve in the other direction, creating the perfect places to tuck in crystals and pearls.

step by step

Centerpiece
[1] On 2 yd. (1.8 m) of Fireline, pick up an 11º seed bead and an 8º seed bead, leaving a 12-in. (30 cm) tail. Working in ladder stitch (Basics, p. 13), make a four-bead ladder with the following bead sequence: 11º, 8º, 8º, 11º. Form the ladder into a ring (Basics), making sure your working thread is exiting an 11º.
[2] Working in tubular herringbone stitch (Basics), pick up an 11º and an 8º for the first stitch, and an 8º and an 11º for the second. Step up after each round. Repeat for a total of 24 rounds.

materials

necklace 16 in. (41 cm)

- 12 mm rivoli
- **18** 10 mm pearls
- **3** 4 mm pearls
- **57** 3 mm bicone crystals
- **15 g** 8º seed beads
- **5 g** 11º seed beads
- **1 g** 15º seed beads
- Fireline 6 lb. test
- beading needles, #12

a

b

c

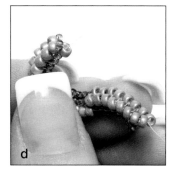

d

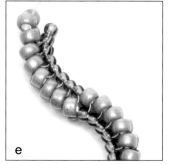

e

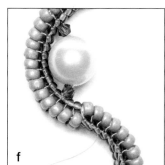

f

[3] Insert the rivoli into the center of the beadwork (**photo a**), and work a tubular herringbone thread path through the beads in the first and last rounds to form a ring (**photo b**). Retrace the thread path of the join.

[4] Sew through the beadwork to exit an 11º on the back of the centerpiece. Pick up three 15º seed beads, skip two 11ºs, and sew through the next 11º in the round (**figure, a–b**). Repeat around, and step up through the first two 15ºs in the first

stitch (**b–c**). Pick up two 15ºs, and sew through the center 15º of the next stitch in the previous round (**c–d**). Repeat around, and step up through the first two 15ºs in the first stitch (**d–e**). Retrace the thread path of the inner ring, then sew through the beadwork to exit an 8º in the outer ring.

[5] Sew under the thread bridge between the next two 8ºs, and pick up a 3 mm bicone crystal and a 15º. Skip the 15º, and sew back through the 3 mm and under the next thread bridge (**photo c**). Repeat around, adding a fringe between all the thread bridges. End the tail (Basics) but not the working thread.

Herringbone rope

[1] On a comfortable length of Fireline, work steps 1 and 2 of "Centerpiece" until you have 16 rounds.

[2] Continue in tubular herringbone, but substitute 8ºs for 11ºs and 11ºs for 8ºs (**photo d**). As you work, your beadwork will begin to curve in the opposite direction (**photo e**). Work a total of

16 rows. Continue in this manner until you have nine curved 16-row sections, ending and adding thread (Basics) as needed. Repeat to make a second rope.

[3] At the end of one rope, work 16 rounds as in step 2, substituting 15ºs for 11ºs and 11ºs for 8ºs. Exiting an 11º, pick up a 4 mm pearl, a 3 mm, a 10 mm pearl, and a 15º. Skip the 15º, and sew back through the remaining beads just picked up and into the adjacent 11º. Sew through the adjacent 15º in the end round, and retrace the thread path of the beads just added. Sew through the remaining 11º and 15º in the end round. Retrace the thread path, and sew through the beadwork to exit the first three 11ºs in the previous curve.

[4] Pick up a 3 mm crystal, a 10 mm pearl, and a 3 mm. Skip 10 11ºs, and sew through the next six 11ºs (**photo f**). Repeat to add crystals and pearls to each curve except the last. End the thread.

[5] Using the tail at the other end of the rope, exit an 8º.

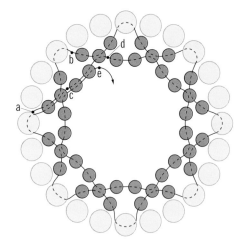

FIGURE

g

h

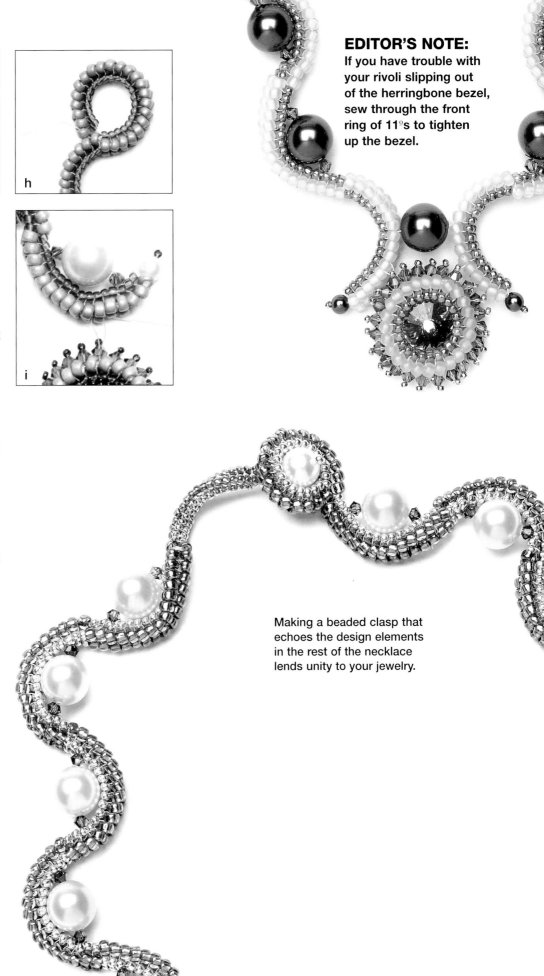

i

Pick up a 4 mm pearl and a 15º, skip the 15º, and sew back through the pearl and the 8º (photo g). End the tail.
[6] On the other rope, work 22 rounds as in step 2, then join to the end round of the previous curve, creating a ring (photo h). Make sure it accommodates the 10 mm pearl at the end of the other rope, adding or removing rounds as needed, and don't end the thread. Sew through the beadwork to exit between the third and fourth pairs of 11ºs below the loop.
[7] Repeat steps 4 and 5 to complete the second rope.

Assembly
[1] Using the working thread from the centerpiece, exit a 15º at the end of a fringe. Sew through the sixth 8º in the last curve of one rope (photo i). Retrace the thread path, then sew through the beadwork to exit the fifth fringe. Connect the centerpiece to the other rope in the same manner.
[2] Sew through the next three 8ºs on the rope, pick up a 10 mm pearl, and sew through the corresponding 8º on the other rope. Retrace the join, and end the thread. ●

EDITOR'S NOTE:
If you have trouble with your rivoli slipping out of the herringbone bezel, sew through the front ring of 11ºs to tighten up the bezel.

Making a beaded clasp that echoes the design elements in the rest of the necklace lends unity to your jewelry.

Daisy

Mix and match components for an endless variety of jewelry

designed by **Cathy Lampole**

materials

necklace 32 in. (81 cm)

- **66** 4 mm fire-polished beads (**15** for each beaded bead, and **6** for assembly)
- **80** 4 mm bicone crystals
- 11º seed beads
  15 g color A
  4 g in each of **3** colors: B, C, D
- 3 g 15º seed beads
- lobster claw clasp
- 20 in. (51 cm) large-link chain
- 6 mm jump ring
- Fireline 6 lb. test
- beading needles, #12
- **2** pairs of pliers
- wire cutters

Modify tubular netting by using two sizes of seed beads, and incorporate clever, colorful rings of beads in the stitches to create a delicate spiral of flowers. Crystal beaded beads add just the right amount of sparkle.

spiral

Use contrasting colors to make the flower motif pop! Cathy's necklace alternates between three flower colors, but you could easily include every color in your stash.

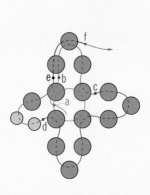

FIGURE 1

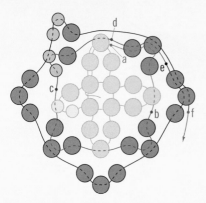

FIGURE 2

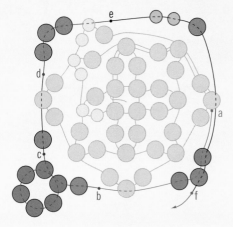

FIGURE 3

stepbystep

Netted tube

[1] On a comfortable length of Fireline, pick up four color A 11º seed beads, and tie them into a ring with a square knot (Basics, p. 13), leaving a 12-in. (30 cm) tail. Sew through the first A in the ring again **(figure 1, a–b)**.

[2] Pick up three As, and sew through the next A in the ring **(b–c)**. Repeat twice **(c–d)**. Pick up two 15º seed beads and an A, and sew through the next A in the ring **(d–e)**. Step up by sewing through the first two As in the first stitch added in this round **(e–f)**.

[3] Pick up three As, and sew through the center A in the next stitch of the previous round **(figure 2, a–b)**. Repeat. Pick up three As, and sew through the center 15º in the next stitch of the previous round **(b–c)**. Pick up two 15ºs and an A, and sew through the center A in the next stitch of the previous round **(c–d)**. Step up by sewing through the first two As in the first stitch added in this round **(d–e)**.

[4] Repeat step 3 **(e–f)**.

[5] Pick up three As, and sew through the center A in the next stitch of the previous round **(figure 3, a–b)**. Pick up one A and six color B 11º seed beads, and sew through the first two Bs just picked up to form a ring **(b–c)**. Pick up an A, and sew through the center A in the next stitch of the previous round **(c–d)**. Pick up three As, and sew through

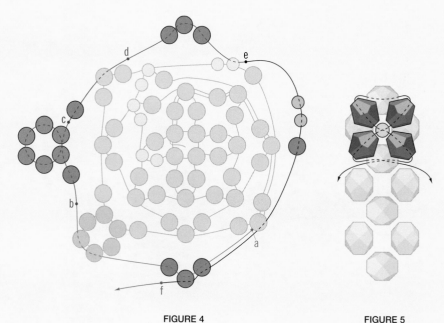

FIGURE 4

FIGURE 5

the center 15º in the next stitch of the previous round **(d–e)**. Pick up two 15ºs and an A, sew through the center 11º in the next stitch of the previous round, and step up through the first two As in the first stitch added in this round **(e–f)**.

[6] Pick up three As, and sew through the two center Bs at the top of the previous ring **(figure 4, a–b)**. Pick up one A and six color C 11º seed beads, and sew through the first two Cs just picked up to form a ring **(b–c)**. Pick up an A, and sew through the center A in the next stitch of the previous round **(c–d)**. Pick up three As, and sew through the center 15º in the next stitch of the previous round **(d–e)**. Pick up two 15ºs and an A, sew through the center A in the next stitch of the previous round,

and step up through the first two As in the first stitch added in this round **(e–f)**.

[7] Continue working as in step 6, cycling through colors B, C, and D to create the rings in each round until the netted tube is about 7 in. (18 cm), ending and adding thread (Basics) as needed.

[8] To end the netted tube, pick up three As, and sew through the two center 11ºs of the previous ring. Pick up three As, and sew through the center bead in the next stitch of the previous round. Repeat. Pick up two 15ºs and an A, sew through the center A in the next stitch of the previous round, and step up through the first two As in the first stitch added in this round.

[9] Pick up three As, and sew through the center bead in the next stitch of the

More project ideas:

- Use the netted section without the beaded beads as a bracelet, or make an entire necklace with an extended netted tube.
- Use 3 mm fire-polished beads and bicone crystals instead of 4 mms to make smaller beaded beads, perfect for a great pair of earrings: On a head pin, string a 3 mm bicone, a beaded bead, and a 3 mm bicone, and make a plain loop (Basics, p. 13). To make a link, string three 3 mm fire-polished beads on wire, and make a plain loop on either end. Open the loops (Basics) of the link, and attach an earring finding to one and the beaded bead to the other. Repeat.
- Make the beaded beads into links by stringing them on wire and making wrapped or plain loops (Basics) on each end of the beaded bead. Attach lengths of chain to the beaded links.
- String beaded beads on beading wire to make a bracelet or necklace using all beaded beads, or space them out by stringing larger crystals, fire-polished beads, or pearls between them. Use crimp beads (Basics) to attach a clasp.

previous round. Repeat twice. Pick up two 15⁰s and an A, sew through the center A in the next stitch of the previous round, and step up through the first two As in the first stitch added in this round.

[10] Repeat step 9.

[11] Pick up an A, and sew through the center A in the next stitch of the previous round. Repeat. Pick up an A, and sew through the center 15⁰ in the next stitch of the previous round. Pick up an A, and sew through the center A in the next stitch of the previous round. Retrace the thread path around the end ring, but don't end the working thread or tail. Make sure the working thread is at least 12 in. (30 cm) long.

Beaded beads

[1] Thread a needle on each end of 2 yd. (1.8 m) of Fireline, and center three 4 mm fire-polished beads. With one needle, pick up a fire-polished bead, and cross the other needle through it.

[2] Continue working in crossweave technique (Basics): With each needle, pick up a fire-polished bead. With one needle, pick up a fire-polished bead, and cross the other needle through it. Repeat twice.

[3] With each needle, pick up a fire-polished bead, and cross the needles through the end fire-polished bead in the first stitch, joining the first and last stitches to form a ring.

[4] With each needle, pick up a 4 mm bicone crystal. With one needle, pick up

an A, and cross the other needle through it. With each needle, pick up a bicone, and cross the needles through the next center fire-polished bead (figure 5). Repeat around the ring, and retrace the thread path to reinforce this round.

[5] With one needle, sew through an edge fire-polished bead. Working with one needle, pick up an A, and sew

through the next fire-polished bead in the ring **(figure 6, a–b)**. Repeat around the ring of fire-polished beads, and exit an A **(b–c)**.

[6] Pick up three As, and sew through the next A **(c–d)**. Repeat around the ring of As, and step up through the first two As in the first stitch added in this round **(d–e)**.

[7] Pick up an A, and sew through the center A in the next stitch of the previous round **(e–f)**. Repeat to complete the round **(f–g)**, retrace the thread path, and end the thread (Basics).

[8] With the remaining needle, repeat steps 5–7 on the other edge of the beaded bead.

[9] Make a total of four beaded beads in crystal colors of your choice.

Assembly

[1] Cut two 10-in. (25 cm) pieces of chain.

[2] Using the working thread from the netted tube, pick up a repeating pattern of a fire-polished bead and a beaded bead twice, then pick up a fire-polished bead, nine As, and the end link of one of the chains. Skip the last nine As, and sew back through the rest of the beads added in this step. Sew through the opposite A in the end round of the netted tube. Retrace the thread path several times to reinforce the join, and end the thread.

[3] Repeat step 2 on the other end of the netted tube using the tail.

[4] Open a jump ring (Basics), and attach the lobster claw clasp and the remaining end link of one of the chains. Close the jump ring. You can hook the lobster claw clasp to any link of the other chain to adjust the necklace length. ●

FIGURE 6

Cutting corners

Incorporating seed beads between the Tila beads allows the tiles to form perfect little hexagons and octagons while rounding the edges and providing a base for the netting that holds the rivoli in place.

Use netting to enclose rivolis in angular bezels

designed by **Michelle Heim**

Netting is versatile in its own right, but when you add Tila beads to the mix, it takes on a whole new look. The flexible netted stitches hug the back of a rivoli to hold it in place while the Tila beads add clean lines to the front of the design.

stepbystep

Rivoli bezels

[1] On 1 yd. (.9 m) of Fireline, pick up a repeating pattern of a 15º seed bead and one hole of a Tila bead six times, leaving a 6-in. (15 cm) tail. To create the inner ring of the front of the bezel, tie the beads into a ring with a square knot (Basics, p. 13). Retrace the thread path, exiting a Tila bead (**figure 1, a–b**), and end the tail (Basics).

[2] To create the outer ring of the front of the bezel, sew through the outer hole of the same Tila bead your thread is exiting (**b–c**). Pick up a 15º, an 11º seed bead, and a 15º, and sew through the outer hole of the next Tila bead (**c–d**). Repeat the last stitch around the ring, and exit an 11º (**d–e**).

[3] To embellish the top of the bezel, pick up a drop bead, sew through the opposite 15º of the inner ring (**e–f**), and sew back through the drop bead and the 11º your thread exited at the start of this step (**f–g**). Sew through the next 15º, Tila, 15º, and 11º in the outer ring (**g–h**). Repeat around the ring.

[4] To create the netting on the back of the bezel, exit an 11º, pick up three 15ºs, an 11º, and three 15ºs, and sew

through the next 11º in the outer ring (**figure 2, a–b**). Repeat around the ring, and step up through the first three 15ºs and center 11º of the first stitch in this round (**b–c**).

[5] To work the next round, pick up two 15ºs, an 11º, and two 15ºs, and sew through the center 11º of the next stitch in the previous round (**c–d**). Using loose tension, repeat to complete the round (**d–e**). Insert a 14 mm rivoli face down into the bezel, and snug the last round of stitches to the rivoli, gently tugging the thread a few times. Step up through the first two 15ºs and center 11º of the first stitch in this round (**e–f**).

[6] To work the last round, pick up a 15º, an 11º, and a 15º, and sew through the next 11º in the previous round (**f–g**). Repeat to complete the round (**g–h**), then retrace the thread path a few times. Sew through the beadwork to the outer ring, and exit a Tila bead. Don't end the working thread.

[7] Make a total of four bezels with 14 mm rivolis.

[8] Make one bezel with an 18 mm rivoli with the following changes:
• In step 1, pick up a repeating pattern of a 15º and a Tila bead eight times instead of six.

materials

gold bracelet 7½ in. (19.1 cm)
• 18 mm rivoli (brandy)
• **4** 14 mm rivolis (golden shadow)
• **5** 8 mm round crystals (topaz)
• 4 mm round crystal (topaz)
• 38 Tila beads
  (TL-455, metallic variegated blue iris)
• 2–3 g 2.8 mm drop beads
  (DP-4202, Duracoat gold)
• 1–2 g 11º seed beads
  (11-2006, matte metallic dark bronze)
• 2–3 g 15º seed beads
  (15-0005L, silver-lined dark topaz)
• Fireline 6 lb. test
• beading needles, #12

green-and-purple bracelet colors:
• 18 mm rivoli (verde)
• 14 mm rivolis (chrysolite)
• 8 mm and 4 mm round crystals (tanzanite)
• Tila beads (TL-468, metallic malachite green iris)
• 2.8 mm drop beads (DP-2035, matte metallic khaki iris)
• 11º seed beads (11-4220, Duracoat eggplant)
• 15º seed beads (15-1558, sparkling amethyst-lined crystal)

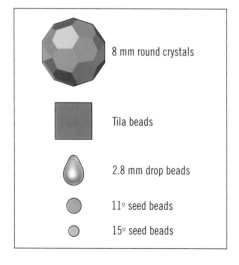

8 mm round crystals

Tila beads

2.8 mm drop beads

11º seed beads

15º seed beads

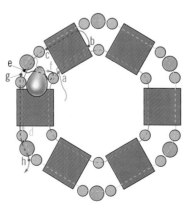

FIGURE 1

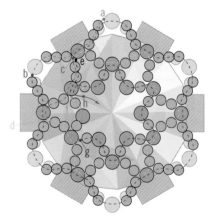

FIGURE 2

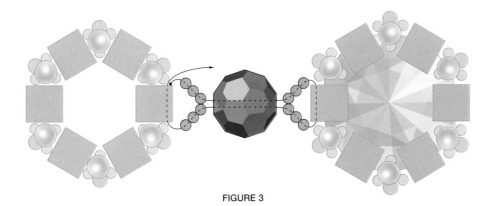

FIGURE 3

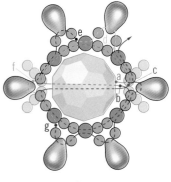

FIGURE 4

• In step 5, work a second round of netting using two 15ºs, an 11º, and two 15ºs per stitch after inserting the rivoli, snugging each round to the rivoli.

Clasp
Toggle ring
Work steps 1–3 of "Rivoli bezels," then retrace the thread path of the inner and outer rings a few times. Don't end the working thread.

Toggle bar
[1] On 1 yd. (.9 m) of Fireline, pick up 20 15ºs, leaving a 6-in. (15 cm) tail. Working in flat even-count peyote stitch (Basics), work a total of eight rows, with four As on each straight edge. Zip up (Basics) the edges to form a tube.
[2] To add a drop bead on each end, sew through the center of the tube, pick up a drop bead, sew back through the tube, pick up a drop bead, and sew back through the tube again. Retrace the thread path, and end the working thread and tail.

Assembly
[1] Place the components on your work surface in the following order: toggle ring, two 14 mm rivolis, 18 mm rivoli, two 14 mms, toggle bar. The working thread from each component will be used to connect the next component, so position each new component with the thread facing away from the previous component. Work the next three steps with the working thread from the toggle ring.
[2] Pick up three 15ºs, an 8 mm round crystal, and three 15ºs. Sew through a Tila bead in the next component. Pick

up three 15ºs, sew back through the 8 mm, pick up three 15ºs, and sew through the Tila bead your thread exited at the start of this step (figure 3). Retrace the thread path a few times.
[3] To embellish the crystal, sew through the first three 15ºs picked up in the previous step and the 8 mm. Pick up a repeating pattern of two 15ºs and an 11º three times, then pick up two 15ºs. Sew through the 8 mm again (figure 4, a–b). Repeat the last stitch (b–c), then sew through the first three beads picked up in this step, exiting an 11º (c–d).
[4] Pick up a 15º, a drop, and a 15º, and sew through the next 11º in the ring (d–e). Repeat, then sew through the next two 15ºs (e–f). Pick up a drop, and sew through the next two 15ºs and an 11º in the ring (f–g). Repeat this step (g–h), and end the thread.
[5] Repeat steps 2–4 to connect the remaining rivolis.

[6] To connect the toggle bar to the end component, pick up four 15ºs, a 4 mm round crystal, four 15ºs, and an 11º. Sew through two center beads of the toggle bar and back through the 11º. Pick up four 15ºs, and sew back through the 4 mm. Pick up four 15ºs, and sew through the Tila bead your thread exited at the start of the step. Retrace the thread path, and end the thread. ●

Add length to your bracelet by picking up more 15ºs in step 2 of "Assembly" to connect the 8 mm round crystals.

Floral memory

A vintage-style garland floats around your neck

designed by **Jacquelyn Scieszka**

Jacquelyn's mother's generation wore beautiful floral costume jewelry designed by Miriam Haskell and others. Inspired by these vintage pieces made with metal, wire, and gemstones, she translated the look into a seed-bead-and-pearl version.

step by step

Flowers

Calyx

[1] On 2 yd. (1.8 m) of thread or Fireline, pick up six color B 8º seed beads, leaving a 20-in. (51 cm) tail. Tie the beads into a ring with a square knot (Basics, p. 13), leaving a small amount of slack between the beads. Sew through the first 8º again **(figure 1, a–b)**.

[2] To work Round 2: Pick up a B, and sew through the next B **(b–c)**. Repeat around the ring, and step up through the first B added in this round **(c–d)**.

[3] Work three rounds (rounds 3, 4, and 5) in tubular peyote stitch (Basics) using Bs. Snug up the beads to form a cup. Exit a B in round 4.

Petals

The first layer of petals will be worked off of calyx round 4, and the second layer of petals will be worked off of calyx round 5.

[1] Pick up three color A 8º seed beads, and sew through the B in the calyx and the first A picked up in this step **(figure 2, a–b)**.

[2] Pick up an A, and sew through the second A picked up in step 1 **(b–c)**. Pick up an A, and sew through the third A picked up in step 1 **(c–d)**. Sew through the B in the calyx and the next two edge As **(d–e)**.

[3] Pick up two As, and sew through the next two As, the B in the calyx, and the following two As **(e–f)**.

[4] Pick up an A, and sew through the first A in the pair picked up in step 3 **(figure 3, a–b)**. Pick up an A, and sew through the second A in the pair **(b–c)**. Pick up an A, and sew through the next two As, the B in the calyx, and the following three As **(c–d)**.

[5] Pick up two As, and sew through the next A **(d–e)**. Pick up two As, and sew through the next three As, the B in the calyx, and the following five As **(e–f)**. Pick up a color C 8º seed bead, and sew through the next five As and the next three Bs in the calyx **(f–g)**.

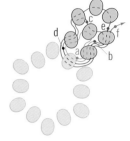

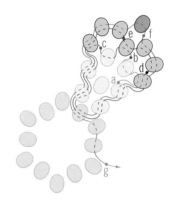

FIGURE 1   FIGURE 2

FIGURE 3

materials

necklace 18 in. (46 cm)

- 10 mm glass pearl
- **15** 6 mm glass pearls
- 8º seed beads
  - 75 g color A (flower petals)
  - 50 g color B (calyxes, flower bases)
  - 16 g color C (petal tips, flower center accents)
- 11º seed beads
  - 6 g color D (leaves)
  - 8 g color E (connector tubes, bud base)
  - 3 g color F (bud petals)
  - 3 g color G (bud petal tips)
- 15º seed beads
  - 3 g color H (leaf picots, bud embellishment)
  - 1 g color I (bud embellishment)
- nylon beading thread or Fireline 6 lb. test
- beading needles, #12

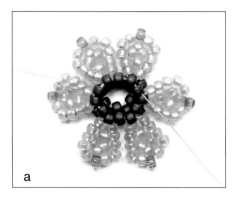

a

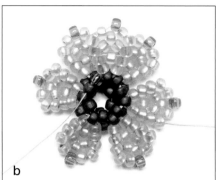

b

c

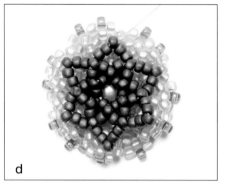

d

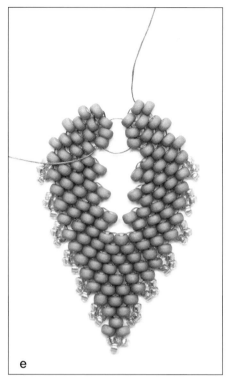

e

[6] Repeat steps 1–5 around the calyx, working a total of six petals (photo a). After completing the sixth petal, step up through a B in calyx round 5.

[7] Work a second layer of petals off of round 5, as in steps 1–5, with the following adjustment: At the end of step 5, after you sew through the five As, pick up a C, and sew through the next B rather than sewing through three Bs (photo b).

[8] Sew through the Bs in round 5 and the Cs added in step 7 to create a ring. Exit a B.

[9] Pick up a 6 mm glass pearl, and sew through a B on the opposite side of the ring (photo c). Retrace the thread path a few times to secure the connection. Sew through the Bs in rounds 4, 3, and 2. End the working thread (Basics).

Base

[1] Using the tail, pick up a B, and sew through the next B in the original ring (figure 4, a–b). Repeat around the ring, and step up through the first B added in this round (b–c).

[2] Pick up three Bs, and sew through the next B in the previous round (c–d), forming a picot. Repeat around the ring, and step up through the first two Bs added in this round (d–e).

[3] Pick up five Bs, and sew through the middle B in the next picot added in the previous round (e–f). Repeat around the ring, and step up through the first three Bs added in this round (f–g and photo d). Retrace the thread path to reinforce the round. End the thread.

[4] Repeat the steps in "Calyx," "Petals," and "Base" to make a total of 15 flowers.

Leaves

[1] On 1 yd. (.9 m) of thread or Fireline, center a stop bead (Basics). Work in peyote stitch as follows:
Rows 1–3: Pick up eight color D 11º seed beads, three color H 15º seed beads, and a D. Skip the last five beads, and sew back through the next D to form a picot (figure 5, a–b). Pick up a D, and sew through the next D. Repeat twice (b–c). Remove the stop bead.
Row 4: Pick up three Ds, and sew back through the first D picked up in this step (figure 6, a–b). Work three stitches with Ds to complete the row (b–c).
Row 5: Pick up three Hs, and sew through the last D picked up in step 4 (c–d). Work three stitches with Ds to complete the row (d–e).
Rows 6–13: Repeat rows 4 and 5 five times. Do not end the working thread.

[2] Using the tail, pick up a D, and sew through the next D (figure 7, a–b). Pick up a D, and sew through the D just added in this step (b–c). Work three stitches with Ds to complete the row (c–d).

[3] Pick up three Hs, and sew through the last D picked up in step 2 (d–e). Work three stitches with Ds to complete the row (e–f).

[4] Work as in rows 4 and 5 of the first side to work the next nine rows of the second half of the leaf. Do not end the thread.

[5] Using the working thread from the first half of the leaf, sew through an inner end D.

[6] Pick up a D, and sew through the next D (figure 8, a–b). Sew through the opposite inner D, pick up a D, and sew through the previous inner D (b–c). Sew through the opposite three Ds (c–d and photo e). Snug up the beads.

[7] Repeat step 6 three times (d–e).

[8] Pick up a D, and sew through the center D at the bottom of the open space, the two adjacent Ds in the next row, and back through the center D and the D added in this step (e–f). Sew through the Ds on the inner edge and the two Ds on the end (f–g).

[9] Pick up a D, and sew through the next D. Repeat (g–h). Pick up three Hs, and sew through the last D added in

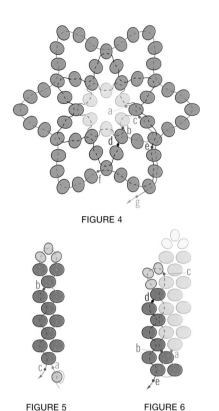

FIGURE 4

FIGURE 5   **FIGURE 6**

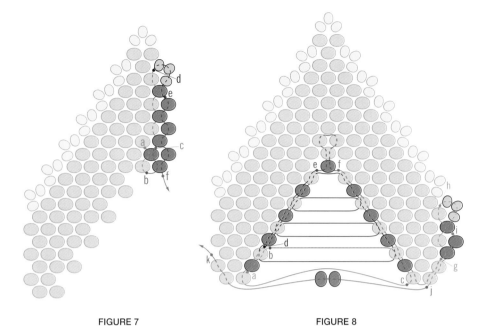

FIGURE 7   **FIGURE 8**

this step **(h–i)**. Pick up a D, and sew through the next three Ds **(i–j)**.

[10] Pick up two Ds, and sew through the two Ds on the opposite end of the leaf **(j–k)**.

[11] Repeat step 9 on the other edge. Do not end the thread.

[12] Repeat steps 1–11 to make a second leaf.

Bud-clasp loop
Calyx

[1] On 1 yd. (.9 m) of thread or Fireline, center three color E 11º seed beads, sew through the Es again to form a ring, then continue through the first E picked up.

[2] Work the following rounds in circular and tubular peyote stitch (Basics), stepping up after each round, and increasing and decreasing (Basics) to form a bud calyx:

Round 1: With one end of the thread, pick up two Es, and sew through the next E in the previous round. Repeat twice, and step up through the first E in the first pair of Es.

Round 2: Pick up an E between each pair of Es and between each bead in a pair (add six beads).

Round 3: Pick up two Es, and sew through the next E in the previous round. Repeat around, and step up through the first E in the first pair of Es.

Round 4: Work 12 peyote stitches with one E per stitch.

Rounds 5–7: Work three rounds of tubular peyote using Es. Snug up the beads to begin forming a cup-like calyx.

Round 8: Work three peyote stitches, then work a decrease by sewing through the next E in round 6 and the next E in round 7. Repeat twice. Step up through three Es.

Round 9: Work two peyote stitches with one E, and work a peyote stitch with two Es over the decrease in the previous round. Repeat twice.

Round 10: Work nine stitches with one E per stitch, sewing through the pair of

Es in the previous round as one bead.

Rounds 11 and 12: Repeat rounds 9 and 10.

Round 13: Work nine peyote stitches with one E per stitch.

Round 14: Work two peyote stitches, and skip a stitch to work a decrease. Repeat twice. Step up through three Es.

Round 15: Work six peyote stitches with one E per stitch.

Round 16: Work one peyote stitch, and skip a stitch to work a decrease. Repeat twice. Step up through three Es.

Round 17: Sew through the three up-beads. Sew through them again, and end the thread.

EDITOR'S NOTES:

- When stitching the bud-clasp petals, anchor the second pair of color F 11ºs in the base color E 11º by picking up two Fs, stitching down through the adjacent F in the first pair, through the base E, and up through the two adjacent Fs before adding the remaining pairs of Fs. This will snug the petal to the base.
- To anchor the connector tubes to the flower bases: Sew through a bead in the end round of the tube and a bead in the flower base. Sew between the tube and the base for two or three stitches. This will prevent the tube from rotating and the single flowers from flipping over.
- Use different colors for each flower petal layer. Repeat your color selection in the beads used for the bud clasp.

f

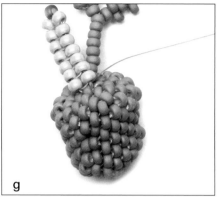

g

h

Loop

[1] Using the tail, pick up eight Es. Then pick up an odd number of Es to make a loop for the clasp bead to fit through (approximately 29), and sew back through the first eight Es. Sew through an E in the calyx's top three-bead round, the eight Es again, and the first E in the loop.

[2] Work a round of peyote stitch around the loop, sew back through the eight Es, and sew through an E in the calyx. Retrace the thread path through the eight Es and the loop, and exit an E in the calyx's top three-bead round **(photo f)**.

Petals

[1] Pick up two color F 11º seed beads, and sew through the E your thread exited at the start of this step and the first F picked up **(figure 9, a–b)**. Pick up the two Fs, and sew through the previous two Fs and the first new F. Repeat five times **(b–c)**.

[2] Pick up a color G 11º seed bead, and sew back through the seven beads in the adjacent column and the base E your thread exited at the start of step 1 **(c–d)**. Sew through an adjacent E **(photo g)**.

[3] Repeat steps 1 and 2, working in a circular pattern to add 24 petals to the top of the calyx. End and add thread (Basics) as needed.

[4] With your thread exiting an E in a round below the petals, pick up two Hs, a color I 15º seed bead, and two Hs, and sew through the next E in the round to form a picot. Repeat around. Exit an E two rounds away from the anchor Es in the first picot round.

[5] Pick up an I, sew through the I in the next picot in the previous round,

pick up an I, and sew through the next E in the round your thread exited at the start of this step. Repeat around. End the thread **(photo h)**.

Connector tubes

[1] On 1 yd. (.9 m) of thread or Fireline, pick up four Es, leaving a 6-in. (15 cm) tail. Sew through the four beads again, and snug them up to form two columns of two beads each.

[2] Working in ladder stitch (Basics), pick up two Es in each stitch to work a two-bead ladder that is eight columns long. Join the ends to form a ring (Basics).

[3] Work eight rounds of tubular herringbone stitch (Basics) using Es. Work a ladder stitch thread path through the last round. You may choose to adjust the length of your necklace by changing the number of rounds in the connector tubes. Do not end the working thread or tail.

[4] Repeat steps 1–3 to make a total of six connector tubes.

Assembly
Flower clusters

[1] Place three flowers face down on your work surface, arranging them in a triangle formation as shown in **figure 10**. Add thread to flower 1. With the thread exiting the center B in a picot, pick up two Bs, and sew through the center B in a picot of flower 2 **(a–b)**. Pick up two Bs, and sew through the center B in a picot of flower 3. Pick up two Bs, and sew through the B exited at the start of this step **(b–c)**. Snug up the beads.

[2] Sew through the next six Bs, exiting the center B in the next picot. Pick up two Bs, and sew through the next four Bs in a picot of flower 2 **(c–d)**.

[3] Pick up three Bs, and sew through the second bead from the center B of flower 1 **(d–e)**.

[4] Sew through the next two Bs, the Bs added in step 2, the next seven Bs in flower 2, the two Bs added in step 1, and the next seven Bs in flower 3, exiting the center B in the second picot **(e–f)**.

[5] Pick up two Bs, and sew through the next three Bs in the adjacent picot of flower 1 **(f–g)**.

[6] Pick up three Bs, and sew through the second bead from the center B of flower 3 **(g–h)**.

[7] Sew through the next two Bs, the two Bs added in step 5, the next seven Bs in flower 1, the first two Bs added in step 1, and the next seven Bs in flower 2 **(h–i)**.

[8] Pick up two Bs, and sew through the next three Bs in the adjacent picot of flower 3 **(i–j)**. Pick up three Bs, and sew through the second bead from the center B of flower 2 **(j–k)**. Sew through the next 14 Bs in flower 2, exiting the center B of the third picot **(k–l)**. Do not end the thread.

[9] Repeat steps 1–8 to make a total of three flower clusters.

Necklace

[1] Using the working thread from a flower cluster, pick up two Bs, and sew through the center B in a picot of another flower cluster **(figure 11, a–b)**. Sew back through the two Bs just added and the B your thread exited at the start of this step **(b–c)**. Retrace the thread path to reinforce the connection. Do not end the thread.

[2] Repeat step 1 to connect the remaining flower cluster to the other edge of one of the flower clusters connected in step 1.

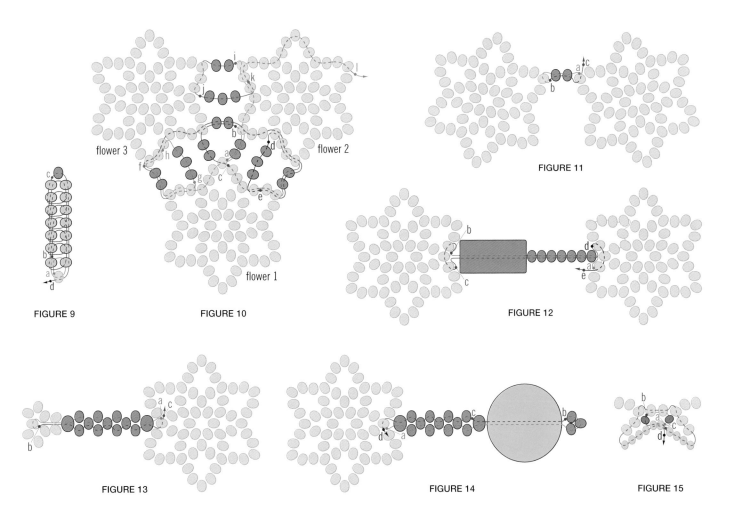

FIGURE 9

FIGURE 10

FIGURE 11

FIGURE 12

FIGURE 13

FIGURE 14

FIGURE 15

[3] Using a working thread in an edge flower cluster, sew through the picot to exit the second B from the center B **(figure 12, point a)**.

[4] Pick up enough Bs to equal the length of a connector tube, then pick up a tube, but do not slide the tube over the Bs yet **(a–b)**.

[5] Sew through three Bs at the base of two picots on a single flower **(b–c)**. Sew back through the tube and the Bs picked up in step 4 **(c–d)**. Snug up the connection, sliding the connector tube over the Bs. Add or remove Bs as needed so the Bs are concealed by the connector tube. Sew through the three Bs at the base of two picots on the flower cluster **(d–e)**. Retrace the thread path twice.

[6] Sew through the single flower base to the opposite edge, and repeat steps 4 and 5 twice to connect two more flowers.

[7] Sew through the last single flower base to the opposite edge, exiting a B at the base of two picots **(figure 13, point a)**.

[8] To attach the bud-clasp loop, pick up a C, seven Es, and a C, and sew through an E in the first round of the calyx **(a–b)**. Sew back through the C, work a row of peyote stitch using Es, and sew back through the C and the B your thread exited at the start of this step **(b–c)**. Retrace the thread path two or three times. End the thread.

[9] Repeat steps 3–7 to stitch the other half of the necklace.

[10] To make the bead toggle, pick up a C, seven Es, a C, a 10 mm glass pearl, and three Es **(figure 14, a–b)**. Skip the three Es, and sew back through the 10 mm and the C **(b–c)**. Work a row of peyote stitch using Es, and sew back through the C and the B your thread exited at the start of this step **(c–d)**. Retrace the thread path two or three times. End the thread.

[11] To attach a leaf, use the working thread exiting the two center Ds in the top row of the leaf. Position the leaf between two flower clusters. Align the two center Ds in the top row of the leaf with the two Bs connecting the flower clusters.

[12] Pick up a D, and sew through the two connector Bs **(figure 15, a–b)**. Pick up a D, and sew through the two center Ds in the top row of the leaf **(b–c)**.

[13] Sew through the top four Ds in the leaf, three Bs in the base picot, the two connector Bs, three Bs in the opposite base picot, the top four Ds on the other top edge of the leaf, and the center two Ds **(c–d)**. Retrace the thread path, and end the thread.

[14] Repeat steps 11–13 to attach the other leaf. ●

Heavy metal bands

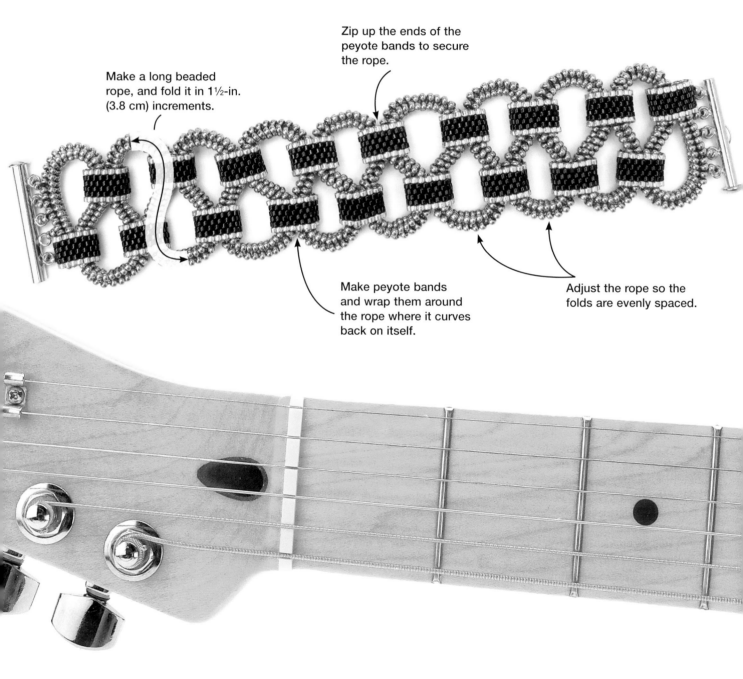

Zip up the ends of the peyote bands to secure the rope.

Make a long beaded rope, and fold it in 1½-in. (3.8 cm) increments.

Make peyote bands and wrap them around the rope where it curves back on itself.

Adjust the rope so the folds are evenly spaced.

Combine a beaded rope with peyote stitch links to make this curvy bracelet

designed by **Jimmie Boatright**

Metallic seed bead ropes and cylinder bead bands give this cuff a chunky chain mail look. Work the rope in herringbone stitch or right-angle weave for slightly different results.

The rope in this bracelet can be made using either herringbone stitch or right-angle weave. The herringbone rope is stiffer, whereas the right-angle weave rope is more pliable. Choose your preferred method, then move on to "Peyote bands" and "Assembly" to complete the bracelet. The instructions are for a 7¼-in. (18.4 cm) bracelet. Increase or decrease the length of the rope by 1½ in. (3.8 cm) to change the length of the bracelet by 1 in. (2.5 cm). This will alter the number of peyote bands required.

Choose monochromatic colors for an elegant look, or go for more drama with contrasting colors.

stepbystep

Herringbone rope
[1] On a comfortable length of nylon beading thread, pick up two 11º seed beads, leaving an 8-in. (20 cm) tail. Sew through both beads again, and position them side by side. Working in ladder stitch (Basics, p. 13), add two more 11ºs. Form the ladder into a ring (Basics).
[2] With your thread exiting the first 11º in the ring, work in tubular herringbone stitch (Basics) with 11ºs to make a 28-in. (71 cm) rope. End and add thread (Basics) as needed. Tie a couple of half-hitch knots (Basics), but do not trim the working thread or tail.

materials

gold-and-black bracelet
7¼ in. (18.4 cm)
- 20 g 11º seed beads (galvanized gold)
- 11º Japanese cylinder beads
  3 g color A (gold)
  7 g color B (opaque black)
- 31 x 6 mm 5-strand slide clasp
- nylon beading thread, size D
- Fireline 6 lb. test
- beading needles, #10

silver bracelet colors:
- 11º seed beads
  (TPF 558, silver galvanized matte)
- 11º cylinder beads
  color A (DB-35, metallic silver)
  color B (DB-26, dark steel)

copper bracelet colors:
- 11º seed beads
  (Toho 222, metallic dark copper)
- 11º cylinder beads
  color A (DB-12, metallic raspberry)
  color B (DB-21, nickel-plated steel)

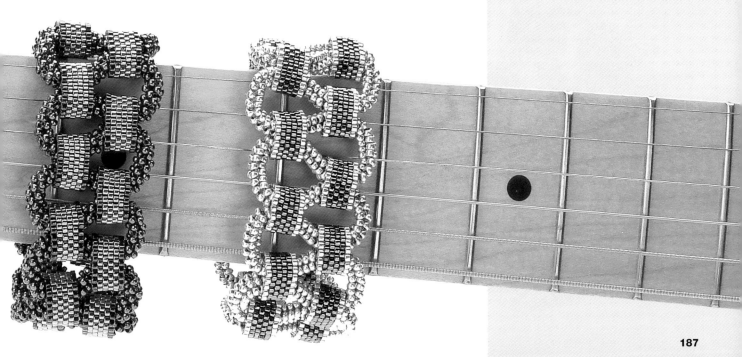

FIGURE

EDITOR'S NOTE:
Use nylon beading thread instead of Fireline for the herringbone rope, and the result will be a very fluid, easy-to-bend piece.

Right-angle weave rope

[1] On a comfortable length of Fireline, pick up four 11º seed beads, leaving an 8-in. (20 cm) tail. Sew through all four beads again, and tie them into a ring with a square knot (Basics, p. 86). Work a flat strip of right-angle weave (Basics) that is three stitches wide.

[2] Form the strip into a ring: Exit the end 11º of the last stitch, pick up an 11º, sew through the end 11º of the first stitch, pick up an 11º, and sew through the 11º your thread exited at the start of this stitch. Retrace the thread path through the connecting stitch.

[3] For subsequent rounds, pick up three 11ºs in the first stitch, two 11ºs in each of the next two stitches, and one 11º in the final stitch. Repeat to make a 28-in. (71 cm) rope. End and add thread (Basics) as needed. Tie a couple of half-hitch knots (Basics), but do not trim the working thread or tail.

Peyote bands

[1] On 24 in. (61 cm) of Fireline, attach a stop bead (Basics), leaving a 6-in. (15 cm) tail. Pick up a color A 11º cylinder bead, four color B 11º cylinder beads, and an A.

[2] Work in flat even-count peyote stitch (Basics) as follows: For each row, work one stitch with an A and two stitches with a B. Work a total of 32 rows (figure). You will have 16 As along each straight edge of the band. Do not trim the working thread or tail.

[3] Make 18 bands for a 7¼-in. (18.4 cm) bracelet.

Assembly

[1] Fold the rope 1½ in. (3.8 cm) from one end. Wrap a peyote band around the rope where it curves back on itself (refer to the photo on p. 186), and zip up (Basics) the ends. End the threads of the band.

[2] Repeat step 1 across the rope, each time folding the rope 1½ in. (3.8 cm) from the previous fold. Adjust the last few folds as necessary so the end of the rope is hidden inside the last peyote band.

[3] Using a thread from the rope, sew through an end peyote band and the rope to secure the band in place. Position the clasp along the end of the bracelet, and exit a cylinder in the peyote band that is closest to the first loop of the clasp. Pick up two 11º seed beads, the loop of the clasp, and two 11ºs, and sew through the peyote band and the rope. Retrace the thread path.

[4] Sew through the rope to exit an 11º near the next loop of the clasp. Pick up two 11º seed beads, the loop, and two 11ºs, and sew through the rope. Retrace the thread path to secure. Repeat to attach the remaining loops of the clasp. End the thread.

[5] Repeat steps 3 and 4 on the other end of the bracelet. ●

Summer's end

Suspend an
art-glass bead
from a tangled vine
of herringbone and
tubular netting

by **Jane Danley Cruz**

materials
necklace 23 in. (58 cm)
- art-glass focal bead
- **7** 4 mm round fire-polished beads
  (jonquil/Montana)
- 10 g 8º seed beads (grape)
- 11º seed beads
  6 g color A (rainbow dark gold)
  6 g color D (matte purple AB)
  40 color F (light yellow)
  40 color G (metallic rainbow bronze)
- 3 g 11º cylinder beads in each of
  3 colors:
  B (opaque luster rainbow
  midnight purple)
  C (silver-lined smoke topaz)
  E (goldenrod-lined topaz)
- 2 g 15º seed beads (metallic
  rainbow bronze)
- 6 mm flower spacer
- **2** 8 x 13 mm filigree cones
- 30 x 6 mm leaf toggle bar
- 30 x 6 mm leaf toggle ring
- Fireline 6 lb. test
- beading needles, #12

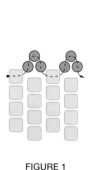

FIGURE 1

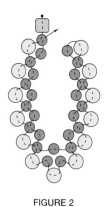

FIGURE 2

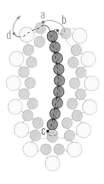

FIGURE 3

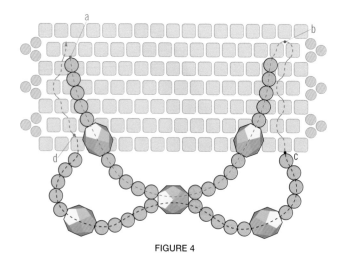

FIGURE 4

The organic look of Sara Sally LaGrand's art-glass bead, created for the 2011 Bead&Button Show, reminded Jane of a garden at the end of the season, with a little treasure hidden among the twisted vines and broken stalks.

stepbystep

Bail
Peyote tube
[1] On a comfortable length of Fireline, attach a stop bead (Basics, p. 13), leaving a 6-in. (15 cm) tail. Pick up 22 color D 11º seed beads. Sew through all the beads again to form a ring, and continue through the first D picked up.
[2] Work in tubular peyote stitch (Basics) until the tube measures 1 in. (2.5 cm).
[3] With your thread exiting an end, pick up three 15º seed beads, and sew through the next up-bead in the tube (figure 1). Repeat around the tube, and sew through the beadwork to repeat on the other end. End the working thread and tail (Basics).

Leaves
[1] On a comfortable length of Fireline, attach a stop bead, leaving a 6-in. (15 cm) tail. Pick up an alternating pattern of a 15º and a color F 11º seed bead for a total of 26 beads.
[2] Work in peyote stitch using 15ºs for five stitches, pick up a 15º, skip the next two 15ºs, and sew through the following 15º. Continue working in peyote stitch to the end of the row (figure 2).
[3] Remove the stop bead, and sew through the first 15º on the opposite end (figure 3, a–b).
[4] Pick up nine 15ºs, and sew through the 15º at the bottom of the leaf (b–c). Sew back through the beads just added, the 15º your thread exited at the start of step 3, and the adjacent F (c–d). Do not end the working thread or tail.

[5] Repeat steps 1–4 to make a total of three leaves.
[6] Position a leaf on the peyote tube. Using either thread, sew through a D in the tube, and then sew through the next F in the leaf. Repeat around the leaf to tack it to the tube. End the threads. Repeat with the remaining leaves.

Focal bead
[1] Add a comfortable length of Fireline to the peyote tube (Basics), and exit a D in the fourth round from one end of the tube (figure 4, point a). Pick up five color G 11º seed beads, a 4 mm fire-polished bead, five Gs, a 4 mm, five Gs, a 4 mm, and five Gs. Sew through the corresponding D at the other end of the tube (a–b).
[2] Sew through the beadwork to exit at point c. Pick up five Gs, a 4 mm, and five Gs, and sew through the center 4 mm from step 1. Pick up five Gs, a 4 mm, and five Gs. Sew through the corresponding D at the other end of the tube (c–d).
[3] Sew through the beadwork to exit the D your thread exited in step 1. Retrace the thread path through the center 4 mm, and pick up the focal bead, a 6 mm flower spacer, and three 15ºs. Sew back through the spacer, the focal bead, the center 4 mm in the same direction as before, and the remaining beads in the strand. Retrace the thread path through both strands several times, and end the thread.

Rope
Twisted herringbone
[1] On 2 yd. (1.8 m) of Fireline, leaving a 6-in. (15 cm) tail, make a ladder (Basics) that is eight beads long in the following pattern: a color A 11º seed bead, three color B 11º cylinder beads,

FIGURE 5

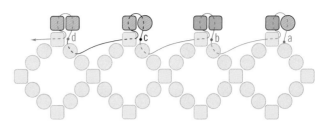

FIGURE 6

an A, and three color C 11º cylinder beads. Form the ladder into a ring (Basics), exiting an A.

[2] Pick up an A and a B, sew down through the next B in the previous round, and sew up through the following B. Pick up two Bs, sew down through the next B in the previous round, and sew up through the following A. Pick up an A and a C, sew down through the next C in the previous round, and sew up through the following C. Pick up two Cs, sew down through the next C in the previous round, and sew up through the next two As in the stack.

[3] Following the pattern in step 2, work in twisted tubular herringbone stitch (Basics) until this section measures 2¼ in. (5.7 cm), stepping up through three As at the end of each round. End and add thread as needed.

[4] Continue in twisted tubular herringbone stitch, but change the beads. Pick up an 8º seed bead and a D in the first stitch, pick up two Ds in the second stitch, pick up an 8º and an A in the third stitch, and pick up two As in the fourth stitch. Sew up through the three beads in the next stack.

[5] Following the pattern in step 4, work in twisted tubular herringbone stitch until this section measures 1½ in. (3.8 cm).

[6] Following the pattern in step 2, work in twisted tubular herringbone stitch for 2¼ in. (5.7 cm).

[7] Following the pattern in step 4, work in twisted tubular herringbone stitch for 4 in. (10 cm).

[8] Following the pattern in step 2, work in twisted tubular herringbone stitch for ½ in. (1.3 cm).

[9] Follow the pattern in step 4 for 4 in. (10 cm).

Tubular netting
[1] Switch to netting: Pick up two Ds, a color E 11º cylinder bead, and two Ds, skip the next D in the previous round, and sew up through the following D **(figure 5, a–b)**. Pick up two Ds, an E, and two Ds, skip the next D in the previous round, and sew up through the following 8º **(b–c)**. Pick up two Ds, an E, and two Ds, skip the next A in the previous round, and sew up through the following A. Pick up two Ds, an E, and two Ds, skip the next A in the previous round, and sew up through the following 8º. Step up through the first three beads added in this round.

[2] Pick up two Ds, an E, and two Ds, and sew through the next E in the previous round. Repeat around, stepping up through the first three beads added in this round. Continue working the
pattern in tubular netting for 4¼ in. (10.8 cm). Step up through the first two Ds in the last round.

Twisted herringbone
[1] Switch back to herringbone: Pick up an A and a B, sew down through the next E in the previous round, skip the next two Ds, E, and D of the previous round, and sew up through the following D **(figure 6, a–b)**. Keep a firm tension, and make sure the thread exits the inside of the tube. Pick up two Bs, sew down through the next E in the previous round, skip the next two Ds, E, and D of the previous round, and sew up through the following D **(b–c)**. Pick up an A and a C, sew down through the next E in the previous round, skip the next two Ds, E, and D of the previous round, and sew up through the following D **(c–d)**. Pick up two Cs, sew down through the next E in the previous

round, skip the next two Ds, E, and D of the previous round, sew up through the following D and step up through the first A added in this round.

[2] Pick up an A and a B, sew down through the next B in the previous round, and sew up through the following B. Repeat the pattern established in step 1, and step up through two As to complete the round.

[3] Following the pattern, work in twisted tubular herringbone stitch for 1¼ in. (3.2 cm), stepping up through three As to complete each round. End the thread.

Assembly
[1] Center the bail on the section of rope from step 8.

[2] On one end of the rope, pick up six As, a filigree cone, a 4 mm, an A, three 15ºs, a 30 x 6 mm toggle ring, and three 15ºs. Sew back through the 4 mm, cone, and As and into the rope. Tie several half-hitch knots (Basics), and retrace the thread path through the toggle ring connection. End the thread.

[3] On the other end of the rope, pick up six As, a filigree cone, a 4 mm, an A, nine 15ºs, a 30 x 6 mm toggle bar, and three 15ºs. Sew back through the toggle bar, and pick up nine 15ºs. Sew back through the 4 mm, cone, and As and into the beadwork of the rope. Tie several half-hitch knots, and retrace the thread path through the toggle bar connection. End the thread. •

(B)ring it

Playful rings include brick stitch, peyote stitch, right-angle weave, netting, embroidery, and fringe

designed by **Kelli Burns**

With or without leaves, these lively rings make a statement. See the Editor's Notes on p. 194 for tips on making rings without leaves.

a

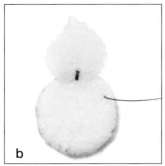

b

c

d

Combine a variety of techniques in one fun ring, mixing and matching the stitches that capture your fancy. The ring band can be worn alone as a sparkling accessory or stacked with leaves, crystal rivolis, and fringe.

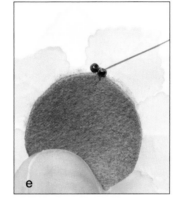

e

stepbystep

Rivoli bezels

[1] Referring to the sidebar, p. 194, and Basics, p. 13, stitch a peyote bezel around a rivoli in the size of your choice, using 11º seed beads and 15º seed beads. If you want to embellish the bezel with crystal fringe, work step 2; otherwise, end the working thread (Basics) but not the tail.

[2] If desired, embellish the outside center round with crystal fringe: Exit an 11º in the outer round, and pick up a 3 mm pearl or bicone crystal and a 15º. Skip the 15º, and sew back through the pearl or crystal and the next 11º in the outer round (photo a). Repeat to complete the round, and end the working thread, but leave the tail.

Ring base

[1] Lay the rivoli bezel on a piece of beading foundation, and trace a circle slightly larger than the rivoli. Cut out the circle. Use the foundation as a template to cut out a piece of Ultrasuede to the same size.

[2] Tie an overhand knot (Basics) at the end of a comfortable length of thread, and trim the tail.

[3] Sew through the foundation from back to front. Pick up a leaf, and position it along the outer edge of the foundation. Sew it in place, then sew through the foundation from back to front so the next leaf will sit right next to the first (photo b). Repeat around the edge of the foundation.

[4] To begin another round, sew through the foundation from back to front, exiting between two leaves in the previous round. Pick up a leaf, and stitch it to the foundation so it overlaps two leaves in the first round (photo c). Repeat to complete the round. Work as many rounds as desired, ending with at least 12 in. (30 cm) of working thread.

[5] Position the rivoli bezel in the center of the ring base, and, using the tail, stitch it to the foundation (photo d). Repeat around the bezel, and end the thread.

[6] Align the Ultrasuede on the back of the foundation, and sew through both layers using the thread from step 4.

[7] Work a modified brick stitch embellishment around the outside edge: Pick up two 15ºs, sew through both layers two bead widths from where your thread is exiting, and sew back through the second 15º (photo e). Pick up a 15º, then sew through both layers and back through the 15º. Repeat to complete the edge. When you reach the first 15º, sew through it and the last 15º, and end the thread.

Ring band

[1] On a comfortable length of thread, pick up 12 15ºs. Sew through the first nine beads again to form a ring (figure 1, a–b).

[2] Working in modified right-angle weave (Basics), pick up nine 15ºs, and sew through the last three 15ºs your thread exited in the previous ring and the next six beads in the new ring (b–c). Repeat until the band is the desired length (c–d). To determine the length you'll need, wrap the band around

materials

ring with leaves

- **12–27** mm rivoli
- **10–28** 7–15 mm Lucite leaves
- **15–32** 3 mm pearls or bicone crystals (optional)
- **20–30** 2.5 or 3 mm pearls or bicone crystals
- 1 g 11º seed beads
- 5 g 15º seed beads
- nylon beading thread, size D, or Fireline 4 lb. test
- beading needles, #12
- Lacy's Stiff Stuff beading foundation
- Ultrasuede

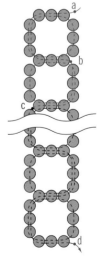

FIGURE 1

These pretty bands are hidden treasures. See the Editor's Notes below to make a ring band without embellishment.

your finger, and place the ring base on top. The ends of the band will be attached to the edges of the ring base, so add or remove stitches as needed.

[3] Exit a center 15º of one of the stitches along one edge of the ring band (figure 2, point a). Pick up five 15ºs, and sew through the center 15º in the next stitch (a–b). Repeat along the edge, and sew through the beads on the end to exit the center 15º in the first stitch on the remaining edge. Repeat.

[4] Exit the three end 15ºs on one end of the band (figure 3, point a). Pick up a 3 mm pearl or bicone crystal, and sew through the opposite three 15ºs in the stitch in the same direction (a–b). Repeat to add a crystal or pearl to each stitch (b–c).

[5] Sew through the next five 15ºs along the edge (c–d). Pick up a 2.5 or 3 mm pearl or bicone crystal, and sew through the three 15ºs in the center of the two adjacent stitches in the band (d–e). Pick up a pearl or bicone, and sew through the opposite

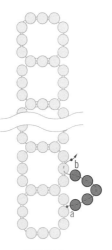

FIGURE 2

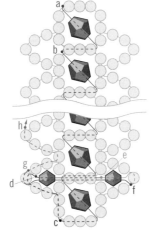

FIGURE 3

15º (e–f). Sew back through the pearl or bicone, the three 15ºs, and the opposite pearl or bicone and 15º (f–g). Sew through the next six 15ºs along the edge (g–h). Repeat to complete the embellishment, exiting the three end 15ºs.

[6] Place the band near the edge of the ring base, and stitch the band in place by sewing through the Ultrasuede, the foundation, and the end three 15ºs again (photo f). Retrace the thread path a few times, and end the thread. Repeat on the other end. ●

Rivoli bezels: How many 11º seed beads do I pick up?

It can be challenging to guess how many beads fit in the initial bezel ring, which makes up the first two rounds of peyote. The initial ring should always have an even number of beads and fit around the widest part of your rivoli or stone. Since beads vary, you may have to adjust the number of beads, but here is a general starting point.

Size of rivoli/ stone	Number of beads
12 mm	28
12 x 18 mm	38
14 mm	34
16 mm	38
18 mm	44
22 x 30 mm	62
27 mm	66

f

EDITOR'S NOTES:

• To make an unembellished ring, simply make the band long enough to wrap all the way around your finger. Form the band into a ring: Pick up three 150s, and sew through the first three end 150s. Pick up three 150s, and sew through the last three end 150s. Retrace the thread path to secure the join, then finish the edges as in steps 4 and 5 of "Ring band."

• You can join the band directly to the bezel if you prefer a ring without leaves. Sew through the beadwork on the bezel instead of the Ultrasuede and foundation.

CUBE
delight

Create the look of tile in a band stitched with cubes and seed beads

designed by **Smadar Grossman**

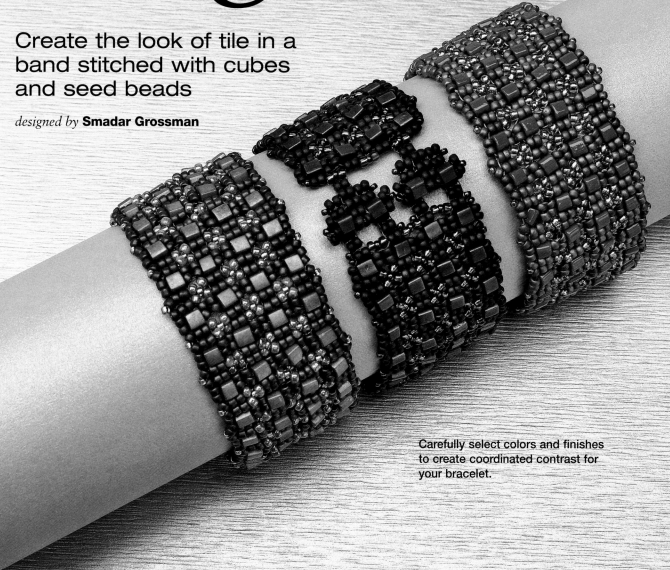

Carefully select colors and finishes to create coordinated contrast for your bracelet.

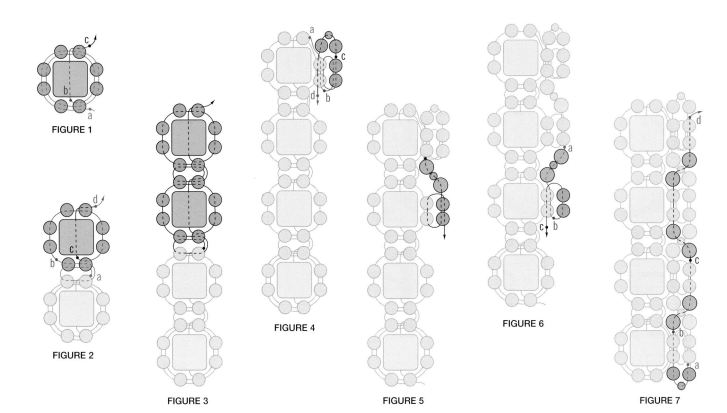

FIGURE 1

FIGURE 2

FIGURE 3

FIGURE 4

FIGURE 5

FIGURE 6

FIGURE 7

materials

bracelet 6½ in. (16.5 cm)

- 4–6 g 3 x 3 mm cube beads
- 11º seed beads
  8–10 g color A
  2–5 g color B
- 1–3 g 15º seed beads
- nylon beading thread, size D, or Fireline 6 lb. test
- beading needles, #12

An ingenious combination of stitches allows you to create this bracelet in one continuous pattern, rather than going back to embellish it later.

stepbystep

Bracelet band
Column 1

[1] On a comfortable length of thread or Fireline, pick up eight color A 11º seed beads, leaving a 30-in. (76 cm) tail. Sew through the beads again to form a ring, and continue through the first A (figure 1, a–b).

[2] Pick up a 3 x 3 mm cube bead, skip four As, and sew through the next A (b–c). There will be two As on each side of the cube.

[3] Working in ladder stitch (Basics, p. 13), pick up two As, and sew through the two adjacent As and the As just picked up (figure 2, a–b).

[4] Working in daisy chain, pick up six As, and sew through the first A picked up in the previous step (b–c). Pick up a cube, skip four As, and sew through the next A (c–d).

[5] Repeat steps 3 and 4 twice (figure 3).

Column 2

[1] Sew through the next two As (figure 4, a–b), and work a ladder stitch with two As (b–c). Pick up an A, a 15º seed bead, and an A, and sew through the two As your thread exited at the start of this step (c–d).

[2] Pick up a color B 11º seed bead, a 15º, a B, and two As. Working in ladder stitch, sew through the pair of As adjacent to the next cube and the two As just picked up (figure 5).

[3] Pick up a B, a 15º, and a B, and sew through the pair of As adjacent to the next cube (figure 6, a–b). Work a ladder stitch with two As (b–c).

[4] Repeat step 2.

[5] Pick up an A, a 15º, and an A, and sew through the pair of As adjacent to the end cube (figure 7, a–b).

[6] Pick up a B, sew through the corresponding 15º, pick up a B, and sew through the next pair of As (b–c). Repeat to the end of the column (c–d), ending and adding thread (Basics) as needed.

Column 3

[1] Pick up six As, and sew through the last two As your thread exited and the first A picked up **(figure 8, a–b)**.

[2] Working in daisy chain, pick up a cube, skip four As, and sew through the opposite A with your needle pointing away from the completed beadwork **(b–c)**.

[3] Work a ladder stitch with two As **(c–d)**.

[4] Sew through the adjacent pair of As in the previous column, pick up four As, and sew through the first A added in the previous step **(d–e)**.

[5] Repeat steps 2–4 twice, and repeat step 2 again to complete the column.

[6] Work steps 1–6 of "Column 2" and 1–5 of "Column 3" until you reach the desired length of the bracelet band (about ¾ in./1.9 cm less than the desired length of the finished bracelet).

Clasp
Toggle rings

[1] Pick up a 15°, and sew through the next pair of As **(figure 9, a–b)**. Pick up a B, a 15°, and a B, and sew through the next pair of As **(b–c)**. Repeat twice **(c–d)**. Pick up a 15°, and sew through all eight As surrounding the end cube **(d–e)**.

[2] Work a ladder stitch with two As **(figure 10, a–b)**. Pick up a 15°, and sew through the pair of As just added **(b–c)**.

[3] Work a ladder stitch with two As **(c–d)**.

[4] Repeat steps 2 and 3, and repeat step 2 again **(d–e)**.

[5] Pick up four As, and sew through the second-to-last pair of As previously added, the last pair of As, and the first two As just added **(e–f)**. Repeat **(f–g)**.

[6] Pick up a 15°, and sew through the last pair of As just added **(g–h)**. Add three pairs of As as in steps 2 and 3 **(h–i)**. When you reach the pair of As adjacent to the next cube, sew through them with a ladder stitch thread path **(i–j)**.

[7] Sew through the beadwork to exit the pair of As adjacent to the next cube. Repeat steps 2–6 to make a second loop, and end the thread.

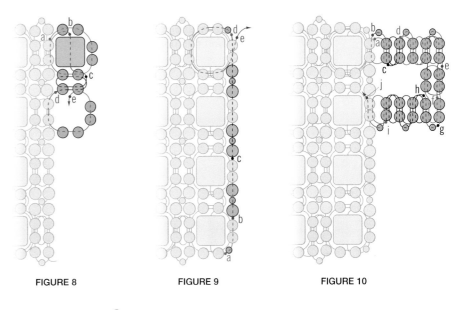

FIGURE 8

FIGURE 9

FIGURE 10

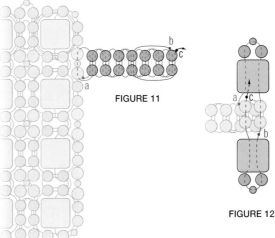

FIGURE 11

FIGURE 12

Toggle bars

[1] Thread a needle on the tail, and repeat step 1 of "Clasp: Toggle rings," but after you pick up the last 15°, sew through the next six As surrounding the end cube.

[2] Sew through the beadwork to exit an end B, 15°, and B just added. Working in ladder stitch, add seven pairs of As **(figure 11, a–b)**. Using a ladder stitch thread path, connect the end pair of As to the middle pair of As **(b–c)**.

[3] Pick up a cube, an A, a 15°, and an A, and sew back through the cube and an adjacent pair of As **(figure 12, a–b)**. Repeat **(b–c)**.

[4] Sew through the beadwork to exit a pair of As that are not connected to a cube, and sew through the cube. Pick up an A, sew through the 15°, pick up an A, and sew through the cube. Sew through the remaining pair of As in the group of four. Repeat on the other side of the toggle bar.

[5] Sew through the beadwork to exit the remaining end B, 15°, and B, and add a second toggle bar as in steps 2–4. End the thread. ●

Square toggle rings mirror the cube theme of the bracelet.

Stitch the ladder strip to fit around any size glass ornament. Just make sure you end up with an even number of four-bugle units.

MULTIPLE STITCHES

Haul *out the* holly

Dress up the holidays with these festive ornaments

designed by **Jamie Cloud Eakin**

DESIGNER'S NOTE:

If the beadwork is too heavy for the ornament, the metal top may pull off when hung. If this happens, remove the metal top, apply E6000 adhesive to the rim of the ornament, and replace the top. Allow the glue to dry overnight.

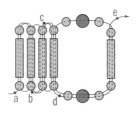

FIGURE 1

FIGURE 2

materials

ornament 2½ in. (6.4 cm) diameter

- 2½-in. (6.4 cm) diameter glass ornament
- 42 7 x 10 mm glass leaves, color B
- 42 8 mm glass flowers, color C
- 42 6 mm round glass beads, color B
- 2 g 6 mm bugle beads, color A
- 42 5 mm metal bicones
- 42 4 mm fire-polished beads, color B
- 98 4 mm fire-polished beads, color C
- 28 4 mm round metal beads
- 20 g 11º seed beads, color A
- 3 g 11º seed beads, color B
- 1 g 11º seed beads, color C
- nylon beading thread, size B
- beading needles, #12
- bobbin or piece of cardboard
- E6000 adhesive (optional)

Combine ladder stitch, fringe techniques, and netting to create an ornament with lots of pizzazz. Substitute colors and styles of seed beads and accent beads to complement your holiday décor.

stepbystep

Ladder strip

[1] Attach a stop bead (Basics, p. 13) to the center of 4 yd. (3.7 m) of thread. Wrap half of the thread around a bobbin or piece of cardboard.

[2] Pick up a color A 11º seed bead, a 6 mm bugle, two A 11ºs, a bugle, and an A 11º. Sew through all the beads again, and snug them up to form two stacks of an A 11º, a bugle, and an A 11º (figure 1, a–b).

[3] Working in three-bead ladder stitch (Basics), pick up an A 11º, a bugle, and an A 11º. Sew through the previous A 11º, bugle, and A 11º, and the new A 11º, bugle, and A 11º (b–c). Repeat (c–d).

[4] Pick up an A 11º, a color C 4 mm fire-polished bead, two A 11ºs, a bugle, two A 11ºs, a C 4 mm, and an A 11º. Sew through the previous A 11º, bugle, and A 11º. Sew through the next six beads (d–e).

[5] Work as in step 3 to stitch a four-bugle unit. Repeat step 4.

[6] Repeat step 5 until you have 14 four-bugle units and 13 C 4 mm units, using the 2-yd. (1.8 m) tail as needed. Zigzag back through the ladder stitches to the other end, and end the working thread and tail (Basics).

Fringe

[1] Add 2 yd. (1.8 m) of thread (Basics) to the ladder, and exit the top of the first stitch of the first four-bugle unit (figure 2, point a).

[2] Pick up an A 11º, and sew through the next A 11º, bugle, and A 11º. Pick up 12 A 11ºs, a color B 4 mm fire-polished bead, a color B 11º seed bead, a 6 mm round glass bead, an A 11º, a 5 mm metal bicone, an A 11º, a C 4 mm, a color C 11º seed bead, a glass flower, a B 11º, a glass leaf, and a B 11º (a–b). Skip the last B 11º, and sew back through the remaining fringe beads

added in this step and the A 11º, bugle, and A 11º (b–c).

[3] Repeat step 2, but begin the fringe by picking up 14 A 11ºs instead of 12 A 11ºs (c–d).

[4] Pick up an A 11º, and sew through the next A 11º, bugle, and A 11º. Pick up five A 11ºs, a 4 mm round metal bead, 12 A 11ºs, a B 4 mm, a B 11º, a 6 mm round, an A 11º, a 5 mm metal bicone, an A 11º, a C 4 mm, a C 11º, a flower, a B 11º, a leaf, and a B 11º (d–e). Skip the last B 11º, and sew back through the next 24 beads to exit the 4 mm round metal bead (e–f). Pick up five A 11ºs, and sew through the first A 11º, bugle, and A 11º in the next four-bugle unit (f–g).

[5] Pick up an A 11º, and sew through the next A 11º, bugle, and A 11º in the unit. Work the next two fringes as a mirror image of the first two (g–h).

[6] Work the next fringe as in step 4, but pick up only one A 11º instead of 12 A 11ºs (h–i).

[7] Add fringe as in steps 1–6, ending and adding thread as needed, to embellish the rest of the ladder strip until you exit the last A 11º, bugle, and A 11º, ending as in step 5. Join the

199

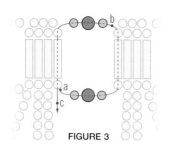

FIGURE 3

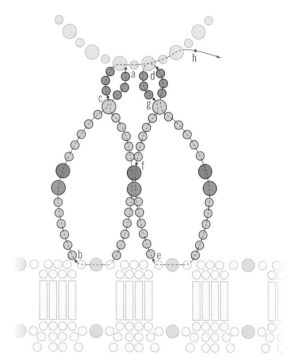

FIGURE 4

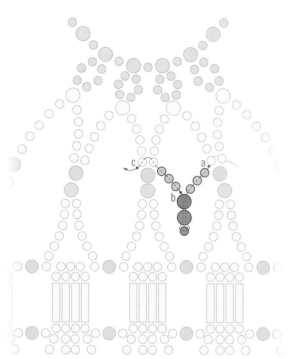

FIGURE 5

ladder into a ring by picking up an A 11º, a C 4 mm, and an A 11º, and sewing through the first A 11º, bugle, and A 11º on the other end of the strip (figure 3, a–b). Pick up an A 11º, a C 4 mm, and an A 11º, and sew through the end A 11º, bugle, and A 11º (b–c). Work the last fringe as in step 4, but pick up only one A 11º instead of 12 A 11ºs. End the working thread and tail.

Assembly

[1] On 2 yd. (1.8 m) of thread or 4 yd. (3.7 m) of doubled thread, pick up a repeating pattern of a B 11º and a B 4 mm 14 times, leaving a 6-in. (15 cm) tail. Sew through the beads again to form a ring, and exit a B 4 mm (figure 4, point a).

[2] Pick up three B 11ºs, a 4 mm round metal bead, five A 11ºs, a C 4 mm, a B 4 mm, and six A 11ºs. Sew through an A 11º, a C 4 mm, and an A 11º on the top edge of the ladder (a–b). Pick up six

A 11ºs, a B 4 mm, a C 4 mm, and five A 11ºs. Sew through the 4 mm round metal bead (b–c). Pick up three B 11ºs, and sew through the B 4 mm your thread exited at the start of this step and the next B 11º and B 4 mm in the ring (c–d).

[3] Pick up three B 11ºs, a 4 mm round metal bead, five A 11ºs, a C 4 mm, a B 4 mm, and six A 11ºs. Sew through the next A 11º, C 4 mm, and A 11º in the ladder (d–e). Pick up six A 11ºs, and sew through the adjacent B and C 4 mms from the previous loop (e–f). Pick up five A 11ºs, and sew back through the 4 mm round metal bead at the top of the new loop (f–g). Pick up three B 11ºs, and sew through the B 4 mm your thread exited at the start of this step and the next B 11º and B 4 mm in the ring (g–h).

[4] Repeat step 3 for a total of 13 loops. Pick up three B 11ºs, a 4 mm round metal bead, and five A 11ºs. Sew

through the first C and B 4 mms in the first loop. Pick up six A 11ºs, and sew through the A 11º, C 4 mm, and A 11º in the ladder. Pick up six A 11ºs, and sew through the B and C 4 mms in the last loop. Pick up five A 11ºs, and sew through the 4 mm round metal bead at the top of the loop. Pick up three B 11ºs, and sew through the B 4 mm your thread exited at the start of this step. End the thread.

[5] Add 1 yd. (.9 m) of thread, and exit the A 11º above a C 4 mm in a loop with the needle pointing toward the fringe (figure 5, point a). Pick up three A 11ºs, a C 4 mm, a B 4 mm, and a B 11º. Skip the B 11º, and sew back through the B and C 4 mms (a–b). Pick up three A 11ºs, and sew through the two A 11ºs above the next C 4 mm (b–c). Repeat around, and end the threads. ●

PEYOTE STITCH / LADDER STITCH / HERRINGBONE STITCH

Tripleplay

Use similar
stitching
techniques to
make a matching
ring, earrings,
and bracelet

designed by **Gohar Breyl**

Metallic-colored seed
beads provide a neutral
background for colorful
bicone crystals.

Crystals light up any piece of jewelry. Wear these pieces as a set for maximum impact or singly for a glittering accent.

step by step

Ring

Band

[1] On 2 yd. (1.8 m) of Fireline, leaving a 6-in. (15 cm) tail, work an even number of ladder stitches (Basics, p. 13) using 11º cylinder beads to make a strip long enough to comfortably fit around your finger. Join the ends to form a ring (Basics).

[2] Work six to eight rounds of tubular herringbone stitch (Basics) to make the band the desired width. Work a ladder stitch thread path through the last round **(photo a)**. End the working thread and tail (Basics).

Medallion base

[1] On 2 yd. (1.8 m) of Fireline, pick up 36 11º seed beads, leaving a 6-in. (15 cm) tail. Tie the beads into a ring with a square knot (Basics), leaving a small amount of slack. Sew through the first 11º again.

[2] Work two rounds of tubular peyote stitch (Basics) using 11º seed beads.

[3] Work three rounds using 10º cylinder beads. Sew through the beadwork to the other edge, and work three rounds using 10ºs **(photo b)**.

[4] Zip up (Basics) the end rounds to form a circular tube, and exit an 11º seed bead in the first round.

[5] Work a round using 11º seed beads **(photo c)**. This round will sit on top of the circular tube. Exit the first 11º added in this step. End the tail but not the working thread.

Crystal inset

[1] On 1 yd. (.9 m) of Fireline, pick up six 11º seed beads, leaving a 6-in. (15 cm) tail. Sew through the beads

materials

all projects
- Fireline 6 lb. test
- beading needles, #12

ring 18.8 mm inside diameter
- 6 4 mm bicone crystals
- 2 g 10º cylinder beads
- 2 g 11º cylinder beads
- 2 g 11º seed beads

pair of earrings
- 110 3 mm bicone crystals
- 4 g 10º cylinder beads
- 4 g 11º seed beads
- pair of earring findings

bracelet 7½ in. (19.1 cm)
- 4 mm bicone crystals
  - **42** color A
  - **6** color B
- 2 g 8º hex-cut cylinder beads
- 6 g 10º cylinder beads
- 8 g 11º cylinder beads
- 2 g 11º seed beads
- 4-loop slide clasp

a

b

c

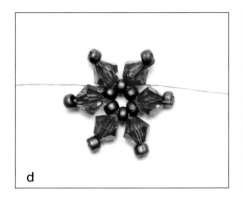

d

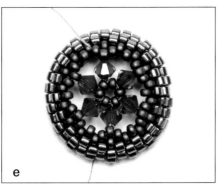

e

f

again to form a ring, and continue through the first bead.

[2] Pick up a color A 4 mm bicone crystal and an 11º. Skip the 11º, and sew back through the A and the next 11º in the ring **(figure 1, a–b)**. Repeat around the ring **(b–c** and **photo d)**. Sew through the first A and 11º picked up in this step **(c–d)**. End the tail but not the working thread.

Assembly

[1] Using the working thread from the medallion base, sew through an 11º at the tip of a 4 mm-and-11º pair on the crystal inset, then sew through the next 11º in the round added in step 5 of "Medallion base." Sew through the next four 11ºs. Repeat around the medallion **(photo e)**. Sew through the beadwork to the back of the medallion base, exiting a 10º in the first round. Do not end the working thread from the medallion base. Using the working thread from the crystal inset, retrace the thread path to secure the connection between the base and the crystal inset. End the working thread from the crystal inset.

[2] Center the medallion base on the ring band. Using the working thread from the medallion base, sew through two cylinders to the left of the middle point of the band with the thread exiting toward the outer edge. Sew through the next 10º in the first round with the thread exiting toward the center of the band **(photo f)**. Sew through the next 10º in the second round and the 10º your thread exited at the start of this step in the opposite direction.

[3] Repeat step 2, working toward the other edge of the band. Retrace the thread path to secure the connection between the medallion and the band.

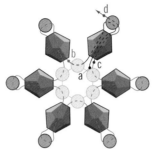

FIGURE 1

[4] Sew through the beadwork to a point opposite where you made the attachment to the band, and repeat steps 2 and 3. End the working thread.

Earrings
Beaded ball

[1] Thread a needle on each end of 1 yd. (.9 m) of Fireline, and center five 3 mm bicone crystals. Cross one of the needles through an end 3 mm to form a ring.

[2] With the left-hand needle, pick up four 3 mms. With the right-hand needle, cross through the last 3 mm picked up **(figure 2, a–b** and **j–k)**.

[3] With the needle that is now the left-hand needle, pick up three 3 mms. With the needle that is now the right-hand needle, sew through the adjacent 3 mm in ring 1, and cross through the last 3 mm picked up **(b–c** and **k–l)**. Repeat twice **(c–d** and **l–m)**.

[4] With the left-hand needle, pick up two 3 mms. With the right-hand needle, sew through the adjacent 3 mms in

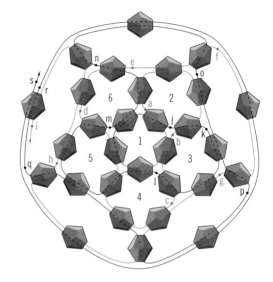

FIGURE 2

rings 1 and 2, and cross through the last 3 mm picked up **(d–e** and **m–n)**.

[5] With the left-hand needle, pick up three 3 mms. With the right-hand needle, sew through the adjacent 3 mm in ring 2, and cross through the last 3 mm picked up **(e–f** and **n–o)**. Snug up the beads to begin forming a ball.

[6] With the left-hand needle, pick up two 3 mms. With the right-hand needle, sew through the adjacent 3 mms in rings 2 and 3, and cross through the last 3 mm picked up **(f–g** and **o–p)**.

[7] Repeat step 6 twice, but sew through the adjacent 3 mms in rings 3, 4, and 5 **(g–h** and **p–q)**.

[8] With the left-hand needle, pick up a 3 mm **(q–r)**. With the right-hand needle, sew through the adjacent beads in rings 5 and 6 and the first 3 mm picked up in step 5, and cross through the 3 mm picked up with the left-hand needle **(h–i)**.

[9] Sew through the top five 3 mms, and snug them up **(r–s)**. Sew through the beads again. End the working thread and tail (Basics).

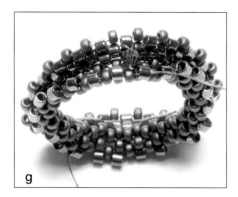

g

h

i

[10] Repeat steps 1–9 to make a second beaded ball.

Medallion base

[1] On 2 yd. (1.8 m) of Fireline, pick up 46 11º seed beads, leaving a 6-in. (15 cm) tail. Tie the beads into a ring with a square knot (Basics), leaving a small amount of slack between the beads. Sew through the first 11º again.
[2] Work two rounds of tubular peyote stitch (Basics) using 11º seed beads.
[3] Work one round using 10º cylinder beads. Sew through the beadwork to the other edge, and work three rounds using 10º cylinders.
[4] Work a round using 11º seed beads. Sew through the beadwork to the other edge, and exit a cylinder.
[5] To connect the end rounds, pick up a 3 mm bicone crystal, and sew through a cylinder on the opposite edge, back through the 3 mm, and through the next cylinder **(photo g)**. Repeat around the ring. Sew through the beadwork, and exit a cylinder on the back edge.

Assembly

[1] Pick up an 11º seed bead, a 3 mm, and the loop of the earring finding, and sew back through the 3 mm. Pick up an 11º, and sew through the base cylinder **(photo h)**. Retrace the thread path two or three times. Sew through the beadwork to exit an 11º opposite the earring finding.
[2] To attach the beaded ball to the base, pick up a 3 mm, sew through a 3 mm in the beaded ball, and sew back through the 3 mm and the base 11º **(photo i)**. Retrace the thread path several times, and end the working thread and tail.
[3] Make a second earring.

Bracelet
Band

[1] On a comfortable length of Fireline, leaving a 12-in. (30 cm) tail, pick up four 11º cylinder beads, and sew through the beads again to form two columns of two beads each. Continue in two-bead ladder stitch (Basics) using two cylinders per stitch for a total of 16 stitches.
[2] Working in flat herringbone stitch (Basics) , make the band the desired length. As you stitch, pick up a 10º cylinder bead as the outside bead on both edges in every other row. End and add thread (Basics) as needed.
[3] Work a ladder stitch thread path through the last two rows.
[4] Center half of the clasp at one end of the band. Sew through the ladder segment, exiting a two-bead column aligned with a clasp loop. Sew through the loop and the adjacent two-bead column. Retrace the thread path twice. Sew through the ladder segment, and repeat to attach the remaining clasp loops. End the thread. Repeat on the other end using the tail.

Crystal inset

[1] On 2 yd. (1.8 m) of Fireline, pick up six 11º seed beads, leaving a 6-in. (15 cm) tail. Sew through the beads again to form a ring, and continue through the first bead.
[2] Pick up a color B 4 mm bicone crystal and an 11º, and sew back through the B, the 11º your thread exited at the start of this step, and the next 11º in the ring **(figure 3, a–b)**. Repeat around the ring **(b–c)**. Sew through the first B-and-11º pair picked up in this step **(c–d)**.

EDITOR'S NOTES:

- To make a smoother transition between the 11º seed beads and the 10º cylinder beads, pick up an alternating pattern of an 11º and a 10º in the appropriate count when you start each project. This will prevent you from pulling the 11ºs too tight. Stitch a round of 10ºs, sew through the beadwork to the other edge, and stitch three rounds of 11ºs, snugging up the 11ºs to reduce the diameter of the inner edge. Complete the remaining rounds as instructed.
- When you stitch the "crystal inset" for the bracelet, work with very snug tension to prevent the beadwork from sagging after it is attached to the medallion base. You may also choose to place a 30 mm glass ring beneath the beadwork to support the crystal inset.

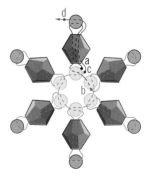

FIGURE 3

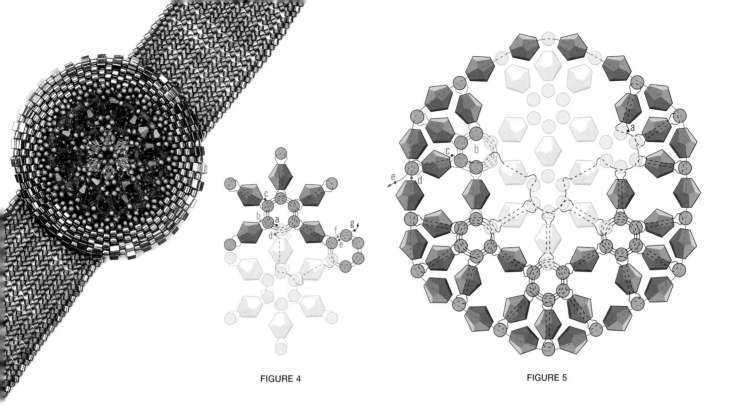

FIGURE 4

FIGURE 5

[3] Pick up five 11ºs, and sew through the 11º your thread exited at the start of this step, all the 11ºs again, and the first 11º picked up in this step (figure 4, a–b).

[4] Pick up a color A 4 mm bicone crystal and an 11º, and sew back through the A, the 11º your thread exited at the start of this step, and the next 11º in the ring (b–c). Repeat four times (c–d). Sew back through the B at the base of this cluster, the next two 11ºs in the center ring, the next B-and-11º pair, and the 11º in the last A-and-11º pair added in this step (d–e).

[5] Pick up four 11ºs, and sew through the next two 11ºs (e–f). Sew through all the 11ºs again, and exit the first 11º picked up in this step (f–g).

[6] Repeat steps 4 and 5 four times (figure 5, a–b), but add four A-and-11º pairs in each cluster.

[7] Pick up three 11ºs, and sew through the next three 11ºs, all the 11ºs again, and the first 11º picked up in this step (b–c).

[8] Pick up an A and an 11º, and sew back through the A, the 11º your thread exited at the start of this step, and the next 11º in the ring. Repeat twice. Sew through the next three 11ºs in the ring and the first A-and-11º pair added in this step (c–d).

[9] Pick up an A, and sew through the 11º in the next A-and-11º pair. Repeat

around the ring (d–e). Retrace the thread path around the outer edge twice. End the working thread and tail.

Medallion base

[1] On 2 yd. (1.8 m) of Fireline, pick up 72 11º seed beads, leaving a 6-in. (15 cm) tail. Tie the beads into a ring with a square knot (Basics), leaving a small amount of slack between the beads. Sew through the first 11º again.

[2] Work two rounds of tubular peyote stitch (Basics) using 11º seed beads.

[3] Work four rounds using 10º cylinder beads.

[4] Work five rounds, alternating a round using 8º hex-cut cylinder beads and a round using 10ºs. Sew through the beadwork to the other edge.

[5] Work four rounds using 10ºs.

[6] Zip up (Basics) the end rounds to form a circular tube, and exit an 11º seed bead in the first round.

[7] Pick up an 11º, and sew through the next 11º in the first round, a 10º in the round of cylinders, and an 11º in the first round. Repeat around the ring, and step up through the first 11º added in this step. Do not end the working thread or tail.

Assembly

[1] With the working thread from the medallion base, pick up an 11º, sew through a 3 mm in the edge of the inset,

pick up an 11º, and sew through the next 11º added in step 5 of "Medallion base." Repeat around the ring. End the threads.

[2] Add a new thread to the back of the medallion base, exiting a 10º. Center the medallion base on the bracelet band.

[3] Sew through a herringbone stitch in the band and the next 10º in the medallion base. Repeat around the curve of the medallion base where it comes in contact with the band. Sew through two rows of stitching, one on the inner and one on the outer curve of the medallion base.

[4] Sew through the medallion base to a point opposite the first connection with the band. Repeat step 3. End the threads. ◗

Other Techniques

Basket bezel

A-tisket, a-tasket, make a woven-wire basket!

designed by **Lisa Barth**

the back of the pendant

A combination of wirework and bead stitching creates a fetching pendant.

stepbystep

Basket weave

[1] Measure the circumference of your 25 x 32 mm cabochon or bead, and add 4 in. (10 cm). Cut five pieces of 20-gauge wire to that length.

[2] Cut 25–30 in. (64–76 cm) of 26-gauge wire. Cross the end of the 26-gauge wire over the end of a 20-gauge wire, leaving about 1 in. (2.5 cm) at the end of each wire. Wrap the 26-gauge wire around the 20-gauge wire three times with the working end of the 26-gauge wire positioned at the top. On the long end of the 20-gauge wire, pick up a color A 11°

seed bead, and snug it up to the wraps **(photo a)**.

[3] On a new 20-gauge wire, pick up an A, and place it just above the previous wire, leaving about 1 in. (2.5 cm) between the A and the end of the wire, and positioning the new A between the previous A and wire wraps. Wrap the 26-gauge wire around the new 20-gauge wire and the previous wire twice, and bring the 26-gauge wire up between the two 20-gauge wires **(photo b)**.

[4] Repeat step 3 three times, but in the last repetition, bring the wire straight down to the first 20-gauge wire. On the end of each 20-gauge

wire, pick up a color B 11° seed bead **(photo c)**, and pull the tips of the wires out a little to leave 1 in. (2.5 cm) at the end of each.

[5] Wrap the 26-gauge wire twice around the first two 20-gauge wires, and bring the 26-gauge wire up between the two 20-gauge wires. Continue the wraps as in steps 3 and 4 **(photo d)**. On the end of each 20-gauge wire, pick up a color C 11° seed bead, and pull the tips of the 20-gauge wires out a little to leave 1 in. (2.5 cm) at the end of each.

[6] Repeat step 5, cycling through A, B, C, and optional D 11° seed beads, hex-cuts, or cylinder beads as desired until the beads reach half the circumference of the cabochon, from top to bottom.

[7] For the turn at the bottom of the cabochon, pick up an 11° on the first three 20-gauge wires, and wrap the 26-gauge wire around the top two 20-gauge wires with the working end of the wire pointing down **(photo e)**.

[8] Pick up an 11° on the first two 20-gauge wires, and continue the wraps as in steps 3 and 4, but work from the top 20-gauge wire to the bottom, then bring the 26-gauge wire to the top of the 20-gauge wires **(photo f)**.

[9] Continue adding 11°s and wrapping the wire as in step 8, cycling through the 11° colors to make a mirror image of the first half of the basket weave **(photo g)**.

[10] When you have made a complete mirror image of the first half, center the 20-gauge

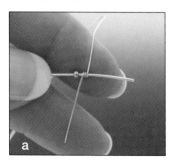

a

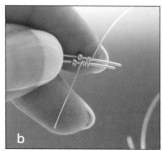

b

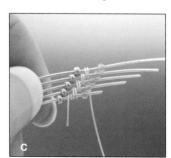

c

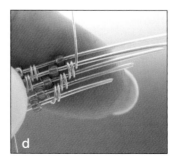

d

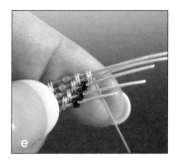

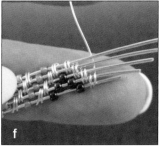

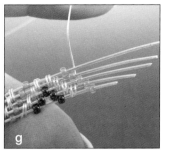

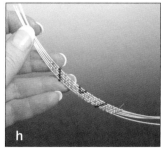

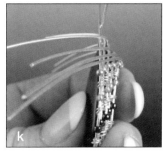

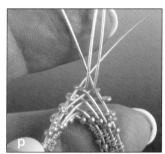

wires in the basket weave (photo h). Wrap the 26-gauge wire three times around the first wire, and trim on the back side of your work. Using chainnose pliers, flatten the 26-gauge wire against the 20-gauge wire. Repeat on the remaining end.

Shaping the bezel
[1] Bend the basket weave in a curve, pressing your finger against the center "V" (photo i). Place the cabochon in the basket weave, and arrange the sides to wrap around the cabochon.
[2] Interlace the ends of the wires. Test the fit, making sure the ends of the innermost wire cross so that the perimeter is slightly smaller than the face of the cabochon, and the ends of the remaining wires fan out so the wires hug the sides of

the cabochon. Bend the ends of the wires so they curve over the opposite side of the bezel (photo j).
[3] Bend the ends of the wires toward the back of the bezel, snugging the cabochon inside it (photo k).
[4] Trim each end of the innermost wire about ¼ in. (6 mm) past each edge of the outermost wire (photo l).
[5] Using roundnose pliers, make a simple loop at each end of the wire trimmed in the previous step, and hook the loops around the outermost wire (photo m).

[6] Repeat steps 4 and 5 with the second and third wires. Do not trim the fourth and fifth wires (photo n).
[7] Bend the ends of the fourth wire so they cross in the back of the bezel (photo o). Then bend them straight up at the center (photo p).
[8] Bend the ends of the fifth wire straight up to align with the ends of the fourth wire,

and string the 8 mm large-hole bead over all four wires (photo q). Test the fit of the cabochon inside the bezel, and bend the wires to adjust them if needed.
[9] Using three-step pliers or roundnose pliers, place the ends of the wires in the jaws so they line up next to each other. Bend the wires back so they touch the 8 mm, and

materials
pendant 1 x 2¼ in. (2.5 x 5.7 cm)
- 25 x 32 mm oval or pear-shaped cabochon or bead (approximate size)
- 8 mm large-hole bead
- 1–3 g 11º seed beads, hex-cuts, or cylinder beads in each of **3–4** colors: A, B, C, (D optional)
- 1 g 15º seed beads
- 25–30 in. (64–76 cm) 20-gauge silver or gold wire, half-hard
- 25–30 in. (64–76 cm) 26-gauge silver or gold wire, half-hard
- Fireline 6 lb. test
- beading needles, #12
- chainnose pliers
- roundnose pliers
- three-step pliers (optional)
- wire cutters

r

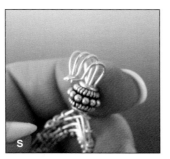

s

t

u

FIGURE 1

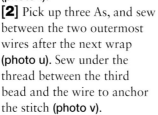

v

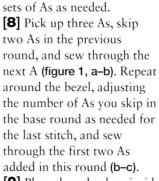

w

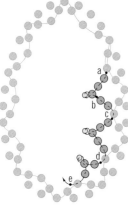

FIGURE 2

FIGURE 3

trim the ends so they end at the midpoint of the 8 mm (photo r).

[10] Using chainnose pliers, grab the ends of the wires, and bend them straight out. Spread the wires so they fan out slightly (photo s), and tuck the end of each wire inside the hole of the 8 mm.

Netting

[1] Center a needle on 2 yd. (1.8 m) of Fireline, and tie an overhand knot (Basics, p. 13) with the ends. Sew between the two outermost wires after the first wrap, and anchor the thread by sewing between the threads next to the knot (photo t).

[2] Pick up three As, and sew between the two outermost wires after the next wrap (photo u). Sew under the thread between the third bead and the wire to anchor the stitch (photo v).

[3] Repeat step 2 until you reach the stitch before the center "V" at the bottom of the bezel.

[4] Pick up five As, sew between the two outermost wires and the two sets of center wraps (photo w), and anchor the stitch.

[5] Pick up five As for the next stitch, and then continue around the bezel as in step 2 with three As per stitch.

[6] At the top of the bezel, pick up three As, and anchor the stitch on the opposite side of the bezel. If needed to complete the round, continue with three As per stitch until you reach the first stitch.

[7] If there are gaps between the sets of As, sew through a set of As, pick up an A, and sew through the next set of As. Continue around the bezel, adding an A between sets of As as needed.

[8] Pick up three As, skip two As in the previous round, and sew through the next A (figure 1, a–b). Repeat around the bezel, adjusting the number of As you skip in the base round as needed for the last stitch, and sew through the first two As added in this round (b–c).

[9] Place the cabochon inside the bezel.

[10] Pick up three Bs and a 15º seed bead. Skip the 15º, and sew back through the last B (figure 2, a–b). Pick up two Bs, and sew through the middle A of the previous round (b–c).

[11] Repeat step 10 to the stitch before the bottom of the bezel (c–d).

[12] Work a stitch as in step 10, but pick up two Bs and a 15º, skip the 15º, sew back through the last B, pick up a B, and sew through the middle A of the previous round (d–e). Repeat.

[13] Repeat step 10 to the top of the bezel, and then repeat step 12.

[14] If any gaps remain, repeat step 10 until you reach the first group of Bs. Sew up through the first three Bs and 15º added.

[15] Pick up three 15ºs, and sew through the next 15º (figure 3, a–b). Repeat around, adding just two 15ºs between the picots at the bottom and top of the bezel (b–c). Sew through the round of 15ºs again, and end the thread and tail (Basics). ●

EDITOR'S NOTE:
If the ratio of your pendant to the wire bezel differs from the designer's, adjust the number of beads per stitch in "Netting," or use 15º seed beads instead of Bs in steps 10–15.

Autumn garland

materials

bracelet 6½ in. (16.5 cm)

- 15º seed beads
  10 g color A (flower, main color)
  3 g color B (flower, accent color)
  3 g color C (leaves, inner-round, light color)
  4 g color D (leaves, inner round, medium color)
  10 g color E (leaves, outer round, dark color)
- 3-strand box clasp
- **21** crimp beads
- 13½–14 ft. (4.1–4.3 m) 26- or 28-gauge craft wire, color A or B
- 17–20 ft. (5.2–6.1 m) 26- or 28-gauge craft wire, color E
- 5 ft. (1.5 m) flexible beading wire, .014–.018
- chainnose or crimping pliers
- wire cutters
- toothpick (optional)

Use one simple technique to make a lush floral garland for your neck or wrist

designed by **Alla Maslennikova**

A profusion of French beaded leaves and flowers makes a pretty-as-a-picture accessory. If you want to make a choker, as shown here, refer to the Designer's Note on p. 213 for suggested adaptations to the bracelet instructions.

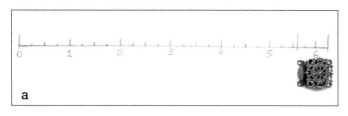

a

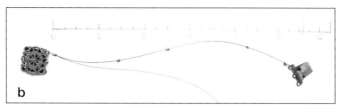

b

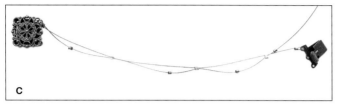

c

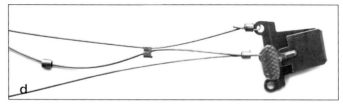

d

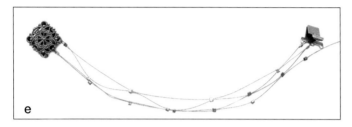

c

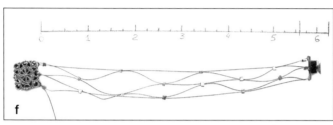

d

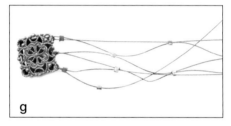

e

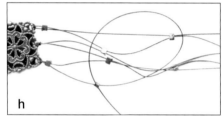

f

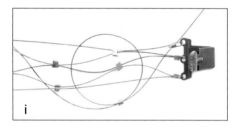

g

h

i

In this simplified version of the French beaded flower technique, loops of seed beads on wire make an adorable array of sweet blossoms and leaves. Arrange them on a base of flexible beading wire for a comfortable, stunning accessory.

stepbystep

Bracelet base

[1] Measure your wrist, add ⅜ in. (1 cm), and mark this length on a piece of paper. Place the clasp at one end, within the marked distance **(photo a)**. Remove half of the clasp, and place it at the other end, aligning it with the other clasp half. The area between the clasp halves will make up the body of the bracelet.

[2] Cut 5 ft. (1.5 m) of beading wire. On one end, string a crimp bead and one clasp loop. Go back through the crimp bead, but don't crimp it.

[3] On the long end, string four crimp beads, then go through the corresponding loop on the other half of the clasp. Go back through the last crimp bead added **(photo b)**. Check that the wire between

the clasp halves is the correct length, and use chainnose or crimping pliers to crimp the crimp bead (Basics, p. 13) your wire just went through.

[4] Pick up a crimp bead, and go through the next crimp bead on the previous strand. Repeat twice. Adjust the tension of the wire so that the working strand forms small swags and the overall piece is slightly curved **(photo c)**, then crimp the three crimp beads on the previous strand that the working strand just went through. The crimp beads on the working strand will remain uncrimped until step 5. Pick up a crimp bead, go through the next loop on the first clasp half, go back through the crimp bead **(photo d)**, and crimp it.

[5] Repeat step 4 twice to make two more strands **(photo e)**.

[6] To add the final strand, go through the crimp beads on the previous strand without adding crimp beads. After going through the last crimp bead on the previous strand, pick up a crimp bead, go through the final clasp loop, and go back through the crimp bead. Adjust the tension so the piece straightens out **(photo f)**, and crimp the crimp bead just added. Do not trim the excess wire, and note that the very first crimp bead added in step 2 is still uncrimped.

[7] To stabilize the base, string a crimp bead, then weave the wire over and under the strands in the base, making sure you've gone past some of the crimped crimp beads **(photo g)**. Loop it around, weave it through the base, and go through the crimp bead added in this step again to form a loop **(photo h)**. Do not crimp it yet.

[8] Repeat step 7 twice to make two more loops, then go through the uncrimped crimp bead from step 2 **(photo i)**. Adjust all the loops, and crimp the four uncrimped crimp beads. Trim the excess wire, and set the base aside.

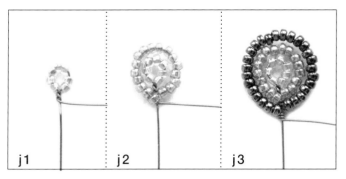

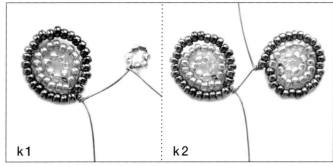

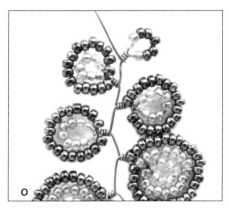

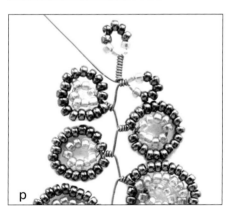

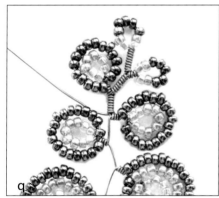

Branches

[1] Cut 20–24 in. (51–61 cm) of color E craft wire. Make a seven-leaf branch as follows:

Leaf 1: Leaving a 2-in. (5 cm) tail, string seven color C 15º seed beads, make a loop, and twist the working wire around the tail **(photo j1)**. If needed, insert a toothpick into the loop to give the loop a nice round shape. Pick up enough color D 15º seed beads to make a loop around the previous loop, and twist the working wire around the tail **(photo j2)**. Repeat with color E 15º seed beads to make a third loop **(photo j3)**.

Leaf 2: Begin another three-loop leaf, securing the first loop of Cs about ¼–⅜ in. (6 mm–1 cm) away from the previous leaf **(photo k1)**. Complete as for leaf 1 **(photo k2)**.

Leaf 3: Continuing with the working wire, make a two-loop leaf: Make the first loop with two Cs, five Ds, and two Cs. Make the second loop with Es **(photo l)**.

Leaf 4: Repeat leaf 3 **(photo m)**.

Leaf 5: Make another two-loop leaf, but make the first loop with two Cs, three Ds, and two Cs **(photo n)**.

Leaf 6: Make a one-loop leaf with one C, one D, five Es, one D, and one C **(photo o)**.

Leaf 7: Repeat leaf 6 **(photo p)**. If needed, reposition the leaves so they zigzag from side to side up the stem.

[2] Coil the working wire around the stems between the top four leaves **(photo q)**, and set the branch aside. Do not trim the wires.

[3] Repeat steps 1 and 2 to make a total of 10–13 branches, varying the size and quantity of leaves as desired and making three branches with Es only.

DESIGNER'S NOTE:
You can use this same technique to make a choker. Begin with 5 yd. (4.6 m) of beading wire to make the base, then make about 33 branches, three large flowers, 10 medium flowers, and 20 small flowers.

r1

r2

s

t

u

v

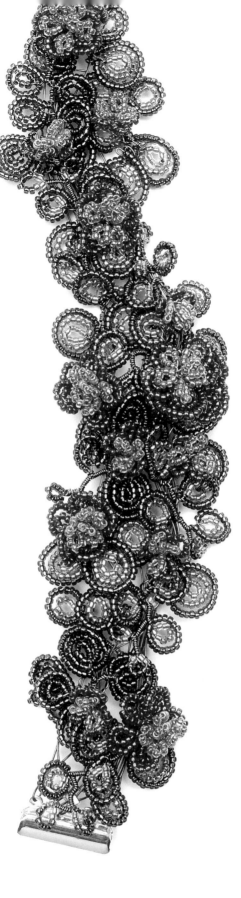

Flowers

[1] Cut 25–28 in. (64–71 cm) of color A or B craft wire, and make a large flower as follows:

Layer 1: Using color B 15° seed beads, make a loop of seven beads, leaving a 2-in. (5 cm) tail. Repeat to make a total of six loops in a row **(photo r1)**. Twist the working wire around the tail, then form a five-petal flower, placing one loop in the center **(photo r2)**.

Layer 2: Using color A 15° seed beads, make a two-loop petal right next to layer 1 the same way you made the two-loop leaves **(photo s)**. Repeat until you have made five two-loop petals **(photo t)**. Twist the working wire around the tail, forming the second layer of petals around layer 1.

Layer 3: Using As, make five three-loop petals **(photo u)**. Twist the working wire around the tail, forming the third layer around the previous layer. Set this large flower aside. Make another large flower if desired.

[2] To make a medium flower, cut 14 in. (36 cm) of wire, and work as in layers 1 and 2. Repeat to make a total of four or five medium flowers.

[3] To make a small flower, work as in step 2, but make only three loops of Bs in layer 1 and make one-loop petals instead of two-loop petals in layer 2. Repeat to make a total of five or six small flowers, but make some with seven-bead loops and some with nine-bead loops **(photo v)**.

Assembly

[1] Figure out where you want to position the branches on the base. Intersperse the one-color branches evenly among the three-color branches **(photo w)**.

[2] Select a branch to attach to the base. Coil the working wire around the stem and a strand in the base near a leaf connection point **(photo x)**. Make two to three coils. Continue coiling the wire around the stem until you reach the 2-in. (5 cm) tail. Coil the tail around a strand in the base two or three times, and bring both the working wire and the tail out to the front of the bracelet. Do not trim.

[3] Repeat step 2 to attach the remaining branches along the base, hiding the crimp beads as well as possible and overlapping the branches somewhat.

[4] When all of the branches have been attached, there will be a pair of wires sticking out from the end of each branch. These wires will be used to attach the flowers, and ideally there will be a pair for each flower you've made. Decide where you want to place each flower **(photo y)**.

[5] Choose a flower, and twist its 2-in. (5 cm) tail together with the pair of wires from the corresponding branch. Start near the base of the flower and branch **(photo z)**.

[6] Wrap the twisted wires three or four times around the neck of the flower where it is attached to the branch **(photo aa)**. Trim the excess wire, and straighten the flower.

[7] Repeat steps 5 and 6 to attach the remaining flowers. If you have flowers left over and no branch to attach them to, simply coil the tails around a branch wire a few times, then secure and finish it as in step 6. ○

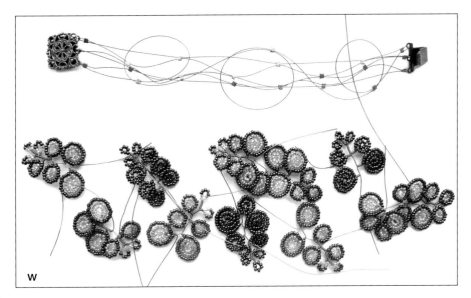

w

x

y

z

aa

Dream weaver

Make a woven-wire bracelet that incorporates a mixture of beads

designed by **Louise Duhamel**

materials

bracelet 8½ in. (21.6 cm)

- **180–200** 2–4 mm beads in a mixture of colors
- **76–80** 2 mm spacers
- 30 in. (76 cm) 16-gauge silver, gold, copper, or craft wire, dead-soft
- 5 yd. (4.6 m) 24-gauge silver, gold, copper, or craft wire
- ½-in. (1.3 cm) diameter mandrel, pen, or marker
- tape
- chainnose pliers
- roundnose pliers
- wire cutters

Use an easy wire-weaving technique to create this funky, eclectic bracelet with an integrated clasp.

step by step

[1] Cut a 20-in. (51 cm) piece of 16-gauge wire. Fold it in half around a ½-in. (1.3 cm) diameter mandrel or the barrel of a pen or marker. Cross the wire ends, and twist them together twice next to the mandrel **(photo a)**.

[2] Cut a 10-in. (25 cm) piece of 16-gauge wire. Using roundnose and chainnose pliers, make a small, tight spiral at one end of the wire, and bend the spiral back to make a hook **(photo b)**.

[3] Cut 1 yd. (.9 m) of 24-gauge wire, and wrap one end around the 10-in. (25 cm) piece of 16-gauge wire, keeping the wraps close together to form tight coils for about ¼ in. (6 mm). Snug up the coils to the spiral, trim the tail of the 24-gauge wire, and flatten it against the 16-gauge wire **(photo c)**.

[4] Overlap the spiral hook of the 10-in. (25 cm) piece of 16-gauge wire on top of the twist in the 20-in. (51 cm) piece of 16-gauge wire **(photo d)**. Tape the wires together to keep them in place, if desired.

[5] Weave the 24-gauge wire around the three 16-gauge wires by wrapping twice around an outer wire, once around the center wire, and twice around the remaining outer wire, keeping the wire bridge between the wraps on the top side of the wire frame. Turn, and repeat the wraps, but keep the wire bridge on the underside of the wire frame **(photo e)**.

a

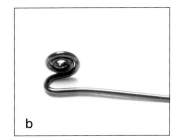

b

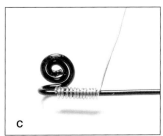

c

d

e

f

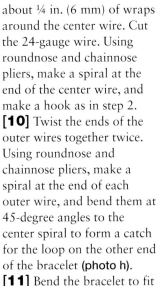

g

h

Continue the wraps for about ¼ in. (6 mm), gradually increasing the distance between the wires of the frame. Every other row of wraps will have a bridge of 24-gauge wire on the top of the frame, while the alternating rows of wraps will have a bridge on the underside of the frame.

[6] With the 24-gauge wire on the top side of the frame, pick up a 2–4 mm bead, and wrap around the center wire. Pick up a 2–4 mm, and wrap around the remaining outer wire. Work a row of wraps with the bridges on the underside. Work a row of wraps without beads, and work another row of wraps with the bridges on the underside (photo f).

[7] Maintaining the gradual increase in the distance between the outer wires, and adding an increasing number of 2–4 mm beads and spacers in each segment, repeat step 6 for about 3¼ in. (8.3 cm) (photo g). The last row should have about seven beads and spacers in each segment. When necessary, end a 24-gauge wire by trimming and flattening the wire close to the frame, and add a new wire by wrapping it around the center wire and

trimming and flattening the tail close to the frame.

[8] Continue as in steps 6 and 7, but gradually decrease the distance between the edges of the wire frame, and decrease the number of beads and spacers so the second half of the bracelet is a mirror image of the first.

[9] Make about ¼ in. (6 mm) of wraps around the end of the frame, and make about ¼ in. (6 mm) of wraps around the center wire. Cut the 24-gauge wire. Using roundnose and chainnose pliers, make a spiral at the end of the center wire, and make a hook as in step 2.

[10] Twist the ends of the outer wires together twice. Using roundnose and chainnose pliers, make a spiral at the end of each outer wire, and bend them at 45-degree angles to the center spiral to form a catch for the loop on the other end of the bracelet (photo h).

[11] Bend the bracelet to fit your wrist. ◗

EDITOR'S NOTE:
If you want to place the bead bridges closer together, omit making the row of wraps without beads between the rows with beads in step 6.

Parisian nights earrings

The bronzy tones of vintage-style chain and filigree complement a faceted crystal bead

designed by **Ann Dee Allen**

materials

pair of earrings
- 2 18 mm large-hole Swarovski crystals (mosaic sand opal)
- 2 6 mm round copper beads
- 10 8º bronze seed beads
- 2 16 mm filigree bead caps
- 7 in. (18 cm) 22-gauge vintage bronze wire
- 12 in. (30 cm) decorative brass chain, 2 mm links
- pair of brass earring findings
- chainnose pliers
- roundnose pliers
- wire cutters

With just a few supplies and 15 minutes, you can whip up these snazzy earrings.

stepbystep

[1] Cut a 1½-in. (3.8 cm) piece of wire, and make a plain loop (Basics, p. 13).

[2] Cut three 1¾-in. (4.4 cm) pieces of chain. Open the plain loop (Basics), and attach a central link of each chain so that it hangs at two lengths. Close the loop.

[3] String five 8º seed beads, an 18 mm crystal, and a filigree bead cap (photo). Snug up the bead cap, crystal, and plain loop, hiding the seed beads inside the crystal. Make a plain loop.

[4] Cut a 1¾-in. (4.4 cm) piece of wire, and make a wrapped loop (Basics). String a 6 mm copper bead, and make a wrapped loop.

[5] Open the plain loop at the top of the crystal unit, and attach it to one of the wrapped loops. Close the loop. Open the loop of an earring finding, and attach it to the other wrapped loop. Close the loop.

[6] Make a second earring. ◗

WIREWORK

Fine-scale earrings

Delicate wraps connect wire components and suspend a focal briolette

designed by **Erin Paton**

Shape, wrap, and weave a gorgeous wire frame to highlight an equally gorgeous briolette.

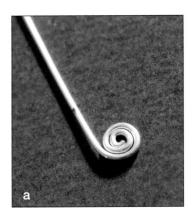

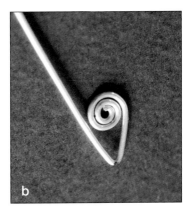

step by step

Earring frame

[1] Cut a 4¾-in. (12.1 cm) piece of 20-gauge wire. Using roundnose and flatnose pliers, make a small, tight spiral approximately 5 mm in diameter at one end of the wire (photo a).

[2] Mark the wire 7 mm from the center of the spiral. Using flatnose pliers, make a sharp bend at this point (photo b).

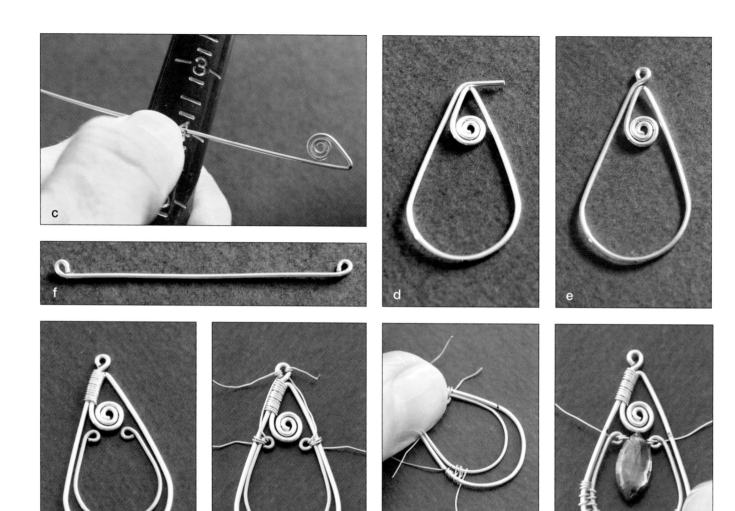

[3] Mark the wire 3.5 cm from the bend. Place this point at the size 4 mark on a ring mandrel (photo c), and bend the wire around the mandrel to form a U shape.

[4] Mark the point where the wire tail meets the top of the frame. Measure 8 mm from the mark, and cut the wire at this point. Using flatnose pliers, bend the wire over the top of the frame (photo d).

[5] Using roundnose pliers, make a small simple loop (photo e).

[6] Gently hammer the frame with a plastic mallet to work-harden the wire.

[7] Cut a 4¾-in. (12.1 cm) piece of 28-gauge wire. Wrap the section of the frame where the wires are parallel to each other, between the loop made in step 5 and the spiral. Trim the tails, and use flatnose pliers to flatten the ends.

[8] Repeat steps 1–7 to make a second earring frame that is a mirror image of the first.

Inner embellishment

[1] Cut a 1⅞-in. (4.8 cm) piece of 22-gauge wire. Make a small loop at each end of the wire, turning them both inward (photo f). Bend the wire around the mandrel at the size 1.5 mark to form a U shape. Place the U-shaped wire inside the earring frame (photo g), and mark where the loops meet the sides of the frame.

[2] Using scrap 26- or 28-gauge wire, wrap the wire around the U and the earring frame through the loops and at the top of the frame to prevent the U from slipping (photo h).

[3] Cut a 14-in. (36 cm) piece of 28-gauge wire. On each side of the frame, mark a point ⅜ in. (1 cm) below the connection of the U and earring frame. At one of these marks, wrap the wire around the earring frame three times. Using a figure-8 motion and keeping an even tension, weave back and forth between the U and the frame (photo i) until you reach the remaining mark. Wrap the wire three times around the earring frame. Trim the tails, and flatten the ends.

[4] Remove the scrap wire added in step 2.

[5] Cut a 4-in. (10 cm) piece of 28-gauge wire. Mark the midpoint of the wire. Slide the wire through one loop of the U from back to front, and position the mark inside the loop. Make a wrap around the inner part of the loop.

[6] String a briolette on the wire, slide the wire through the opposite loop from

k

l

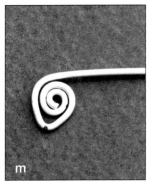

m

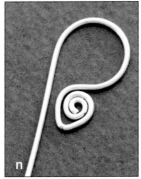

n

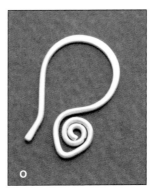

o

materials

pair of earrings

- 2 10 x 5 mm briolettes
- 2 3 mm round beads
- 4 2 mm round beads
- 15 in. (38 cm) 20-gauge wire
- 3¾ in. (9.5 cm) 22-gauge wire
- 1.5 yd. (1.4 m) 28-gauge wire
- scrap 26- or 28-gauge wire
- 8 mm dowel (optional)
- anvil or bench block
- file or emery board
- plastic mallet
- ring mandrel
- washable marker
- flatnose pliers
- roundnose pliers
- flush wire cutters

back to front, and make a wrap around the inner part of this loop (photo j).

[7] With the wire on the underside of the frame, make two or three wraps around the earring frame. Repeat on the other side of the frame using the tail from step 5 (photo k). Trim the wire to the underside of the frame.

[8] Cut a 4-in. (10 cm) piece of 28-gauge wire. Mark the midpoint of the lower edge of the earring frame. Make two wraps 2 mm to one side of the midpoint mark.

[9] String a 2 mm round bead, a 3 mm round bead, and a 2 mm on the wire. Make two wraps 2 mm to the other side of the midpoint mark. Trim the wire to the underside of the earring frame (photo l).

[10] Repeat steps 1–9 to embellish the second earring frame.

Earring finding

[1] Cut a 2¾-in. (7 cm) piece of 20-gauge wire. Using roundnose and flatnose pliers, make a 4 mm diameter spiral. Mark 3 mm from the spiral, and bend the wire to form a V at the base of the spiral (photo m).

[2] Wrap the wire around an 8 mm mandrel or dowel (photo n). Cut the wire to the desired length, make a slight bend about 3 mm from the end, and file the end (photo o). Hammer the earring finding if desired.

[3] Repeat steps 1 and 2 to make a second earring finding.

Assembly

[1] Slide the end of an earring finding through the loop at the top of a frame.

[2] Repeat step 1 to assemble the second earring. ●

WIREWORK

Free-form
for all

Use a clever tool to coil wire,
and then wind it through a
free-form necklace

designed by **Leah Hanoud**

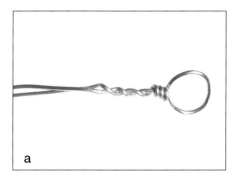

a

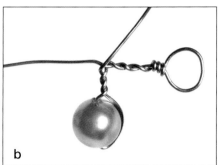

b

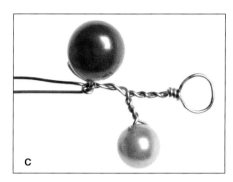

c

d

e

f

Can't keep the symmetry out of asymmetrical designs? A randomly winding wire coil has an abstract effect in this beaded collar.

stepbystep

Necklace frame

[1] Cut a 4-ft. (1.2 m) piece of 24-gauge craft wire. At the center of the wire, make a wrapped loop (Basics, p. 13), but do not trim the wrapping wire. Instead, bend the wrapping wire down to make it parallel to the other wire. Twist the wires together for ¼ in. (6 mm) to begin the twisted "core" of the necklace frame (photo a).

[2] On one wire, string a 6–8 mm bead, and slide it down to within ¼ in. (6 mm) of the core. Bend the wire around the bead and back toward the core. Holding the wire against the bead, twist the bead a few times. This creates a twisted "branch" connecting the bead to the core (photo b). Twist the wires together for ¼ in. (6 mm) to continue the core.

[3] Using the longer of the two wires, repeat step 2, positioning the new bead on the opposite side of the core as the previous bead (photo c). Repeat for the length of the necklace frame, keeping in mind the following:

• Gradually increase the size of the beads as you work toward the center of the necklace frame.

• To help the necklace lie properly when worn, add smaller beads to one side of the core and larger beads to the other side. When you add a large bead

to one side of the core, you may need to add two or three smaller beads on the opposite side to balance it.

• As you work, curve the necklace frame so the smaller beads are on the inside of the curve and the larger beads are on the outside of the curve.

• When your wires get short, cut a new 4-ft. (1.2 m) piece of 24-gauge craft wire. Fold the wire in half, creating two parallel wires. Starting 1 in. (2.5 cm) back from where your previous wires ended, thread the new parallel wires between two branches so the core rests in the fold (photo d). Wrap the two new parallel wires around the core one at a time. Where the two previous wires end, begin twisting the two new wires together to continue the core (photo e). Using chainnose pliers, tuck the ends of the previous wires into the core.

• When your necklace frame is 7–8 in. (18–20 cm) long, gradually decrease the size of the beads, working the second half of the necklace frame as a mirror image of the first. Reserve two 6–8 mm beads for the clasp.

[4] Make a wrapped loop, and trim the excess wire. Bend the twisted branches to create the desired look.

Coil embellishment

[1] Cut a 4-ft. (1.2 m) piece of 24-gauge craft wire. Wrap one end around the wraps of the wrapped loop on one end of the necklace frame (photo f).

[2] Cut a piece of 24-gauge craft wire appropriate to the coiling tool you're using, and coil the wire on a 2 mm mandrel. Remove the coil from the mandrel.

materials

necklace 15–17 in. (38–43 cm)

- **5** 20 mm round gemstone beads
- **6** 16 mm round gemstone beads
- **10–12** 12 mm round gemstone, crystal pearl, or wood beads
- **14** 10 mm round gemstone, crystal pearl, or wood beads
- **12–16** 10 mm faceted gemstone lentil beads or coin pearls
- **8** 8 x 14 mm faceted gemstone rondelles, or a mixture of **15–20** 8 mm round gemstone beads and **15–20** 6 mm round crystal pearls
- **20–40** 8 mm faceted gemstone rondelles or button pearls
- 2 in. (5 cm) 18-gauge wire
- spool of 24-gauge craft wire
- 2½ in. (6.4 cm) chain, 15–17 mm links
- 1½-in. (3.8 cm) head pin
- **2** 6 mm jump rings
- coiling tool with 2 mm round mandrel, such as the Twist 'n' Curl or Coiling Gizmo
- chainnose pliers
- roundnose pliers
- wire cutters

EDITOR'S NOTES:

- **When you reserve two 6–8 mm beads in "Necklace frame" step 3, test to make sure that one of the beads' holes will accommodate the 18-gauge wire you'll use for the clasp.**
- **Try using colored craft wire to give your necklace an extra pop of color.**

g

[3] Slide the coil onto the wire added in step 1. Wrap the coil around the beads as desired **(photo g)** until you run out of coil. Wrap the wire from step 1 once or twice around the core where the coil ends.

[4] Repeat steps 2 and 3 until you reach the other end of the necklace frame. Wrap the end of the wire around the wraps of the wrapped loop, and trim the excess wire.

Clasp

[1] Cut an 18-in. (46 cm) piece of 24-gauge craft wire, and use the coiling tool and 2 mm mandrel to make a 1-in. (2.5 cm) coil.

[2] Cut a 2-in. (5 cm) piece of 18-gauge wire. Make a plain loop (Basics) on one end. String a 6–8 mm bead and the 1-in. (2.5 cm) coil, and make another plain loop perpendicular to the first. Curve the coil into a hook clasp **(photo h).**

[3] Open a 6 mm jump ring (Basics), and attach the loop of the hook clasp just below the 6–8 mm bead and the wrapped loop on one end of the necklace frame.

[4] Cut a 2½-in. (6.4 cm) piece of chain. Open a jump ring, and attach an end link of the chain and the wrapped loop on the other end of the necklace frame.

[5] On a head pin, string a 6–8 mm bead, and make the first half of a wrapped loop. Slide the remaining end link of chain into the loop, and complete the wraps. ●

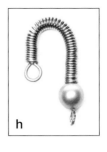

h

A coiled clasp continues the necklace design.

Whether you hammer or file your tubing, adding texture takes copper to a whole new level.

Can't-beat-copper earrings

A hardware-store staple goes glam with texture and a no-fuss patina

designed by **Kimberly Berlin**

materials

pair of earrings

- at least 6 in. (15 cm) copper tubing, ¼–⅜-in. (6 mm–1 cm) diameter
- **4–6** 6–8 mm metal, gemstone, or crystal rondelles, round beads, or bicone beads
- 7 in. (18 cm) 22-gauge wire (optional)
- **2** 2-in. (5 cm) head pins
- pair of earring findings
- bench block or anvil
- clear, non-yellowing satin urethane spray for metals, such as Minwax Helmsman Spar Urethane Clear Satin spray or Rust-Oleum Ultra Cover Satin clear spray
- metal file
- permanent marker in the color of your choice
- polishing cloth or paper towel
- scrap flexible beading wire
- texture hammer, cross-peen hammer, or ball-peen hammer
- wire clothes hanger
- chainnose pliers
- roundnose pliers
- tube-holding or tube-cutting pliers (optional)
- tube cutter
- wire cutters

Copper tubing and tube cutter may be found at hardware stores.

With silver and gold prices still inflated, it's smart to harvest copper tubing from your local hardware store. Texture and trim the metal to make tube beads, then have some fun coloring to create a patina in the recesses. Now you're set to string simple earrings!

step by step

[1] Place one end of the tubing on a bench block or anvil. Using a texture hammer or the peen (back end) of a cross-peen or ball-peen hammer, gently strike the end of the tubing to texture the metal **(photo a)**. Hammer up to ¼–½ in. (6 mm–1.3 cm) from the end, then slowly rotate the tubing to texture all the way around. Reposition the tubing on the bench block or anvil to add texture from another direction. Alternatively, file the tubing with even strokes to create a subtle texture.

[2] Using tube-holding pliers, tube-cutting pliers, or your fingers, grasp the tubing above the texture. Place the tubing in the tube cutter so the blade is positioned at the end of the texture. Tighten the screw of the cutter until the blade touches the tubing **(photo b)**, then tighten the screw a quarter turn more.

[3] Holding the tubing still, rotate the tube cutter twice around the tubing. You should notice the blade scoring the surface of the metal. Tighten the screw a quarter turn more, and repeat. Continue tightening the screw and rotating the cutter until the end of the tubing falls off. File the ends of the textured tube.

[4] Color the textured tube with a permanent marker **(photo c)**, then quickly rub it off with a polishing cloth or paper towel, leaving the color in the texture marks. Color the ends of the tube if desired.

[5] Repeat steps 1–4 to make a second textured tube bead.

[6] String a tube bead on a piece of scrap beading wire, and tie the ends of the wire together. Repeat with the other bead. String each beading wire loop over the neck of a clothes hanger, and arrange the beads so they do not touch. In a well-ventilated area, evenly spray the beads with clear satin urethane. This seals the copper, protecting it from oxidation. Let the beads dry overnight.

[7] For a short earring dangle: On a head pin, string a 6–8 mm bead, a tube bead, and a 6–8 mm bead. Make a wrapped loop (Basics, p. 13). Open the loop (Basics) of an earring finding, attach the wrapped loop, and close the loop.

a

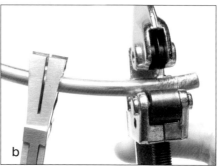

b

c

EDITOR'S NOTE:
If your pliers mark up the metal in step 2, place a small square of non-slip drawer liner in the jaws before grasping the tubing.

For a longer earring dangle: On a head pin, string a 6–8 mm bead, and make a wrapped loop. Cut a 3½-in. (8.9 cm) piece of 22-gauge wire, and make the first half of a wrapped loop. Slide the dangle into the loop, and complete the wraps. String a 6–8 mm bead, a tube bead, and a 6–8 mm bead, and make a wrapped loop. Open the loop of an earring finding, attach the top wrapped loop, and close the loop.
[8] Repeat step 7 to make a second earring. ○

DESIGNER'S NOTES:
• Hammering too hard in step 1 could cause the tubing to collapse.
• If using a file to texture the tubing, larger file grooves will produce a rougher texture, which will show the marker better.
• If you are using tubing finer than ¼ in. (6 mm), use a jeweler's saw to cut the tubing. Also, consider using tube-cutting pliers (like the ones shown in photo b). They have a slit through the jaws to accommodate the saw blade.

Fine-gauge tubing may be too delicate to hammer, but it makes for a smooth and dainty version of these earrings.

Mio cuore

Mio cuore means "my heart," but this copper pendant requires no translation

designed by **Linda Fordyce**

a

b

Shape copper wire into a heart, add some loops, and adorn with seed beads to create a lovely pendant.

stepbystep

[1] Cut an 8–10-in. (20–25 cm) piece of 16-gauge wire. Mark the center of the wire with a permanent marker.

[2] Position the largest part of the roundnose pliers on the center mark, and curve the ends around the top jaw of the pliers to make a loop (photo a).

[3] Using your fingers, curve the wire ends to begin forming the heart shape. Make one lobe slightly larger than the other (photo b).

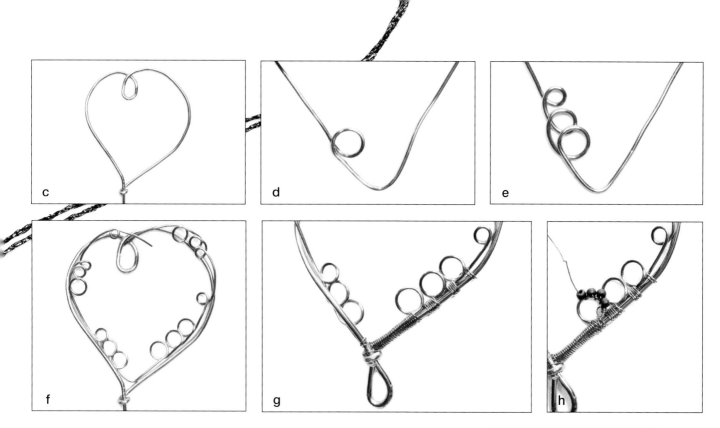

c

d

e

f

g

h

[4] Straighten one wire where the two wires intersect at the bottom of the heart frame. Wrap the other wire around the straight wire, and trim the excess wrapping wire **(photo c)**.

[5] Using roundnose pliers, make a loop at the end of the straight wire, and trim the excess wire.

[6] Cut a 24-in. (61 cm) piece of 20-gauge wire. Mark the center of the wire with a permanent marker, and bend the wire at that point to form a V. Position the roundnose pliers ¼ in. (6 mm) from the bend, and wrap the wire around the pliers to make a loop **(photo d)**.

[7] Reposition the roundnose pliers next to the previous loop, and make another loop. Repeat to make a series of slightly stacked loops **(photo e)** long enough to fit around one lobe of the heart frame to the center loop at the top. Vary the size and spacing of the loops as desired.

[8] Repeat step 7 with the other half of the wire. Place the series of loops in the heart frame so that the bend is aligned with the point of the heart and the ends meet near the center loop at the top **(photo f)**.

[9] Cut a 1½-yd. (1.4 m) piece of 28-gauge wire. Starting at the bottom of the heart and leaving a 3-in. (7.6 cm) tail, wrap the 28-gauge wire around

the heart frame and the looped wire **(photo g)**. Continue all around the heart, connecting the loops to the frame. Trim the excess wire from each end, and press the ends close to your work.

[10] Cut a 12-in. (30 cm) piece of 28-gauge wire. Leaving a 2-in. (5 cm) tail, wrap the wire twice around the first loop. String an 11º seed bead, and wrap the wire around the loop. Continue adding 11ºs around the loop **(photo h)**. To finish the ends, twist the tail and working wire together four or five times, trim the ends, and press them close to your work.

[11] Repeat step 10 for the remaining loops, cycling through all the colors of 11ºs.

[12] Cut a 2-in. (5 cm) piece of 20-gauge wire. Make a plain loop (Basics, p. 13) on one end, string an 11º, an 8 mm round crystal, and an 11º, and make another plain loop.

[13] Open the loop (Basics) at the top of the dangle, and attach it to the loop at the bottom of the heart frame. Close the loop.

[14] Open the 5 mm jump ring, attach the large lobe of the heart frame, and close the jump ring. String as desired. ✿

materials

pendant 2½ in. (6.4 cm)
- 8 mm round crystal
- 1–3 g 11º seed beads in each of **2–5** colors
- 8–10 in. (20–25 cm) 16-gauge copper wire
- 26 in. (66 cm) 20-gauge copper wire
- 3 yd. (2.7 m) 28-gauge copper wire
- 5 mm jump ring
- permanent marker
- chainnose pliers
- roundnose pliers
- wire cutters

EDITOR'S NOTE:

Use this pendant as an embellishment when wrapping a special gift or designing a scrapbook page.

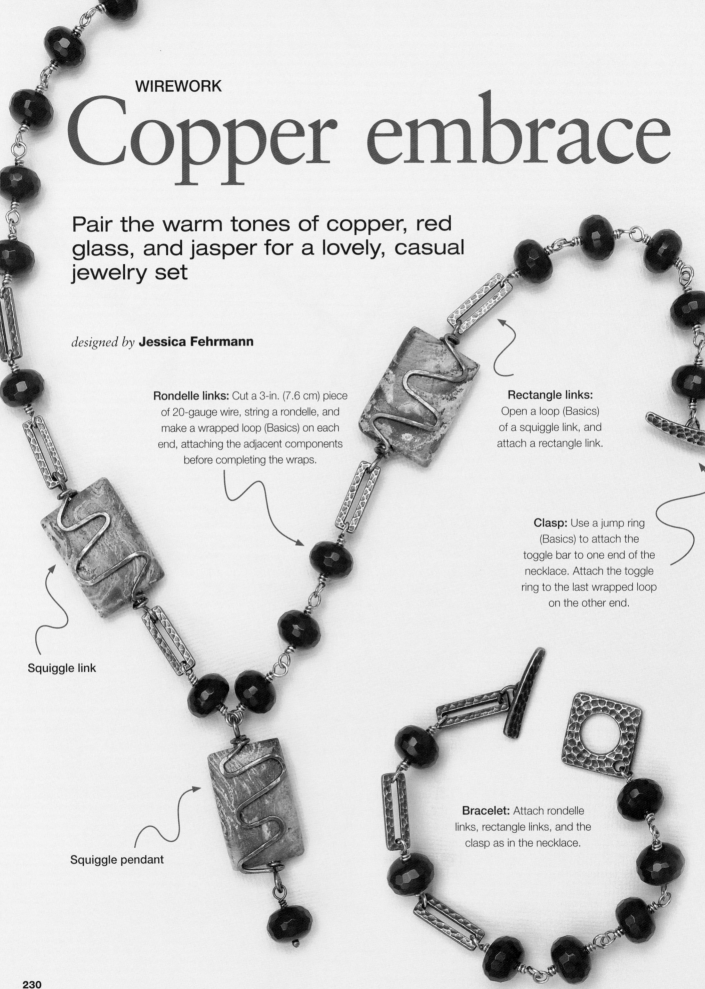

WIREWORK
Copper embrace

Pair the warm tones of copper, red glass, and jasper for a lovely, casual jewelry set

designed by **Jessica Fehrmann**

Rondelle links: Cut a 3-in. (7.6 cm) piece of 20-gauge wire, string a rondelle, and make a wrapped loop (Basics) on each end, attaching the adjacent components before completing the wraps.

Rectangle links: Open a loop (Basics) of a squiggle link, and attach a rectangle link.

Clasp: Use a jump ring (Basics) to attach the toggle bar to one end of the necklace. Attach the toggle ring to the last wrapped loop on the other end.

Squiggle link

Squiggle pendant

Bracelet: Attach rondelle links, rectangle links, and the clasp as in the necklace.

Squiggly arms of wire hold gemstones in place, making them easy to use in a necklace of wrapped loops. Use leftover beads for a matching bracelet.

stepbystep

Squiggle links

[1] Cut a 5-in. (13 cm) piece of 16-gauge wire, and make a plain loop (Basics, p. 13) on one end.

[2] Using roundnose pliers, grasp the wire ¼ in. (6 mm) below the plain loop. Pull both ends of the wire around the pliers, making a U-shaped turn in the same plane as the loop.

[3] Continue making U-turns to create a "squiggle," making sure it is no wider than the 20 x 30 mm rectangle beads. When your squiggle is the same length as the bead (not counting the plain loop made in step 1), trim the wire to ½ in. (1.3 cm), and make another plain loop **(photo a)**. Adjust the loops as necessary so they align with the holes of the rectangle bead.

[4] Repeat steps 1–3 to make a second squiggle component, but in step 3, make the squiggle 2–3 mm longer than the rectangle bead.

[5] Place a squiggle component on an anvil or bench block, and hammer both sides of the squiggle. Do not hammer the plain loops. Hammer the other squiggle component.

a

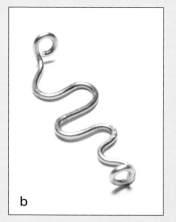

b

c

d

[6] Using chainnose pliers, grasp a plain loop on a squiggle component, and bend it perpendicular to the squiggle. Repeat with the other plain loop, bending it parallel to the first **(photo b)**. Repeat to bend the loops of the other squiggle component.

[7] Place the shorter squiggle component from step 3 on a rectangle bead. Since hammering may have lengthened the component, you might need to adjust the squiggle: Using roundnose pliers, grasp a U-turn, and pull to the side. Repeat until the plain loops on each end of the component are snug against the bead holes.

[8] Holding the shorter squiggle component against one side of the rectangle bead, place the longer squiggle component on the other side. Adjust the squiggle as in step 7 until the plain loops are snug against the plain loops of the shorter squiggle component.

[9] Cut a 4-in. (10 cm) piece of 16-gauge wire, and make a plain loop on one end. String a loop of the longer squiggle component, a loop of the shorter squiggle component, and a rectangle bead. Position one squiggle component on each side of the rectangle bead, then string the remaining loops of

materials

both projects
- chainnose pliers
- roundnose pliers
- wire cutters

necklace 19 in. (48 cm)
- **3** 20 x 30 mm rectangle beads (striped jasper)
- **16** 8 x 12 mm faceted glass rondelles (red)
- **5** 6 x 18 mm hammered rectangle links
- toggle clasp
- 42 in. (1.1 m) 16-gauge wire (copper)
- 45 in. (1.2 m) 20-gauge wire (copper)
- 1½-in. (3.8 cm) head pin (copper)
- 5–6 mm jump ring (copper)
- anvil or bench block
- hammer

bracelet 8 in. (20 cm)
- **7** 8 x 12 mm faceted glass rondelles (red)
- **3** 6 x 18 mm hammered rectangle links
- toggle clasp
- 21 in. (53 cm) 20-gauge wire (copper)
- 5–6 mm jump ring (copper)

the squiggle components. Trim the wire to ½ in. (1.3 cm), and make a plain loop **(photo c)**.

[10] Make a total of three squiggle links.

Squiggle pendant

On a head pin, string an 8 x 12 mm rondelle, and make the first half of a wrapped loop (Basics). Attach a plain loop of a squiggle link, and complete the wraps **(photo d)**. ●

Twisted lantern pendant

Adjust a custom-woven cage to surround any size focal bead

designed by **Lisa Barth**

materials

pendant

- 25 x 15 mm focal bead
- **2** 6 mm round accent beads
- **10** 4 mm round sterling silver beads
- **10** 3 mm round beads to match focal bead
- **2** 10-hole bead caps
- 5 in. (13 cm) 18-gauge round sterling silver wire
- 20 in. (51 cm) 21-gauge round sterling silver wire, half-hard
- 2½ yd. (2.3 m) 26-gauge round sterling silver wire, half-hard
- Fireline 6 lb. test
- embroidery needles, #12
- chainnose pliers
- roundnose pliers
- wire cutters

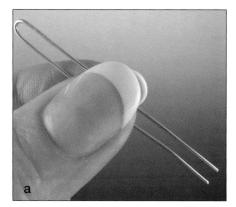
a

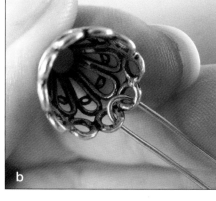
b

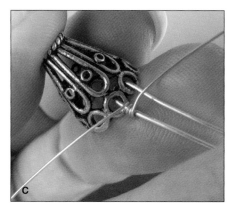
c

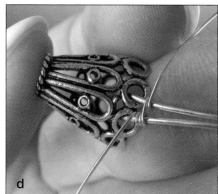
d

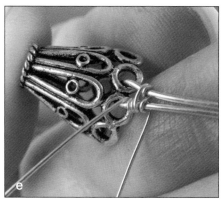
e

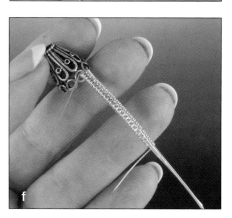
f

Embellish a pair of filigree bead caps with accent beads to enhance a gemstone or lampworked focal bead.

stepbystep

[1] Cut a 4-in. (10 cm) piece of 21-gauge wire. Using roundnose pliers, fold the wire in half **(photo a)**.

[2] Push the ends of the folded base wire through two holes in a bead cap **(photo b)**.

[3] Cut an 18-in. (46 cm) piece of 26-gauge wire. Leaving a 1-in. (2.5 cm) tail, wrap it three times around the lower base wire next to the bead cap. End with the weaving wire positioned on top of the upper base wire **(photo c)**.

[4] Wrap once around the upper base wire, pulling the weaving wire between the two base wires. End with the weaving wire positioned upward **(photo d)**.

[5] Pull the weaving wire under the upper and lower base wires, then wrap once around the lower base wire. End with the weaving wire positioned downward **(photo e)**.

[6] Repeat steps 4 and 5 24 times **(photo f)**. Do not trim the wires.

g

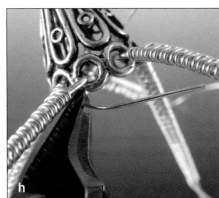

h

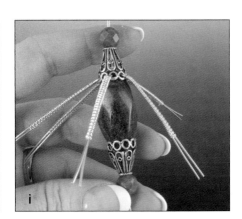

i

j

k

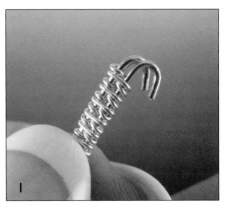

l

m

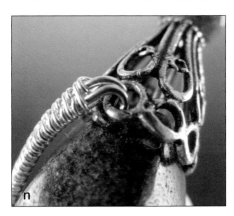

n

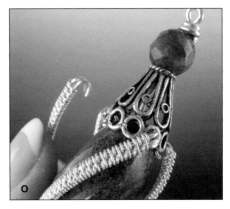

o

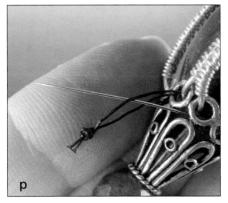

p

q

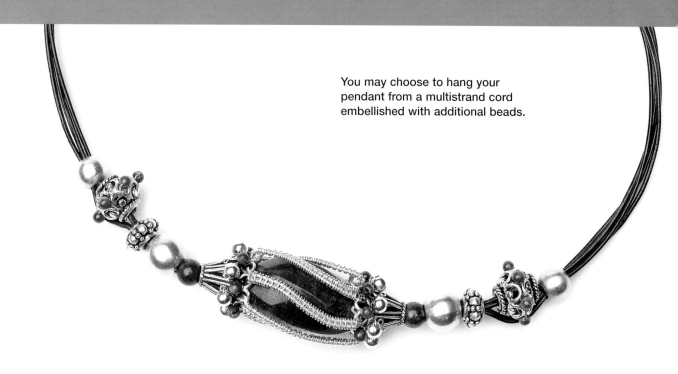

You may choose to hang your pendant from a multistrand cord embellished with additional beads.

DESIGNER'S NOTES:

- If you are using a different size focal bead, lengthen or shorten the base wires. Lay the bead caps next to your focal bead, and measure the distance between them. Make the base wire ½ in. (1.3 cm) longer than that measurement.

- To wear the pendant, thread two 16-in. (41 cm) pieces of leather cord through each wrapped loop, slide an 8 mm large-hole round sterling silver bead and a large-hole spacer over the doubled cords, and attach a clasp.

[7] Repeat steps 1–6 for a total of five woven prongs (photo g). If you are using a six- or eight-hole bead cap, repeat two or three more times as appropriate. Trim the tails of the weaving wires next to the bead cap (photo h), and press them close to the base wires. Repeat to trim the weaving wires at the other end of the base wires.

[8] Cut a 5-in. (13 cm) piece of 18-gauge wire. String a 6 mm round accent bead, the bead cap with the woven prongs, the focal bead, the remaining bead cap, and a 6 mm, and center them on the wire (photo i).

[9] Make a wrapped loop (Basics, p. 13) on each end (photo j).

[10] Position a woven prong next to the focal bead. Grasp the unattached ends with chainnose pliers, and gently pull the woven prong toward an opening in the opposite bead cap offset by one opening from the connection point on the other bead cap (photo k).

[11] Trim the ends of the base wires, leaving ¼-in. (6 mm) tails between the weaving and the end of the wire. Using roundnose pliers, make a small hook on the end of each wire (photo l).

[12] Tuck both hooks into a hole in the bead cap. Using roundnose pliers, pull the wire beneath the bead cap base

(photo m), and rotate each hook into a loop (photo n).

[13] Repeat steps 10–12 to attach the remaining woven prongs (photo o).

[14] Center a needle on 2 yd. (1.8 m) of Fireline, and tie an overhand knot (Basics) with the ends. Sew through an opening in the bead cap, pulling the knot next to it. Sew back through the doubled Fireline (photo p), and pull to tighten.

[15] Pick up a 3 mm round bead, and sew through the next opening in the bead cap, positioning the bead on top of the ends of the prong. Repeat around the bead cap (photo q).

[16] Repeat step 15 to add the 4 mm round sterling silver beads between the beads added in step 15 (photo r). End the working thread (Basics).

[17] Repeat steps 14–16 on the other bead cap. ◕

Chain of command

Forge a chain mail bracelet with copper jump rings and a burst of colorful beads

designed by **Arja Aalto-Viittala**

Make a handmade clasp like the designer's, or use a ready-made clasp from the store.

a

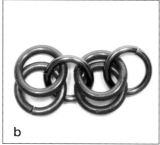

b

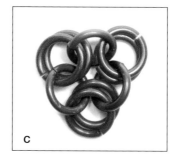

c

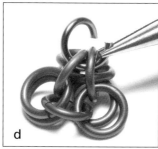

d

e

f

g

An easy chain mail weave called round mail works up fast in this gratifying bracelet. Beaded wire links add a pleasing dash of color.

stepbystep

Bead links

[1] Cut a 3-in. (7.6 cm) piece of 21-gauge copper wire, and make a wrapped loop (Basics, p. 13). String an 8 mm bead, and make another wrapped loop.

[2] Repeat step 1 for a total of nine bead links, and set them aside.

Chain mail

[1] Open 123 4.8 mm jump rings (Basics), and close four.

[2] Slide an open jump ring through the four closed jump rings, and close it.

[3] Position the five-ring chain so the first and last pair of jump rings are parallel to the work surface on either side of the single jump ring **(photo a)**.

[4] Slide an open jump ring through the last two closed jump rings in the chain, and close it **(photo b)**.

[5] Slide two open jump rings through the jump ring added in step 4, and close them.

[6] Slide an open jump ring through the first two jump rings and the last two jump rings in the chain, and close it to form a ring **(photo c)**.

[7] Position the single jump rings on top. Cut a 6-in. (15 cm) piece of 21-gauge wire, and weave it through the remaining six jump rings to stabilize your work.

[8] Slide an open jump ring through two of the adjacent single jump rings, and close it **(photo d)**. Repeat twice to connect the second and third single jump rings and the third and first single jump rings.

[9] Repeat step 8 seven times.

[10] Slide an open jump ring through two adjacent rings and a loop of a bead link, and close it. Repeat twice for a total of three bead links.

[11] Slide an open jump ring through the remaining loop of a bead link, and close it. Repeat for the remaining two bead links.

[12] Repeat steps 8–11 twice.

[13] Repeat step 8 eight times.

Clasp

[1] Cut a 4-in. (10 cm) piece of 17-gauge wire. Using roundnose pliers, turn up one end. Using chainnose or flatnose pliers, press the end to the wire **(photo e)**.

[2] About ¼ in. (6 mm) from the first bend, use roundnose pliers to bend the wire back toward the first bend, making a small hook as shown **(photo f)**.

[3] About ½ in. (1.3 cm) from the curve of the hook, use flatnose pliers to bend the wire straight back toward the hook, and squeeze it together to make a tongue **(photo g)**.

materials
bracelet 8½ in. (21.6 cm)
- **9** 8 mm beads
- **127** 4.8 mm inside-diameter (ID) copper jump rings, 17-gauge
- 3 in. (7.6 cm) 16-gauge copper wire
- 6 in. (15 cm) 17-gauge copper wire
- 2 yd. (1.8 m) 21-gauge copper wire
- liver of sulfur (optional)
- chainnose pliers
- flatnose pliers
- roundnose pliers
- wire cutters

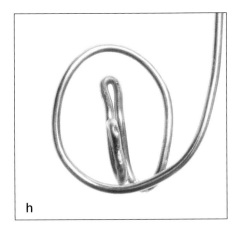

h

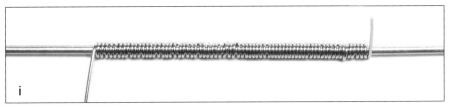

i

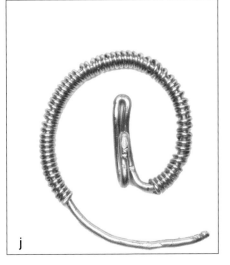

j

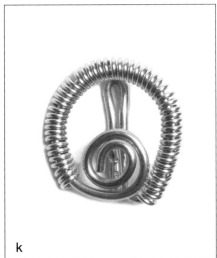

k

[4] Using your fingers, form the wire into a ½-in. (1.3 cm) loop **(photo h)**, leaving a 3-in. (7.6 cm) tail.

[5] Cut a 3-in. piece of 16-gauge wire and a 1-yd. (.9 m) piece of 21-gauge wire. Center the 21-gauge wire on the 16-gauge wire, and coil half of the 21-gauge wire around it, keeping the coils straight and snugging them right next to each other. Repeat with the other half of the 21-gauge wire until the coil is 2 in. (5 cm) long **(photo i)**.

[6] Slide the coil off the 16-gauge wire, and slide it onto the ½-in. loop **(photo j)**. Trim the coil if it extends past the ½-in. loop.

[7] Using roundnose pliers, make a decorative spiral with the tail of the wire **(photo k)**.

[8] Cut a 2½-in. (6.4 cm) piece of 17-gauge wire. With roundnose pliers, form a decorative spiral on one end of the wire. Place the roundnose pliers ¼ in. (6 mm) from the coil, and bend the wire back toward the coil. Place the roundnose pliers on the wire below the coil, and make a gentle right-angle bend

back toward the coil. Make a plain loop (Basics and **photo l**).

Finishing

[1] Remove the scrap wire from the chain mail portion of the bracelet.

[2] Open and remove a jump ring from each pair of jump rings added in steps 1–6.

[3] Slide an open jump ring through two adjacent jump rings on one end of the bracelet and through the coiled loop of the first half of the clasp, and close the jump ring. Repeat to connect a different pair of adjacent jump rings to the coiled loop.

[4] Repeat step 3 on the other end of the bracelet with the other half of the clasp. ◉

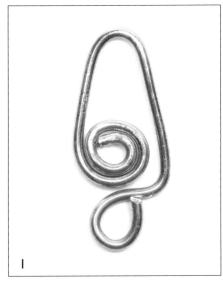

l

EDITOR'S NOTE:
To patinate your jump rings, you can submerge them in liver of sulfur, following the manufacturer's instructions. Polish the surface to bring out more of the copper color.

Reversible chain reaction

Make a striking bracelet with a hybrid pattern of interlocking chain mail weaves

designed by **Vanessa Walilko**

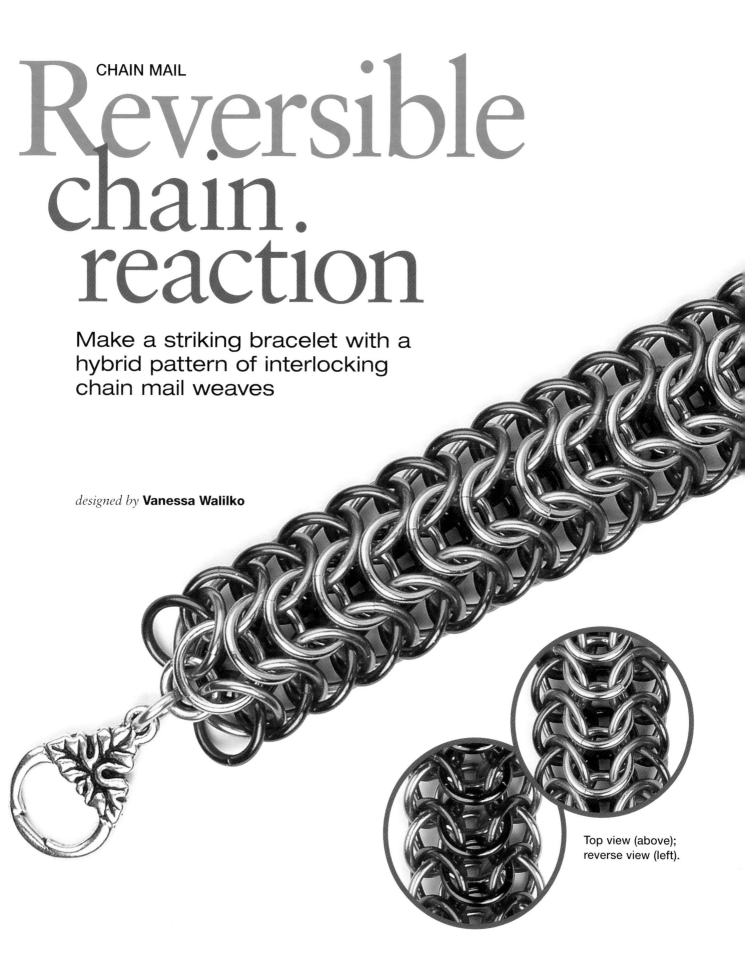

Top view (above);
reverse view (left).

materials

warm-tone bracelet
7 in. (18 cm)

- 6 mm inside-diameter (ID) anodized aluminum jump rings, 18-gauge
  62 color A (orange)
  62 color B (red)
  30 color C (gold)
  30 color D (brown)
- 3.9 mm ID anodized aluminum jump rings, 18-gauge
  4 color C (gold)
  2 color D (brown)
- 2 3 mm ID anodized aluminum jump rings, 18-gauge (brass)
- toggle clasp (gold plated)
- **2** pairs of pliers

cool-tone bracelet colors:

- color A (black)
- color B (blue)
- color C (silver)
- color D (gray)

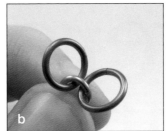

Begin with a basic European 4-in-1 chain, add half-Persian edging, and connect the edges to create a double-sided bracelet.

stepbystep

4-in-1 base

[1] Close all of the color A 6 mm jump rings, and open all the remaining jump rings (Basics, p. 13).
[2] Slide a color C 3.9 mm jump ring through two As, and close it (photo a).
[3] Hold the C added in the previous step so the As flare out above the C (photo b). Slide a color C 6 mm jump ring through two new As, then slide it down through the front of the right-hand A and up through the back of the left-hand A added in the previous step, and close it (photo c).
[4] Repeat step 3 to add the remaining As.

[5] Slide a C 3.9 mm down through the front of the last right-hand A and up through the back of the last left-hand A, and close it (photo d).

Half-Persian edging

[1] At the starting end of the 4-in-1 base, begin working on the right-hand side of the chain. Slide a color B 6 mm jump ring up through the back of the second A and down through the front of the first A, and close it (photo e).
[2] Slide a B up through the back of the third A and down through the front of the second and first As, and close it (photo f), making sure you are placing the new B behind the previous B added. Repeat this step to the end of the base.

[3] At the end of the right-hand side, slide a B through the front of the last two As, and close it (photo g).
[4] Go back to the starting end of the base to work on the left-hand side. Slide a B up through the back of the first A and down through the front of the second A, and close it (photo h).
[5] Slide a B up through the back of the first and second As and down through the front of the third A, and close it (photo i), making sure you're placing the new B behind the previous B.

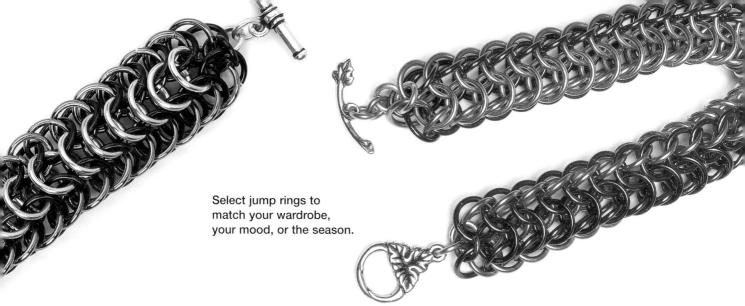

Select jump rings to match your wardrobe, your mood, or the season.

Repeat this step for the length of the base.

[6] At the end of the left-hand side, slide a B through the back of the last two As, and close it (photo j).

Joining the edges

[1] Go back to the starting end of the bracelet, and flip it over. Run your finger down the spine of As to make the Bs flip in toward the center. This is the position they need to be in as you join them. Slide a color D 3.9 mm jump ring down through the end B on the right-hand side and up through the end B on the left-hand side, and close it (photo k).

[2] Slide a color D 6 mm jump ring down through the first and second Bs on the right-hand side and up through the second and first Bs on the left-hand side, and close it (photo l).

[3] Slide a D 6 mm down through the second and third Bs on the right-hand side and up through the third and second Bs on the left-hand side, and close it (photo m). Continue in this manner to connect the remaining edge links.

[4] At the end of the bracelet, slide a D 3.9 mm down through the last B on the right-hand side and up

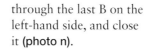

through the last B on the left-hand side, and close it (photo n).

Toggle clasp

[1] Slide a C 3.9 mm through the toggle ring and the D 3.9 mm and C 3.9 mm on one end of the bracelet, and close it (photo o).

[2] Slide a C 3.9 mm through the D 3.9 mm and C 3.9 mm on the other end of the bracelet, and close it.

[3] Slide a 3 mm jump ring through the C 3.9 mm added in the previous step, and close it. Slide another 3 mm jump ring through this 3 mm and the toggle bar, and close it (photo p). ❍

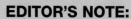

EDITOR'S NOTE:
It's important to work with the same surface facing up for the 4-in-1 base and half-Persian edging. To make sure you're always working on the right side, mark the first 3.9 mm ring with a twist tie: Fold the twist tie in half, guide the fold through the ring, and pull the twist tie ends through the fold to make a lark's head knot with the folded loop on the top surface of the chain. Then, if you drop the chain, you'll be able to figure out which surface is the top.

Layered chains

Make a classic bracelet with an easy chain mail weave

designed by **Anne E. Mitchell**

Two plus two equals one great gift idea in this elegant and easy bracelet (and yes, it's okay to give it to yourself!).

Process photos by Anne E. Mitchell

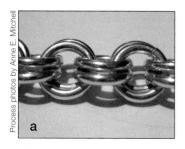

a

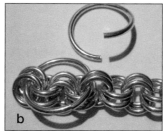

b

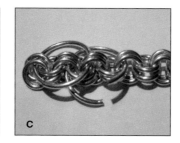

c

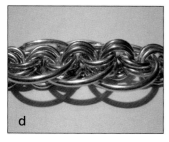

d

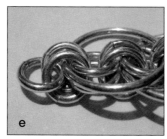

e

f

materials

bracelet 8 in. (20 cm)
- **21** 12 mm inside-diameter (ID) jump rings, 16-gauge
- **92** 4.5 mm ID jump rings, 16-gauge
- lobster claw clasp
- **2** pairs of pliers

EDITOR'S NOTE:

If you want to make a mixed-metal version of this chain, it can be hard to find these exact jump ring sizes in other metals. Our editors experimented a bit and found a different combination of sizes that worked (below): ⁹/₆₄ in., 18-gauge raw copper rings and 4 mm, 18-gauge matte gold-colored niobium rings for the 2+2 chain. Instead of the 16-gauge 12 mm rings, this bracelet uses 17-gauge 10 mm sterling rings, linking them through the niobium rings.

A basic 2+2 chain gets an upscale look with the addition of a second layer of rings. This fast-and-easy bracelet provides instant gratification, even for absolute chain mail beginners.

stepbystep

[1] Open 44 and close 46 4.5 mm jump rings (Basics, p. 13). Slide two closed rings onto an open ring, and close it. Slide another open ring through the same two closed rings, and close it. This is called doubling. Spread out the rings to make the start of a 2+2 chain.
[2] Slide an open ring through a pair of rings, slide on two more closed rings, and close the open ring. Double the new ring. Continue in this manner **(photo a)** until the

2+2 chain is 45 pairs long or the desired length.
[3] Open all the 12 mm jump rings.
[4] Slide a 12 mm ring through the first pair of 4.5 mms on one end. Skip the next three pairs, slide the ring through the fifth pair of 4.5 mms, and close the 12 mm **(photo b)**.
[5] Guide an open 12 mm under the previous 12 mm, and slide it through the third and seventh pairs of 4.5 mms **(photo c)**. Close the 12 mm. Notice that the 12 mms go through the vertical pairs of

4.5 mms and skip over the horizontal pairs.
[6] Repeat step 5, sliding the new ring through pairs five and nine **(photo d)**. Continue in this manner, moving down the chain by one pair of vertical 4.5 mms for each repetition, until you have attached all the 12 mms.
[7] Open a 4.5 mm ring, and attach it to an end pair of 4.5 mms **(photo e)**.
[8] Open a 4.5 mm ring, and attach the other end pair of 4.5 mms and a lobster claw clasp **(photo f)**. ◗

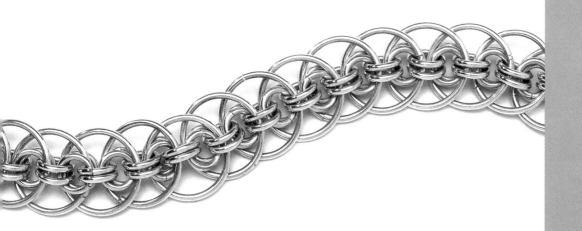

243

Scale the heights

Dating back to third century Japan, magatamas are comma-shaped jade beads believed to have derived from prehistoric animal-tooth pendants.

Combine traditional kumihimo with 8º seed beads and long magatamas for a study in textural beading

designed by **Paula Juvinall**

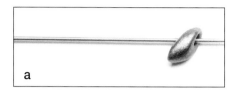

a

b

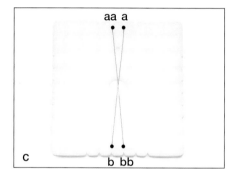

c

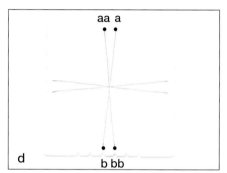

d

This technique results in a rope that resembles bead crochet but with the ease of kumihimo and a simple wrapped loop/ bead cap closure.

The hole through each magatama is on an angle. On one side, the hole is near the center of the bead; on the other, it's closer to the end of the bead. For this project, string the magatamas going through the side with the hole near the center of the bead and exiting the side with the hole near the end of the bead (photo a). Make sure the magatamas are all facing the same direction when strung (photo b).

stepbystep

Setup

[1] Cut four 3-yd. (2.7 m) lengths of Super-lon or #18 nylon cord.
[2] Thread a Big Eye needle on each end of one of the cords. With each needle, pick up eight 8º seed beads, 36 color A magatamas, and 45 8ºs, and center the beads on the cord. Remove the needles, and tie an overhand knot (Basics, p. 13) at each end to keep the beads from sliding off. Repeat for another length of cord.

[3] Repeat step 2 for the other two cords, but use color B magatamas.
[4] On each cord, find the center of the beads, and push the beads to each end so you have the same number and type of beads on each end of the cord. Center a cord with color A magatamas vertically over the hole of the kumihimo disk. Position one end in the inner slit at the top-right of the disk, and position the other end in the inner slit at the bottom-left (photo c, a–b).
[5] Repeat step 4 for the other color A magatama cord, but position one end of the cord in the inner slit at the top-left, cross the center hole at an angle, and position the other end in the inner slit at the bottom-right (aa–bb).
[6] Rotate the kumihimo disk ¼ turn, and repeat steps 4 and 5 with the color B magatama cords (photo d, a–b and aa–bb).
[7] Wrap each cord end around a bobbin, and secure, leaving about 2 in. (5 cm) of each cord to work with.

materials

black-and-silver necklace 18 in. (46 cm)
- 4 x 7 mm long magatamas in **2** colors:
  144 color A (galvanized silver)
  144 color B (metallic luster gunmetal)
- **2** 3 mm round beads (silver)
- 18 g 8º seed beads (hematite)
- clasp
- **2** 8 mm bead caps
- **2** 6 mm jump rings
- 8 in. (20 cm) 20-gauge wire
- Super-lon or #18 nylon cord
- **2** Big Eye needles
- **8** bobbins and a Bead Stopper or clip
- G-S Hypo Cement
- kumihimo disk with small weight (12–14 oz)
- **2** pairs of chainnose pliers
- roundnose pliers
- wire cutters

black-and-gold necklace (p. 246) colors:
- 4 x 7 mm long magatamas
  color A (metallic gold iris)
  color B (matte black)
- 8º seed beads (matte mauve)

green bracelet (p. 246) colors:
- 4 x 7 mm long magatamas (matte metallic patina iris)
- 8º triangle seed beads (matte metallic dark)

EDITOR'S NOTE:
To make an 8-in. (20 cm) bracelet like the one shown on p. 246, substitute 8º triangles for the 8º seed beads. On each cord end, pick up four 8ºs, 20 4 x 7 mm long magatamas, and four 8ºs, and work as you would the necklace.

DESIGNER'S NOTE:
To mark your place while braiding, move the cord at the top right to the bottom right. Having three cords on one side will indicate where you left off.

Experiment with a variety of threads, cords, and wire to make beautiful kumihimo jewelry.

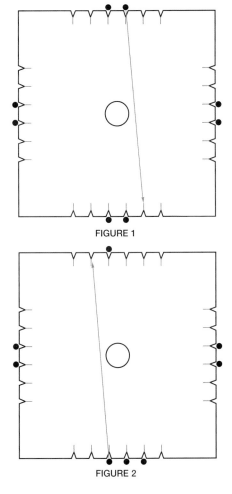

FIGURE 1

FIGURE 2

[8] Cut a 4-in. (10 cm) piece of 20-gauge wire. Make the first half of a wrapped loop (Basics) on one end. Slide the center of each cord into the loop. Complete the wraps. Use a Bead Stopper or clip to attach a small weight to the wire stem.

Making the braid

[1] Without moving any beads, pick up the cord at the top-right position, and bring it straight down to the right of the cord at the bottom-right **(figure 1)**. Pick up the cord at the bottom-left position, and bring it straight up to the left of the cord at the top-left **(figure 2)**. Turn the disk ¼ turn, and repeat.

[2] Repeat step 1 four times.

[3] Continue working as in step 1, but as you pick up each cord, slide down an 8° seed bead so it rests under the horizontal cord in the center hole, then position the working cord in the correct slot on the opposite side of the disk. Repeat for all the remaining beads on the cord, keeping a firm tension and making sure each bead sits under the horizontal cord. As you work, try to keep the point of the braid (where the cords are crossing) almost level with the top surface of the disk.

[4] Continue working as in step 1 for a total of three full rotations of the disk Cut a 4-in. (10 cm) piece of 20-gauge wire. Form the wire into a U-shape, and place it over the braid in the center of the hole. This wire will become the wrapped loop you attach the clasp to. Work three more rotations of the disk to capture the wire.

[5] Pick up the two horizontal cords on each side of the disk, bring them to the center, and tie a square knot (Basics). Repeat with the vertical cords. Dot the knots with glue, allow to dry, then trim the cords directly above the knot.

Assembly

[1] On the end of the necklace with the cut cords, keeping the wire in place, wrap one end of the wire tightly around the cord several times just below the knot, and trim.

[2] On the other end of the wire, string an 8 mm bead cap and a 3 mm bead, and make a wrapped loop. Repeat on the other end of the necklace.

[3] Open a 6 mm jump ring (Basics), and attach a wrapped loop and half of the clasp. Close the jump ring. Repeat on the other end of the necklace. ●

STRINGING
Intertwined
elements

Create an interesting necklace by crossing strands above your favorite pendant

designed by **Anna Elizabeth Draeger**

Use small chain links as a secret structure in this pretty necklace with intersecting strands.

materials

necklace 15 in. (38 cm)

- 1¼-in. (3.2 cm) pendant
- 1¾-in. (4.4 cm) curved metal tube
- 11º seed beads (11-459H, emerald green metallic iris)
- clasp
- 19 in. (48 cm) medium-link chain
- approx. 2 in. (5 cm) small-link chain with figure-8 links
- **2** 6 mm jump rings
- **4** crimp beads
- **4** crimp covers
- flexible beading wire, .010
- Bead Stoppers or tape
- crimping pliers
- **2** pairs of pliers
- wire cutters

stepbystep

Centerpiece

[1] Cut the small-link chain as necessary to remove eight intact figure-8 links.

[2] Cut five 12-in. (30 cm) strands of beading wire.

[3] On one strand, center the curved metal tube, and string the pendant on the tube. On each end, string seven 11º seed beads, one hole of a figure-8 link, seven 11ºs, a link, 13 11ºs, a link, 13 11ºs, a link, and three 11ºs. On each end, temporarily secure the beads with a Bead Stopper or a piece of tape next to the 11ºs.

[4] With another strand, go through the open hole of the first link next to the tube on one side of the centerpiece. Fold the wire in half, and string 55 11ºs over both wire ends. Using both wire ends, go through the open hole of the third link from the tube on the opposite side of the centerpiece. Pick up 18 11ºs, snug up the beads to the link, and temporarily secure the wire ends. Repeat on the other side of the centerpiece.

[5] With another strand, go through the open hole of the second link from the tube on one side of the centerpiece. Fold the wire in half, and string 65 11ºs over both wire ends. Using both wire ends, go through the open hole of the fourth link from the tube on the opposite side of the centerpiece. Pick up three 11ºs, snug up the beads to the link, and temporarily

secure the wire ends. Repeat on the other side of the centerpiece.

Neck straps

[1] Subtract the length of the centerpiece and the clasp from the overall desired length of the necklace. Cut two pieces of medium-link chain to that length.

[2] On one end of the centerpiece, string a crimp bead over two strands, then go through an end link of one of the chains. Go back through the crimp bead, and crimp it (Basics, p. 13). Repeat with the remaining three strands and the other end link of the same piece of chain. Close a crimp cover over each crimp.

[3] Repeat step 2 on the other end of the centerpiece.

[4] On one end of the necklace, open a jump ring (Basics), and attach half of the clasp to one of the chains. Repeat on the other end of the necklace. Close the jump ring. ●

Bunches of buttons

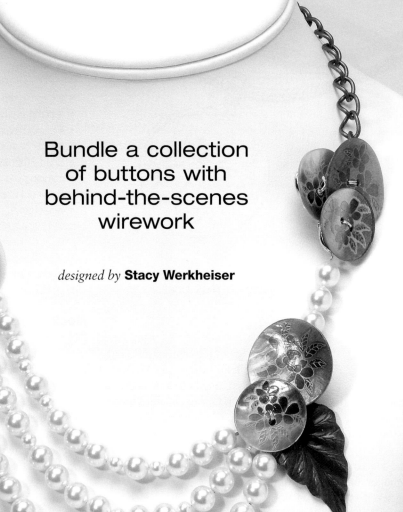

Bundle a collection of buttons with behind-the-scenes wirework

designed by **Stacy Werkheiser**

Brass chain, crystal pearls, and a leaf component lend a vintage look to this necklace.

materials

necklace 19 in. (48 cm)

- **4** 1¹/₁₆-in. (2.7 cm) cupped agoya shell or mother-of-pearl sew-through buttons
- **4** ⅞-in. (2.2 cm) cupped agoya shell or mother-of-pearl sew-through buttons
- 38 x 23 mm leaf component
- 16-in. (41 cm) strand 8 mm crystal pearls
- **14–20** 5 mm crystal pearls
- **8** 18 x 12 mm oval links
- hook clasp
- 32 in. (81 cm) 24-gauge wire, half-hard
- 9 in. (23 cm) chain, 10–11 mm links
- **4** 8 mm jump rings
- **7** 5 mm jump rings
- 8 microcrimp beads
- flexible beading wire, .010
- **2** pairs of pliers
- wire cutters

As soon as Stacy saw these sew-throughs, she imagined them clustered together in little button bouquets. You likely won't find buttons identical to hers, but search the Internet for "shell," "agoya," or "mother-of-pearl" buttons to find a sea of options.

stepbystep

Button clusters

[1] Cut a 4-in. (10 cm) piece of 24-gauge wire. With the tip of your chainnose pliers, grasp the center of the wire, and bend both ends downward. Feed each end of the wire through a hole of a sew-through button, front to back. Cross the wires close to the back of the button. With one end, go through the opposite hole, back to front, then go through the first hole again **(photo a)**.

[2] Over both ends, string an oval link. Using chainnose pliers to guide the wire, wrap each end around a side of the link three or four times. Trim the wire, and press the ends close to the link **(photo b)**.
[3] Repeat steps 1 and 2 with the remaining buttons.
[4] To make a two-button cluster, layer two buttons as desired so that the ends of the oval links are touching. Open a 5 mm jump ring (Basics, p. 13), attach the oval links, and close the jump ring **(photo c)**. To make a three-button

cluster, use 5 mm jump rings to attach the oval link of a third button to each of the previous two links **(photo d)**. Adjust the buttons until they lock into a solid cluster (see Designer's Note, p. 250). Make one two-button cluster and two three-button clusters.

Necklace

[1] Cut an 8-in. (20 cm) piece of beading wire. String a microcrimp bead and a link of a three-button cluster. Go back through the crimp bead, tighten the wire, and flatten the crimp bead with chainnose pliers. String a pattern of 8 mm and 5 mm pearls for 4¼ in. (10.8 cm), covering the wire tail left from crimping. String a crimp bead and a link of the two-button cluster. Go back through the crimp bead and two or three pearls, tighten the wire, flatten the crimp bead, and trim the excess wire.

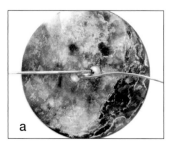

a

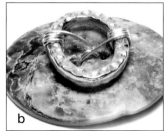

b

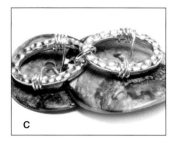

c

d

These oval links do double duty connecting the buttons as well as the pearl strands and chain.

[2] Repeat step 1 using a 9-in. (23 cm) piece of beading wire and stringing 5½ in. (14 cm) of pearls. Repeat again using an 11-in. (28 cm) piece of beading wire and stringing 7¼ in. (18.4 cm) of pearls. Attach both strands to the same two links as the first strand.

[3] Cut a 3½-in. (8.9 cm) piece of beading wire. String a crimp bead and the remaining link of the two-button cluster. Go back through the crimp bead, tighten the wire, and flatten the crimp bead. String three 8 mm pearls, covering the wire tail left from crimping, then string a crimp bead and a link of the remaining three-button cluster. Go back through the crimp bead and one or two pearls, tighten the wire, flatten the crimp bead, and trim the excess wire.

[4] Cut a 4½-in. (11.4 cm) and a 3¾-in. (9.5 cm) piece of chain. Open an 8 mm jump ring, and attach an end link of the 4½-in. (11.4 cm) chain and an oval link

of the three-button cluster connected to the three strands of pearls. Close the jump ring. Use another 8 mm jump ring to attach the 3¾-in. (9.5 cm) chain and an oval link of the other three-button cluster. Use a third jump ring to attach

the remaining end link of the 3¾-in. (9.5 cm) chain and a hook clasp.

[5] Open an 8 mm jump ring, and attach the leaf component and a link of the two-button cluster. Close the jump ring. ●

DESIGNER'S NOTE:

Your buttons may form a solid cluster on the first try, or they may need some encouragement. Try any of the following to make your cluster more stable:

- **Combine buttons with different degrees of the cupped shape.**
- **Mix up the sizes of buttons in the cluster.**
- **Layer the buttons in different arrangements.**
- **Open the 5 mm jump rings attaching a link, turn the link, and attach the jump rings to the other end of the link.**
- **Add more jump rings between 5 and 8 mm in diameter. Oval jump rings may also prove useful.**
- **If you still find that a button is prone to popping out of the cluster, avoid attaching the chain or pearl strands to that button.**

Get loopy

String a necklace with a turnabout trick *designed by* **Tea Benduhn**

Make loops of seed beads and accent beads for a fast and fun necklace.

stepbystep

[1] Cut 2 yd. (1.8 m) of beading wire.

[2] Center a 10 mm rondelle. On each side, string 25 15º seed beads. On one side, string an 8 mm twisted round crystal, and cross the other end of the wire through it. Temporarily secure one end with a Bead Stopper or tape, and work steps 3–11 with the other end.

[3] String six 15ºs, a color A 4 mm bicone crystal, and six 15ºs.

[4] String a color B 6 mm bicone crystal, 12 15ºs, an A 4 mm, and 12 15ºs. To form a loop, go through the B 6 mm again, then repeat step 3.

[5] String an 8 mm, 18 15ºs, a 10 mm, and 18 15ºs. To form a loop, go through the 8 mm again, then repeat step 3.

[6] String a color B 4 mm bicone crystal, nine 15ºs, an A 4 mm, and nine 15ºs. To form a loop, go through the B 4 mm again, then repeat step 3.

[7] String a color A 6 mm bicone crystal, 15 15ºs, a 6 mm coin, and 15 15ºs. To form a loop, go through the A 6 mm again, then repeat step 3.

[8] String a color C 4 mm bicone crystal, nine 15ºs, an A 4 mm, and nine 15ºs. To form a loop, go through the C 4 mm again, then repeat step 3.

[9] String an A 4 mm, 12 15ºs, a B 6 mm, and 12 15ºs. To form a loop, go through the A 4 mm again, then repeat step 3.

[10] String a 6 mm coin, nine 15ºs, an A 4 mm, and nine 15ºs. To form a loop, go through the 6 mm coin again, then repeat step 3.

[11] String a B 6 mm, six 15ºs, an A 4 mm, six 15ºs, a C 4 mm, six 15ºs, an A 4 mm, 12 15ºs, a crimp bead, 15 15ºs, and half of the clasp. Go back through the crimp bead to temporarily secure this end, but do not crimp the crimp bead.

[12] Remove the Bead Stopper or tape, and repeat steps 3–11 on the remaining end.

[13] Test the fit, and add or remove beads if necessary. Crimp the crimp beads (Basics, p. 13), and trim the wire on both ends. ●

materials

necklace 18 in. (46 cm)

- **3** 10 mm rondelles
- **3** 8 mm twisted round crystals, color A
- 6 mm bicone crystals
  2 color A
  6 color B
- **4** 6 mm coin beads
- 4 mm bicone crystals
  30 color A
  2 color B
  4 color C
- 2–3 g 15º seed beads
- **2** crimp beads
- clasp
- flexible beading wire, .015
- Bead Stopper or tape
- crimping pliers
- wire cutters

You can change the look of this necklace by substituting bead colors and styles. Also, experiment with bead counts in the loops and between them.

Contributors

Arja Aalto-Viittala is a jewelry artist from Tampere, Finland. See more of Arja's work at arjasuni.etsy.com, or contact her via email at aalto.arja@gmail.com.

Ann Dee Allen is formerly the editor of *Bead&Button* magazine. Contact her in care of Kalmbach Books.

Mark Avery has been a jewelry designer and bead maker for over 15 years. Mark enjoys coming up with new ways to make beads in his studio in Lansing, N.Y. Contact him via email at youngalby@yahoo.com, or visit etsy.com/people/MillcreekDesign.

Diane Baker started beading when she received a bead loom set as a gift when she was a girl. She learned to make her own lampworked beads at the Pratt Fine Arts Center in Seattle, Wash. When she's not beading, Diane sells brush covers and cleaning kits for cosmetic brushes through thebrushguard.com. Contact her via email at 1dianebaker@gmail.com.

Lisa Barth has been a creative person all her life. A wire jewelry artist and a certified metal clay instructor living in Atlanta, Ga., she began designing wire jewelry in 2003. Contact Lisa at ibelisab@yahoo.com, or visit her website, lbjewelrydesigns.com.

Contact **Tea Benduhn** in care of Kalmbach Books.

Kimberly Berlin, a retired educator, has taught for over 30 years and has been working with wire since childhood. She is now a full-time jewelry artist, teaches wireworking classes in San Antonio, Texas, and is the author of *Build Your Own Wire Pendants*. Contact Kimberly via email at berlik@flash.net.

Jimmie Boatright is a retired school teacher and lifelong crafter who teaches jewelry making at the Atlanta Bead Market in Buford, Ga. Contact Jimmie via email at atlantabeadmarket@hotmail.com, or see a list of her classes at atlantabeadmarket.com.

Gohar Breyl enjoys designing jewelry — everything from daytime casual to evening fancy — and teaching beading master classes in Petah Tikva, Israel. She also sells and rents her jewelry for special occasions through her own shop. Visit her website, gohardesign.com, or contact her at gohar.gm@gmail.com.

Kelli Burns owns The Hole Bead Shoppe in Bartlesville, Okla. She has been beading for over eight years, concentrating on designs using Lucite, but also loves to incorporate crystal into her work. Visit her website, theholebeadshop.com, or contact her at (918) 338-2444 or theholebeadshop@aol.com.

Contact **Juanita Carlos**, or **"Jaycee"** as she is known in the beading world, via email at juanita.carlos@gmail.com, or visit her website, jayceepatterns.com.

Mary Carroll is a graphic designer and self-taught beaded-jewelry designer who resides near Denver, Colo. She's been beading since 2003, and loves mixing color and texture in her designs. Visit her website, desertrosecreations.biz.

Aurelio Castaño started working in metal more than a decade ago, but craved the bright colors of his Latino heritage. Beads gave him that palette while allowing him to create the look of metal when he wanted to. He was born in Manizales, Colombia, and now teaches at the Westchester Community College Center for the Arts in White Plains, N.Y. To see more of Aurelio's work, visit clau-art.com.

Jane Danley Cruz is an associate editor at *Bead&Button* magazine. Contact her at jcruz@beadandbutton.com.

Marcia DeCoster makes her living and derives much pleasure from pursuing a beady life. She has been beading and teaching worldwide since 1999. Her book, *Marcia DeCoster's Beaded Opulence*, is part of the Beadweaving Master Class series. Visit her website, marciadecoster.com.

Seed bead weaving instructor **Donna Pagano Denny** lives in Fayetteville, N.C., where she teaches at All Things By Hand. She also sells her finished work at Lush Beads in her hometown of Lowell, Mass. Contact her via email at lacetatter@aol.com.

Anna Elizabeth Draeger is an associate editor at *Bead&Button* magazine and author of *Crystal Brilliance*. Contact her via email at adraeger@beadandbutton.com, or visit her website, http://web.mac.com/beadbiz.

Louise Duhamel has been beading since 1997. Her current focus is on metal clay, metalsmithing, and wirework, which she finds relaxing and meditative. When she's not beading, Louise is recuperating from the jet lag she gets traveling between Los Angeles and Sydney, Australia, as a flight attendant. Contact Louise by email at enchante@roadrunner.com, and visit her website at louiseduhamel.com.

Jamie Cloud Eakin is a professional bead artist and teacher. Her designs have appeared in numerous publications and books, and she is the author of *Beading with Cabochons*, *Bugle Bead Bonanza*, and *Dimensional Bead Embroidery*. Contact Jamie via email at jamie@studiojamie.com.

Jessica Fehrmann is a full-time massage therapist in Wisconsin and enjoys the creative outlets of making jewelry, especially with PMC and stitching. She recently started a business for jewelry design and participates in local art and craft fairs. Contact her at jessyemt@yahoo.com, or visit her website, sparklingc.com.

Diane Fitzgerald is an internationally recognized teacher, designer, and author. Among her numerous awards, she received the Spun Gold Award from the Textile Center of Minnesota for her lifetime commitment to fiber art. Diane has written 10 beading books; her next book, *Diane Fitzgerald's Favorite Bead Projects*, will be published in March 2012. Diane teaches classes at many locations, listed on her website at dianefitzgerald.com.

Linda Fordyce has been fascinated by beads since she was a child and now teaches classes in both wirework and seed beads. Contact Linda via email at sissybeads@yahoo.com.

Julie Glasser has been beading since 1980, when she inherited her grandmother's wire and seed beads. Now she focuses on bead-weaving techniques and teaches beading classes at an art school in Atlanta, Ga. She is also an accomplished metalsmith, combining sterling silver and seed beads in a lot of her work. Visit Julie's website at julieglasser.com.

Melissa Grakowsky has been beading since 2007 and now teaches workshops on the national and international level. Beading is a natural fit for Melissa, who feels that the art form combines her backgrounds in both science and art. Contact Melissa via email at grakowsky@gmail.com, or visit her website, grakowsky.net.

Gretchen Grammer is a self-taught bead artist who finds inspiration in antiquity and the natural world. A marine scientist by profession, she balances science with art through her beadwork, preferring to work primarily with seed beads and crystals. Contact Gretchen via email at g_waggy@hotmail.com, or follow her on Facebook, facebook.com/SilverPerchDesigns.

Smadar Grossman lives in Israel. She fell in love with bead weaving in 2005 and has been exploring its endless possibilities ever since. Visit Smadar's website, smadarstreasure.blogspot.com.

Leah Hanoud has been beading for more than 15 years and has a B.F.A. with a concentration in jewelry and metalsmithing from the University of Massachusetts. She has worked her entire beading career at Turquoise-StringBeads in Fall River, Mass. Contact Leah at (508) 677-1877 or turq2000@turquoise-stringbeads.com, or visit turquoise-stringbeads.com.

Michelle Heim co-owns her shop, Beadalotta, in Fond du Lac, Wis., where she's been surrounded by her addiction since 2006. Contact her at michelle@beadalotta.com, or visit her website, beadalotta.com.

Diane Hertzler specializes in off-loom bead-weaving techniques and teaches her original designs throughout the country. She also contributed several projects to the book *Beaded Ornaments for the Holidays and Beyond*. Contact her via email at dianehertzler@verizon.net, or visit her website, dianehertzler.com.

Jonna Ellis Holston is a full-time beader and teacher of beaded arts both privately and as a faculty member at the Sawtooth School of Visual Arts in Winston-Salem, N.C. You can contact her at gianabijou@yahoo.com.

Collette Hunt specializes in whimsical ornaments and adornments. Contact her in care of Kalmbach Books.

Diane Hyde specializes in designing vintage styles with a contemporary twist. For more than 30 years, she has been combining her skills as a graphic artist, beader, and seamstress to create her intricate jewelry pieces. Contact her via email at dianehyde@mac.com, or visit her websites, designersfindings.net, beadpunk.net, and dianehyde.com.

Contact **Amy Johnson** via e-mail at amy@amyjohnsondesigns.com, or visit amyjohnsondesigns.com.

Paula Juvinall lives in Dunedin, Fla. She began beading about 10 years ago and enjoys many techniques, but kumihimo has become one of her favorites. She shares her passion and skill with others through teaching classes at Dunedin Beads. Contact Paula at pjuvinall@gmail.com.

Sandra Lamoureux has been beading since 2009 and has been designing since 2010. Her designs are featured at Beadiful in Cumming, Ga., where she also teaches classes. Contact her via email at sjlamoureux@mindspring.com.

Cathy Lampole of Newmarket, Ontario, Canada, enjoys the fine detail that can be achieved with bead weaving, especially with crystals. Besides designing jewelry, Cathy owns a bead shop, That Bead Lady. Visit her website, thatbeadlady.com, or email her at cathy@thatbeadlady.com.

Linda K. Landy has been teaching bead weaving for 10 years and was a finalist in Bead Dreams 2010. She jokes that beads "speak to her" and loves to share her joy of beading. Contact Linda at lindaleeoriginal@bellsouth.net.

Shirley Lim resides in Singapore and has been beading since 2000. She loves combining peyote with herringbone, her favorite stitch. Contact Shirley at beadingfantasy@me.com, visit her online at web.me.com/beadingfantasy, etsy.com/shop/beadingfantasy, or beading-fantasy.blogspot.com.

Glorianne Ljubich began beading 10 years ago and quickly fell under its spell. Incorporating bead weaving, wireworking, and stringing, she designs and teaches in Seattle, Wash. Contact her via email at info@fusionbeads.com.

Alla Maslennikova lives in Moscow, Russia, where she works for the largest Russian bead show, Beading Design. Visit her website, beadlady.ru, or email her at to@beadlady.ru.

Laura McCabe has been beading for a lifetime and enjoys using unconventional materials. In addition to her own books, her work appears in the recently released *Beading Across America: Jewelry Inspirations from Coast to Coast*. Visit her website, justletmebead.com, or email her at justletmebead@gmail.com.

Anne E. Mitchell is a popular jewelry designer and teacher. Besides making chain mail jewelry, she is also a metalsmith and metal clay artist who specializes in low-tech and environmentally friendly studio practices. Visit her website, annemitchell.net.

Samantha Mitchell teaches beading classes and designs jewelry as a way to express her creativity when she's not busy caring for her young son. Contact her at samantha@crystyles.com, or visit her website, crystyles.com.

Deb Moffett-Hall designs heirloom peyote stitch ornament patterns and fun ornament, bracelet, and earring kits-of-the-month. She also invented the Quick Start Peyote starter card system to help even beginners enjoy peyote stitch. Deb lives with her family in Hatfield, Pa. Email her at beadpatterns@aol.com, or visit her website, patternstobead.com.

Grace Nehls is a jewelry designer who teaches her creations at Bead Haven in Las Vegas. She finds inspiration for designs in her everyday surroundings. Contact her via email at gnehls@beadmegracefully.com.

Julie Olah lives in Temecula, Calif. Contact her in care of Kalmbach Books.

Erin Paton lives in Nowra, New South Wales, Australia. She likes incorporating various techniques into her jewelry designs, such as the figure-8 weaving used in her "Fine-scale earrings" featured in this book. Contact her at earringsbyerin@gmail.com.

Pascal Pinther is a self-taught artist who resides in Dortmund, Germany. Since 2006, he has been creating lampworked beads and combining them with metalsmithing. Contact Pascal at pascal-pinther-querbead@gmx.de, or visit querbeads-beads.blogspot.com.

Cynthia Poh is an international jewelry designer and instructor based in Perth, Australia, who takes inspiration from places she has lived and taught. Contact her via email at info@beadygirl.com, or visit her website, beadygirl.com.

The author of *Beading with Right-Angle Weave*, **Chris Prussing** specializes in designing and teaching two-needle projects. Visit her website, bead-patterns.com.

Maggie Roschyk is an accomplished beadwork artist who teaches at many venues, including the Bead&Button Show in the U.S. and the Bead Art and Jewelry Accessory Fair in Germany. Maggie is a contributing editor to *Bead&Button* magazine, the author of an online column called "Maggie's Musings," and the author of the book *Artistic Seed Bead Jewelry*. Contact her via email at blueroses@wi.rr.com.

Marcia Rose finally has time to do the things she loves since selling the mail-order computer/electronics company she co-founded. She discovered the art of French beaded flowers and became completely hooked on beads. Contact Marcia at mnrgorr@yahoo.com.

Nancy Sebestyen has been beading for more than four years. After teaching stitching techniques to customers in the bead store where she worked, Nancy started designing her own pieces. Contact Nancy by email at nancyseb@verizon.net or by phone at (909) 590-2976.

Jacquelyn Scieszka lives in Birmingham, Mich., and is a member of the Great Lakes Beadworkers Guild. Contact her at jmscieszka@aol.com, and visit her website at jacquelynscieszka.com.

Sue Sloan, a self-taught beader based in Portland, Ore., has been experimenting with color, texture, and technique for over 20 years. Contact Sue in care of Kalmbach Books.

Lynne Soto teaches bead jewelry making to individuals and groups through her business "Lessons with Lynne." She also teaches her original designs at the Bead&Button Show. Contact her via email at mscalto2@att.net.

Eileen Spitz sells her designs through her favorite bead store, Crystal Creations/Beads Gone Wild in West Palm Beach, Fla. Contact her at eileenspitz@comcast.net.

Liz Stahl lives in Chelmsford, Mass., and has been beading since 2006. She is a bead hobbyist who enjoys creating with seed beads in her free time. Contact Liz via email at liz.stahl@comcast.net.

Sylvia Sucipto was eight years old when her grandmother passed on to her the craft of making *kasut manik* — beaded Chinese-Peranakan slippers — and she's been beading ever since as a hobby. Sylvia developed her own style, mixing traditional techniques with modern influences and using beadwork as a way to express her creativity. Contact Sylvia in care of Kalmbach Books.

Kimie Suto is a popular beading teacher in Japan, where she teaches more than 100 students per month. She discovered beading as a child and became a certified beading teacher in 2002. To see more of Kimie's work, visit her website, kimiyell.com, or email her at info@felice-jewelry.com.

Liisa Turunen, Head Designer and Instructor at Crystal Creations Bead Institute in West Palm Beach, Fla., has been beading for over 15 years. Contact Liisa at (561) 649-9909 or via email at info@beadsgonewild.com, or visit beadsgonewild.com.

A microbiologist and jewelry designer based in Huntington Beach, Calif., **Jenny Van** is a frequent contributor to *Bead&Button* magazine. Contact her via email at jenny@beadsj.com, or visit her website, beadsj.com.

Vanessa Walilko is a jewelry and fashion designer who has been making chain mail for more than five years. Her chain mail has taken top prizes in the Bead Dreams competition and the British Bead Awards, and her pieces have been featured in shows around the country. Visit her website, kalibutterfly.com.

Stacy Werkheiser is an associate editor of *Bead&Button* magazine. Contact her at swerkheiser@beadandbutton.com.

Index

Pursue Your Passion

Make hundreds of
CREATIVE JEWELRY PIECES
with the techniques and projects in these volumes

Each volume contains more than
80
projects and is just $29.95!

This stunning collection of hardcover volumes contains hundreds of fabulous step-by-step projects and fresh ideas selected from the pages of *Bead&Button* magazine. Be a creative beader with the thorough Basics sections, project sections grouped by technique, and a range of editor-tested stringing, wirework, embroidery and crochet designs.

From easy strung bracelets to sleek crocheted bead ropes, there's a project to excite and inspire everyone.

Creative Beading
62288

Creative Beading, Vol. 3
62625

Creative Beading, Vol. 4
62892

Creative Beading, Vol. 5
62922

Creative Beading, Vol. 6
64193

Available at your favorite bead or craft shop!
Order online at www.KalmbachStore.com or call 1-800-533-6644
Monday–Friday, 8:30 a.m. – 4:30 p.m. Central Time. Outside the U.S. and Canada, call 262-706-8776 x661.

 www.facebook.com/KalmbachJewelryBooks   www.twitter.com/KalmbachBooks   2XBB

KB KALMBACH BOOKS

P16125